National Variations in
JEWISH IDENTITY

National Variations in
JEWISH IDENTITY

Implications
for Jewish Education

EDITED BY

Steven M. Cohen and
Gabriel Horencyzk

STATE UNIVERSITY OF NEW YORK PRESS

DS
143
.N27
1999

Published by
State University of New York Press, Albany

© 1999 State University of New York

Printed in the United States of America

For information, address State University of New York
Press, State University Plaza, Albany, N.Y., 12246

Production by Diane Ganeles
Marketing by Patrick Durocher

Library of Congress Cataloging-in-Publication Data

National variations in Jewish identity : implications for Jewish
    education / edited by Steven M. Cohen and Gabriel Horencyzk.
        p.   cm.
    Includes index.
    ISBN 0-7914-4371-X. — ISBN 0-7914-4372-8 (pbk. : alk. paper)
    1. Jews—Identity—Congresses.   2. Jews—United States—Identity—
Congresses.   3. Jews—Israel—Identity—Congresses.   I. Cohen,
Steven Martin.   II. Horencyzk, Gabriel, 1954–   .
DS143.N27   1999
305.892´4—dc 21   99–19029
                                                                 CIP

10 9 8 7 6 5 4 3 2 1

Contents

Introduction

Steven M. Cohen

Throughout the world, Jews in different locations share certain key elements in their subculture and group identity. The most obvious similarities are found in their holidays, liturgy, religious implements, ceremonies, and religious literature. The preponderance of Jews worldwide also seem to share certain distinctive attitudes. Among the most notable are involvement in middle- to high-brow cultural pursuits; a sense of minority status and victimization; familylike conceptions of their relations with one another; identification with Israel; and solidarity with oppressed Jewry; as well as self-images (whether accurate or not) of intellectual acuity, ambition, industriousness, social achievement, close-knit families, and moral sensitivity. Politically, they lean toward the democratic left of their respective societies' political centers, and, often, their most politically active are overrepresented in movements for social change. Demographically, Jews outside of Israel are characterized by relatively late marriage, low birthrates, mounting rates of intermarriage, and long life expectancy.

Moreover, some groups of Jews are more alike than others. In particular, the extent of similarity is especially pronounced when comparisons are restricted to the primarily Ashkenazi Jews now living in societies regarded as part of the "West" (Western Europe, North America, the former British commonwealth, and parts of Latin America). In contrast with Israelis, all these Jewries live as minorities. As opposed to most Sephardim who encountered the full force of modernity only in the twentieth century, all experienced the onset of "modernity" at roughly the same time—the mid- to late-nineteenth century.

Certainly the commonalities among Jewries—especially Western, Ashkenazi Diaspora Jewries—are not at all hard to come by. Undoubtedly, the items mentioned easily could be extended and elaborated upon. When one thinks about it, for such a geographically far-flung religio-ethnic group, this is quite a remarkable list of shared features.

Notwithstanding the many shared elements, various contemporary Jewries present several crucial points of distinction as well. In ways ranging from the readily apparent to the highly subtle, modern Jews in different societies—and even those separated only by regions within the same countries—are characterized by crucial differences in their identities as Jews, differences that extend beyond such immediately obvious variations as language and dress. They go to matters of what Jews believe they share and what sets them apart from others; what specific elements of Judaism, which conceptualizations, and which interpretations acquire special emphasis; the extent to which, and the manner in which, Jews are to function as part of the larger societies in which they dwell; and more.

These considerations raise a key question. Simply stated it reads: How do patterns of Jewish identity vary across modern societies—and why? This, in essence, is the question addressed in a conference held in January 1994 at the Melton Centre for Jewish Education in the Diaspora of The Hebrew University. Entitled,"National and Cultural Variations in Jewish Identity and Their Implications for Jewish Education," the conference featured the participation of nearly two dozen scholars from disciplines as varied as history, anthropology, sociology, psychology, demography, political science, philosophy, and literature. The chapters collected in this anthology are based on the lectures delivered at that conference.

In a manner of speaking, the chapters can be seen as elaborating upon each of the key terms in the title of the conference. Several authors present a general understanding of modernity and how it wrought profound and far-reaching changes on Jews and Judaism. Others, implicitly critical of this approach, emphasize the uniqueness of social circumstances in particular societies, and of the varying outcomes that serve to distinguish modern Jewries in different times and places. Some seek to illuminate the distinctive character of Judaism in particular societies, in effect, expanding the meaning of the term,

Jewish identity. One chapter seeks to explore and refashion the understanding of *identity* itself. All of these issues bear elaboration.

It would be fair to say that this entire enterprise takes place against the backdrop of what may be called, "the Jewish modernity model," linked to the European Enlightenment and the Jewish Emancipation. All the chapters here implicitly or explicitly take the Jewish encounter with modernity as a fundamental framing device. They portray contemporary variations in Jewish identity today as diverse responses to the confrontations of Jews and Jewish life with dramatically changing cultural, economic, and political environments that took place primarily during the nineteenth century in Western Europe and North America.

The well-known analysis of the Jewish encounter with modernity can be quickly summarized (see Katz 1971 and 1978 for an overview). Jews and Judaism in premodern times were adapted to a world radically different from our own in terms of both social structure and culture. Structurally, Jews tended to reside for relatively long periods in smaller communities, situated often in commercial villages. They often worked as merchants and artisans. They maintained politically autonomous communities, with a highly developed institutional infrastructure, generally under the rubric of localistic governing authorities. In these communities (*kehillot*), religious authorities, in conjunction with the more affluent Jewish families, exercised significant political influence and social control. They functioned amid larger (generally Christian) societies whose cultures legitimated key aspects of traditional life generally and, by extension, traditional Jewish life in particular. These elements included mutually shared antagonism and distrust between Jews and Gentiles; a reverence for the past, ancient texts, and ancient thinkers; a powerful, ubiquitous and exclusivist religious symbol system (of course, Christians, Moslems, and Jews had different ideas about whose interpretations were correct); the circumscription of life chances by such ascribed characteristics as sex, age, and social status at birth; and a premium on collectivist obligations over individual self-fulfillment, as well as license—if not the obligation—to treat members of one's own group more favorably than others. Such terms as *past-orientation, ascription, parochialism, particularism*, and *collectivism* are frequently applied to describe the culture, values, and consciousness of the premodern societies in which traditional Jews and Judaism dwelled for centuries.

In this world (whose highly generalized description ignores inevitable variations over numerous societies), Judaism lived and

developed. It was a Judaism highlighted by self-rule; rabbinic authority; an ancient (though organically changing) religious legal system that—in modern eyes—regulated the most private spheres of
one's life; patterns of socializing demarcated by age and sex; and,
not least, suspicion of the socially distant Gentiles coupled with dis-
dain for their culture.

The world in which this Judaism was built, of course, came to
an end. The cultural and intellectual changes embraced in the term
Enlightenment, along with the political and economic changes subsumed under the label *Emancipation*, meant that Jews, Judaism,
and their relations with the societies around them would be revolu-
tionized. Either modernity came to the Jews, or—in the great migrations of the nineteenth and twentieth centuries to expanding
cities and Western countries—millions of Jews moved to modernity.
Either eventuality meant the demise of the self-governing *kehillot*
(communities), with their coercive powers over individuals, and a
host of other new circumstances for Jews and Judaism. Inevitably,
these changes demanded a wide diversity of responses and formulations of what it means to be a Jew in the modern world.

The articles in this volume differ in the extent to which they partake of this general model of modernity. But they are uniform in accepting—if not always highlighting—those cultural and social
structural tendencies in modernity that are seen as having the most
significant impact upon Jews, Jewish communities, Judaism, and, ultimately, Jewish identity. Among the most salient cultural elements
are individualism, secularism (be it in terms of church leaders' diminished influence or the reduced prominence of religion in the culture), voluntarism (especially, the freedom to choose whether and how
to be a member of a religious or ethnic group), pluralism (and tolerance), futurity (the valuing of the new and improved), nationalism,
and a variety of modern political ideologies and movements.

This entire anthology presumes the centrality of the encounter
of Judaism with these values. However, given the familiarity of
the argument in the scholarly literature (written in part by some
of the contributors to this volume), none of the authors felt compelled to cover well-trodden ground again. Rather, presuming at
least a cursory familiarity with the basic outline of Jews' encounter with modernity, this collection explores the consequences
of that encounter, both globally and specifically for certain times
and places.

From four perspectives and four disciplines, the first group of
authors in the volume describe the fragmentation, fracturing, and

diversification of Judaism that ensued from the encounter with modernity.

The first section of the book leads off with an essay by the modern Jewish historian Michael A. Meyer in which he explores how modernity has engendered several classic responses by Jews throughout the Western world. One such reaction is "contraction," or the reduction of the scope and power of Jewish identity. Another response is *fragmentation*, a term that takes on several meanings for Meyer. It includes the selection of particular elements within historic Jewish culture that are to be retained and elaborated upon in the post-Enlightenment era, even as many other elements are abandoned as unsuitable to modernity. Fragmentation also connotes the disentangling of the ethnic dimension of being Jewish from the religious dimension of Judaism. And, along with these developments, comes another sort of fragmentation: increasingly sharp and antagonistic relations among Jewish partisan factions and ideological movements.

Beyond fragmentation, the Emancipation means that Jews, who had been marginalized and excluded, could and would seek entry into wider societies which, in effect, issued conditional invitations—often reluctantly—to the former pariahs. Under such circumstances, to legitimate and promote their acceptance, Jews understandably develop techniques and claims of "justification," entailing their calling attention to their distinctive contributions to the society at large.

As they win their acceptance (or not), Jews are torn by the cultural contradiction of present-day modern society and by their traditional religious culture, albeit reformed in line with the new reality.

Meyer delineates four broad strategies that Jews have used to cope with this: incompatibility (rejecting modernity in favor of maintaining ancient Jewish folkways as much as is possible); compartmentalization (creating separate spheres to insulate the modern public life from the Jewish private life); harmonization (adjusting Judaism to comport with modernity); and equivalency (downplaying tensions between the two cultural systems). As we shall see, other authors in this volume derive parallel schemata to comprehend widespread similar phenomena.

Peter Berger's many writings on modernity emphasize the movement from fate to choice as pivotal to the modernization experience. In the religious sphere, this movement translates into the unavoidable necessity of committing a type of heresy, which, as Berger points out, is the word for "choice" in Greek (hence: "Heretical Imperative"

[1979] as the title of one of his books). Modernity means that the given is removed, that choice is unavoidable. All moderns need to construct their religious perspectives in terms of some mix of the modern culture, traditional religion, and personal experience.

These themes—the expansion of options and the requirement to choose—resonate throughout Daniel J. Elazar's formulation of the Jewish entry into modernity. In premodern Jewish history, Elazar notes, Jews hardly ever experienced problems of identity. "Jews knew who was a Jew and how." What modern Jews would come to define as distinctive religious, ethnic, and national identities were—before the Emancipation—inseparable and nearly indistinguishable. With modernity, identity became "subjective and voluntary, as distinct from objective and communal, if not compulsory." In contrast with their ancestors, modern Jews can "make any claims, adopt any practices" (Charles Liebman, in like fashion, writes of "voluntarism" and "personalism" as two hallmarks of modern Judaism; see Liebman and Cohen 1990). As a result, the Jewish group definition is fragmented, taking on different emphases in different places. Being Jewish, as Elazar notes in his survey of world Jewry, is defined as principally national in Israel, religious in the United States, and ethnic in most other parts of the world.

Arthur Ruppin, the pioneering early twentieth-century Jewish demographer, anticipated linkages between demographic modernization and outright and eventual assimilation. He predicted that Jews' geographic and social mobility, along with accompanying changes in family-formation patterns, would inevitably diminish the communal ties and cultural features that served to maintain Jewish distinctiveness. Sergio DellaPergola's scan of worldwide Jewish demographic trends finds high levels of urbanization and suburbanization, and professionalization. Confirming and echoing Ruppin, he demonstrates that these trends—in several societies today—are associated with high rates of intermarriage and low rates of religious commitment. Israel, of course, provides a dramatic counterexample, again in keeping with the predictions and predilections of Ruppin.

If modernity brings about fragmentation, diversity, factionalization, and turbulence, it stands to reason that all of these unsettling developments will be felt keenly on the personal level. The anthropologist Harvey E. Goldberg, reflecting on his Jewish autobiography, explores the predicament of "middle-of-the-road" Jewish families, those who seek religiously serious lives and who fully participate in their modern societies. Goldberg observes that such families are fated to establish schools and synagogues that are in a constant state of ideological turmoil. The cultural and ideological fragmentation of Jewish life, coupled with high rates of geographic mobility, generate Jews with highly individuated and differentiated Jewish autobiographies. Lacking the common ground that arises out of similar socialization experiences, these highly differentiated Jews nevertheless are drawn to one another to establish institutions to serve their educational and religious needs. Yet, given these circumstances, not only are they compelled to work together, but they must turn to educators, rabbis, and functionaries with whom they often share little ideologically. The result is constant bickering, repeated splits, and an ongoing search for new alternatives. For Goldberg, the constant churning within the middle-of-the-road institutions are not happenstance. They are endemic to Jewish modernity.

No serious scholar would deny that, for Jews, the modern social structure and consciousness constitute a clear and definable break with their traditional or *premodern* counterparts (no term is readily available for that which preceded modernity). But the particular mix of modern cultural elements, their potency, and their timing differ across both time and space. Recent literature on Jewish Emancipation and its aftermath delves deeply into details; rather than generalizing across time and space, it plays up the distinctive factors, processes, and outcomes that characterize dynamic transformations among Jews in particular societies at particular moments in history. In their recently published anthology (*Paths to Emancipation*), Pierre Birnbaum and Ira Katznelson state the matter succinctly in their respectful criticism of Jacob Katz's influential understanding of European Jewish modernization. They claim that his "unitary and linear perspective pushes far too hard in the direction of singularity. One goal . . . is to underscore just how wide a perspective, and just how much of a flattening of variations, is required to sustain Katz's landmark formulation" (Birnbaum and Katznelson 1995: 17).

The chapters in this volume situate themselves on both sides of this controversy. The four chapters gathered in the first section, while keenly aware of variations, can be seen as functioning with a general model of Jewish modernization, à la Katz. In contrast, the remaining chapters of this anthology highlight the variations and focus upon the peculiar processes that have emerged in specific societies.

Paula E. Hyman's leadoff piece in this section emphasizes the fact that Jewries in different times and places encountered different forms of modernity, at different levels of intensity, and with different

consequences. Some Jewries modernized sooner and faster, others
later and slower. In Hyman's view, the application of an overarching
model of modernization to all Western Jewry obscures important
variations among American, British, and French Jewries. Despite
many real and significant similarities, these three Western Ashkenazi Jewries, all living as religious minorities in countries with relatively low levels of anti-Semitism, exhibit key variations. The Jews
of Great Britain did not achieve unusually high levels of education.
Native French Jewry is extraordinarily secularized. American
Jews—in contrast with the other two Jewries—are unusually decen-
tralized, localistic, and congregational. These variations are not the
exception to the rule, but are central to a nuanced understanding of
how modernity differentially influenced different Jewish communities at different times.

Further elaboration of the themes can be found in the subsequent five chapters that explore aspects of British, Canadian, and
American Jewry.

Geoffrey Alderman's historical survey of British Jewry picks up
on the themes of diversification and fragmentation presented earlier, and offers a narrative of the ongoing tensions between British
Orthodoxy and Reform. More broadly, it points to the dynamic
processes of Jewish identity formation and reformation as a result
of migration and of the relaxation of the social pressure to conform.

Undoubtedly, the extent to which the larger society demands
conformity or allows for (and even formally sanctions or financially
supports) cultural diversity directly impinges on the nature and potency of Jews' group identity. The conformity/diversity dimension explains (in part) both international and overtime variations in Jewish
identity, and it lies at the heart of Stuart Schoenfeld's analysis of distinctive aspects of the Jewish situation in Canada. He begins with a
quandary: Why are Canadian Jews so much more Jewishly active (in
all measurable respects) than American Jews just over the porous
border? The sociodemographic explanation (Canadian Jews arrived
from Europe more recently) is only part of the answer. Rather,
Schoenfeld looks to three key characteristics of Canadian society.
Perhaps most critical is its multicultural self-definition, necessitated
by the long-standing and increasingly sharp division between En-
glish- and French-speaking segments of the Canadian population.
The cultural legitimacy available to the major subcultural groups extends to smaller minorities including Jews (although, politically,
Jews and other smaller minorities may enjoy less influence than the
British- and French-stock population groups). Schoenfeld also points

to a growing "globalism" that stresses Canada's involvement with the international community. This tendency lends a global perspective to Canadian Jewish identity, reinforcing notions of world Jewish peoplehood. Last, Schoenfeld points to growing integration with the United States, a trend that lends Canadian Jewry some of the benefits of a larger continental Jewish population. But it also brings with it certain cultural elements that serve to undermine collectivist Jewish identity.

About America's receptivity to Jewish distinctiveness—or lack thereof—Henry L. Feingold has much to say. Indeed, for Feingold, the United States presents an unusual, and potentially highly destructive, form of secularism. The peculiarly "hard" form of secularism found in America is characterized by an extraordinarily high degree of individualism and libertarianism. "It is that hardness which creates the powerful solvent that poses a survival challenge to all religious and ethnic cultures in America. The former is desacralized, the latter, denuded." American secularism—at least that which Jews experience or think they experience—exerts a special pull upon American Jews as it is abetted by, and associated with, the "drive to rise out of the ghetto." For American Jews, according to Feingold, these processes translate into Jewish cultural ignorance, low ritual observance, high intermarriage, "cultural dilution," and, most broadly speaking, "loss of communal memory." (One wonders whether the French secularism noted by Hyman is as hard and—in line with Feingold's theoretical assumptions—whether its impact on Jewish identity and community is as destructive.)

Inter alia, many of the chapters in this volume describe how the word "Jewish" in the term *Jewish identity* has acquired new, clearly nontraditional meanings. Milton Gordon in *Assimilation in American Life* (1964) distinguished between intrinsic and extrinsic ethnic characteristics. Intrinsic ethnic traits are those that are totally identified with the ethnic group. Examples might include ethnic churches for European-origin Christians, or kosher dietary laws for Jews. Extrinsic characteristics are those that could conceivably be shared by many groups, but that tend to be concentrated among members of a particular group (or groups) and come to be identified in some way with that group. Examples include the putative American patriotism among the Irish, the drive for home ownership among Italian-Americans (Glazer and Moynihan, 1963), or political liberalism among American Jews.

Where these chapters contributed to expanding the meaning of the word "Jewish," they did so primarily by adding to the extrinsic compartment of Jewish identity. Riv-Ellen Prell, for example, in writing about Jewish immigrants to the United States and their children in the first half of the twentieth century, provides evidence of the striking extent to which the drive for social mobility influenced Jewish self-perceptions. "Being Jewish in America came to be associated by Jews with remarkably specific types of work and success, consumption patterns, and styles of life." The need to achieve materially, the evaluations of one another based on achievement, and the gender-based and age-oriented family roles associated deeply affected relations between the sexes and between the generations. Women were defined as consumers, men as producers. Women were primarily responsible for the functioning of families, and families were responsible for shaping and maintaining morality. "The family . . . increasingly redefined Jewishness in relationship to work, family loyalty, and community, but not necessarily in relationship to Judaism." The impact was so profound and so far-reaching that one is forced to conclude that the press for upward social mobility constituted an outstanding (extrinsic) component of Jewish identity for American Jews in the first half of the twentieth century.

If Jewish identity takes on different colorations in different countries, then, by extension, regional variations should emerge as well. One would expect regional diversity to be especially pronounced in societies that are geographically large, span culturally diverse regions, and provide homes to large Jewish populations. Clearly, societies that fit these requirements include contemporary Russia (or, more broadly, the former Soviet Union), and the United States. The two chapters that constitute the third section of this volume—one that focuses on southern California and the other on New York Jewry—clearly point to the influence of region upon Jewish identity.

Deborah Dash Moore's account (a revised extract from her monograph on Jewish migration to the American Sun Belt) analyzes the origins of the Brandeis Camp Institute, a Jewish educational retreat center for young adults and families. She clearly points to the larger regional subculture as essential to the directions the camp took, and by extension, the shape of Jewish identity in southern California. The educational approach, which Moore labels, "spiritual recreation," is uniquely attuned to the spirit of Los Angeles, a metropolitan area noted for leisure, Hollywood, and, in general, that which is "eclectic, experiential, experimental, popular." Central to the educational thinking of Shlomo Bardin (the camp's founder and director for decades) was the notion that in this land of leisure, people should feel good about being Jewish and feel good in general. Reflecting the influence and resource of Hollywood, he made extensive use of drama, theatrics, music, and dance. "The Brandeis Camp Institute implicitly understood Judaism and Jewishness to be leisure-time activities; it blended drama and music, because of their ability to transform observers into participants, to produce Shabbat . . . a distinctive form of Shabbat that provided meaning, community and religious experience."

From southern California of the 1950s, we move to metropolitan New York of the 1990s. And here too, the influence of region is clear and paramount. Bethamie Horowitz seeks to understand how and why New York area Jews differ from those elsewhere in the United States. In the aggregate, they are somewhat more observant, more socially embedded (more Jewish friends, lower intermarriage), more ready to define themselves as Jews by religion, and—perhaps owing to the large size of New York Jewry—*less* likely to affiliate with formal institutions of Jewish life. One reason for some of these differences lies in the higher proportions of Orthodox Jews and of earlier generation Jews in New York. But, these alone are insufficient to fully account for the "New York effect," as both the Orthodox and non-Orthodox in New York are more observant than their counterparts elsewhere, as are third-or more generation New Yorkers when compared with those elsewhere.

In seeking to explain New York's distinctiveness, Horowitz points to the "propinquity of large masses of Jews there," and to the consequent diversity of Jewish subcultures made possible by the large Jewish population, as well as by the wide array of Jewish communal services. She also makes note of the long history of a large and influential Jewish population in the city, and of the wider recognition of, and comfort with, the sustained, substantial, and influential Jewish presence in New York.

If New York's Jewry is characterized by greater size, concentration, influence, diversity, Orthodoxy, infrastructure, and closeness to European origins, then—on a certain level—Israel can be regarded as a more extreme version of New York. Of course, the major distinctions between Israel and the rest of Jewry lie in the fact that Israel is a complete society, with a Jewish majority, and Jewish sovereignty. As such, Jewish identity in Israel is more collective in nature and more multilayered in complexity. The three chapters in the concluding section of this volume testify to these and to other distinctive features of Jewish identity in Israel.

Israel's distinctiveness can even be seen on the level of philosophical thought. Jonathan Cohen's analysis of the approaches of Joseph B. Soloveitchik (for decades, America's premier Orthodox thinker) and Eliezer Schweid (one of Israel's most prominent philosophers) points to differences that grow out of the very different environments that surround each of these thinkers. Both men's work tackle a similar problem: how Jews (and people in general) are to overcome individuality, cope with existential angst, and provide for elusive meaning in their lives. But the sources of this quandary, and its resolution, differ for Soloveitchik and Schweid. For the former, the problem of radical individuality is rooted in an ambivalence toward modernity generally, and technological achievement and the success ethic in particular. For Shweid, the starting point is his compatriots' readiness to sacrifice for the Jewish state combined with a resistance to infusing "their lives with positive Jewish content by way of a serious confrontation with Jewish sources." As opposed to Soloveitchik, Schweid "accords virtually no legitimacy to individuality as such." Rather, he argues for the reinvigoration of the individual's ties with the concentric circles of family, tribe, people (a family of tribes), culture, history, literary sources, and, ultimately, God. Schweid's Jew is inextricably bound with these larger social and cultural entities; Soloveitchik's "Lonely Man of Faith" is "endemically homeless." The contrast between the two is a parable on the key distinctions between Israeli and American Jewries. Perhaps unintentionally, perhaps not, Cohen's comparative analysis of these two leading Jewish thinkers sheds an indirect but very illuminating light on key distinctions between Israeli and American Judaism.

In a study that seeks to examine the patterns of Jewish identity characterizing the perceptions of Israeli youths toward Jewish texts, Asher Shkedi analyzes the tension between modernity and Judaism—a subtheme of this entire volume—in the context of Israeli Jewish education. He reports the results of an ethnographic investigation in which Israeli students of varying backgrounds offered their reactions to a small piece of traditional Jewish text. Shkedi delineates a variety of reactions that remarkably resemble those offered by Meyer in the first chapter of this collection. At one extreme, students manifest a distancing from the text, rejecting any personal connection therewith. At the other, some of the more religious students manifest "isolation" wherein they close off any perspectives on the text outside of the Jewish tradition. Between these two poles lie various other reactions, including belonging, ideational, academic, and theocentric. Clearly, the religious-secular dimension, seen as crucial and distinctively Israeli by members of the society, is a crucial axis of social differentiation that makes itself felt in shaping students' reactions to a classic Jewish text. While the reactions may be substantively different, all contend with modernity's challenge to Judaism, one that is readily apparent even in Israel, the one society where Jews are sovereign, and where they constitute the numerically overwhelming and culturally dominant majority. Even (or especially?) here, as Shkedi details, Jewish youngsters display the full spectrum of responses to the modern Jewish predicament.

The fully textured Israeli society, and the multiple waves of immigration from a wide variety of native lands set the stage for the development and maintenance of several levels of Jewish group and subgroup identity. In the concluding chapter of this volume, Stephen Sharot argues that "Jewish identity in Israel is differentiated from but interpenetrates and overlaps with, other national and ethnic identities." Among them are those based on national origin, as well as on the multinational categories of Ashkenazi and Sephardi identities. Sharot analyzes the factors that influence the perpetuation of these identities and delineates several configurations. Rather than seeing these layers in competition, he argues that "people [including Israeli, and no doubt, other Jews as well] may have more than one identity based upon common descent."

None of the authors is particularly happy with the term *identity* (although their dissatisfaction was more apparent at the conference than in this book). The chief problem is that the term *identity*, tends to connote a highly individualist phenomenon, sounding like something that the individual carries around with him or her. The term fails to automatically convey the notion of an ongoing social interaction in which individuals, acting and interacting as members of a group in a larger social context, shape their own images of themselves even as they shape the images held by others of themselves. The processes of identity formation, projection, and negotiation are intertwined empirically and are nearly inextricable analytically. Yet "identity" lacks that dynamic, interactionist quality, and it seems, at first blush, to reside within individuals rather than within groups in a social context.

Notwithstanding the widespread dissatisfaction with the term *identity*, no participant at the conference could offer an acceptable substitute. Perhaps, we are not yet totally capable of stepping out of our "individualistic" skins and fully adopting a more contextualized and interactionist approach to culture and Jewishness for our thinking and writing. Moreover, the English language (and very probably French, Hebrew, and others) contains no single word that would immediately convey the social, communal, and fluid nature of identity. Thus, for want of a better term, the chapters in this volume are stuck with *identity*, when, in fact, they almost universally refer to something richer, more nuanced, more malleable, and decidedly more interactive. Perhaps *culture* would do, but then, how would it be applied to the individual? Would one speak of someone being more or less Jewishly "enculturated," or enculturated in a fashion different from another or a member of a different society?

As a first step toward a contextualized and interactionist study of Jewish and other group identities particularly within the context of Israeli society and culture, Gabriel Horenczyk and Zvi Bekerman ground themselves in social constructivist perspectives, especially in the Social Representations approach. Within this framework, Horenczyk and Bekerman propose a theoretical conceptualization and a methodology aimed at exploring the meanings people assign to their ethnic and national identities, and the role ethnicity and nationality play in the construction of their social and cultural worlds. In order to understand the social and cultural anchoring of the social representations of ethnic and national identities, they developed the "associations grid" as a quantitative research tool for investigating the associative meanings attached to ethnic and national concepts. Using multidimensional scaling techniques, they describe the different social constructions of ethnicity, nationality, and religion among different subcultures of Israeli society (secular Jewish Israelis, Arabs, and newcomers from the former Soviet Union). The configuration obtained from the secular Israelis, for example, portrays the complex nature of their Jewish identity. Jewishness is, on the one hand, seen as part of the "religious other," sharply differentiated from Israeliness that is associated with Western modern values. On the other hand, Jewishness and Israeliness seem to come together when facing the "political other" represented primarily by Arabs and Islam.

Horenczyk and Bekerman also put forward the notion of the "constructivist" aspect of ethnic or national identity—the extent to which individuals use ethnicity and nationality to construe their social and cultural worlds. They claim that this notion of the constructivist use of Jewishness is increasingly relevant for the understanding of modern Jewish identity, especially for the study of the identity of those Jewish individuals and groups who do not tend to grant behavioral or attitudinal expression to their Jewishness in the ways usually measured by pollsters and social scientists.

We can now return to the key question: how does Jewish identity vary and why? A synthesis of the chapters contained here provide the beginnings of an answer.

First, let's deal with the "how."

One theme cursing through many of the chapters is the distinction between ethnic, religious, or national definitions of being Jewish. Jews in different lands vary in the extent to which they place primary emphasis on each of these principal alternative conceptualizations. It should be noted, however, that the meanings of these labels also vary significantly across cultures; for example, *nationality* is understood (and politically used) in a markedly different way in the former Soviet Union and in Israel; the term *ethnic*, carries different meanings in Israel, the former Soviet Union, and in the United States. Even the word "religion," is interpreted very differently by American and Israeli Jews. It is the ambiguity of these labels that leads very often to "communication breakdowns" in the efforts to bring together Jews from different cultures and nationalities to discuss aspects of their cultural identities.

A second variation entails the investment of one's circumstances, condition, or environment with Jewish meaning. American Jews equate social justice with being Jewish, and see social achievement as a defining feature of Jewishness. For all but the more religious French Jewry, and now perhaps for a more ethnically assertive segment, commitment to laicity and secularism is intrinsic to Judaism.

Why do Jews define themselves in terms of one or another dimension? The larger societal context is clearly the key factor. Jews are defined nationally where they are a nation (Israel). In many Western countries, which are ultimately inhospitable to enduring ethnic differences, the religious definition is the only one that is socially acceptable (even desirable). (Of course, in places like California where, for middle-class whites, neither religion nor ethnicity are particularly attractive, one wonders whether Jews can sustain a strong Jewish group definition.) The ethnic dimension is strongest in countries riven with ethnic strife or where nationalities, races, tribes, or immigrant groups are officially—or unofficially—recognized social entities.

However, individual or subgroup differences should also be taken into account. While the religious definition for Jewishness is widely accepted by American Jews, for example, many Jews see themselves as "Jewish in an ethnic sense" or tend to adopt a cultural or national-Zionist interpretation of their Jewish identity. This type of intragroup variation can also be attributed in part to societal factors, differentially affecting the various Jewish subgroups within larger cultural and national contexts. It seems to us, however, that a more complete understanding of Jewish definition and identity will also need to address individual factors, such as family socialization, Jewish schooling, as well as the person's values and beliefs.

Political and social fractures within the societies within which Jews reside, and are part of, have led Jews to align with one or another political, cultural, or social tendency. If the fractures are enduring enough (as they frequently are), if the issue(s) are those that can be interpreted as Judaically meaningful, and if Jews tend to cluster in one part of the cultural or political map, then that choice can, over time, acquire Jewish meaning. In other words, Jews can come to believe that advocating abolition of apartheid, or democratic reforms, or separation of church and state, or relaxation of immigration restrictions are reflective of, or even part and parcel of, traditional Jewish values, as they come to understand (and reinterpret) them.

These processes are but a special case of a more general phenomenon. Jews in various societies often take meaningful aspects of their condition, their environment, or their characteristics and invest them with Jewish meaning. Thus, as Prell notes, social mobility and achievement become associated with being Jewish in America. Involvement in the arts, literature, music, and other cultural pursuits are seen as quintessentially Jewish by Central European and Russian Jews. Israelis see the army experience, and more generally, their support for the state, as intimately bound up with their idea of the good Jew. And on and on. While this reformulation and reconstruction of Jewishness and Jewish values is an important accomplishment of modern Jews in their various national and cultural contexts, the cultural and ideological context of these formulations should be seriously taken into account. Many secular Israelis may point to the army when asked "How do you express your Jewishness?" as part of their rhetorical stance in the cultural struggle taking place within Israeli society over the meanings of Jewishness and Israeliness. They may not, however, refer to their Jewishness when asked "What are the values you associate with your service in the army?" The analysis of the argumentative function of Jewish discourse seems thus crucial for our understanding of the cultural (and subcultural) variations in modern Jewish identity.

Certainly, as we stated at the outset, Jews worldwide share numerous features. But, most assuredly, insofar as Jews are geographically dispersed, and insofar as they participate in, and are influenced by, their various national and cultural environments, and to the extent to which they incorporate elements from those cultures and their lives into their conceptions of being Jewish, Jews around the world will also display significant variations in their Jewish identities.

References

Berger, Peter. (1979) *The Heretical Imperative: Contemporary Possibilities of Religious Affirmation*. Garden City, New York: Anchor Books.

Birnbaum, Pierre, and Ira Katznelson, eds. (1995) *Paths to Emancipation*. New York: Oxford University Press.

Glazer, Nathan and Patrick Moynihan. (1963). *Beyond the Melting Pot*. Cambridge: MIT Press.

Gordon, Milton. (1964) *Assimilation in American Life*. New York: Oxford University Press.

Katz, Jacob. (1961; reprint, 1971) *Tradition and Crisis: Jewish Society at the End of the Middle Ages*. New York: Schocken.

———. (1973; reprint, 1978) *Out of the Ghetto*. New York: Schocken.

Liebman, Charles, and Steven M. Cohen. (1990) *Two Worlds of Judaism: The Israeli and American Experiences*. New Haven: Yale University Press.

Part I

Jewish Responses to Modernity

Chapter 1

✑

Being Jewish and. . . .

Michael A. Meyer

The dynamics of Jewish identity since the eighteenth century is best understood by the interplay of three forces—rationalism, anti-Semitism, and Zionism. These served to define, as well as to strengthen or weaken it. Here, however, I would like to concentrate less on causes and effects and more on the nature and substance of Jewish identity. My first task will be to show how modernity both fragmented Jewish identity and prompted the creation of a survival mechanism in the form of an ideologized Jewish relevance beyond the circle of Judaism itself. My focus will then shift to the nature of the borders between the Jewish identity of the Jew and the non-Jewish identities that a particular environment offers. My examples here will be taken mainly from Central Europe and from the United States. Finally, I shall try to draw out the implications of Jewish identity structures for contemporary Jewish education.

Contraction

If one compares modern with premodern Jewish identity, one is struck, above all, by its greater narrowness. Self-consciously or not, modern Jews appropriated only a portion of the totality available to them. What had been encompassing became segmental. One no longer identified fully with all Jews or with all elements that made up Judaism. This holds true for identification both with the Jewish past and with the Jewish present.

The first modern Jews to study their past critically and from a distance did so, in large measure, in order to liberate themselves from it. A studied past became a mastered past, a desacralized past. Once put into the historical context of their origins, norms tend to lose the binding force that they possessed before such examination. In the end they may regain it, but only after renewed affirmation. As historical analysis and critique, Wissenschaft des Judentums (The Scientific Study of Judaism) was a destroyer of continuity. As it raised consciousness of the Jewish past as variegated and diverse, it necessarily also raised questions of identification with it. What was still binding and what not? What was Jewish and what was really foreign, imported as the result of an earlier encounter of Jews with non-Jews? In short, studying the past led to throwing out at least some of it, declaring it not part of one's own Jewish identity even if it had been part of one's ancestors' Jewishness.

Needless to say, this was not an objective process. What state or society or intellectual fashion regarded as harmful or simply inappropriate very much affected what Jews cast out. This influence of the environment is most obvious in the comparison between the Jews of Eastern and Western Europe. In the East, ethnic differences were acceptable in the multinational empires of the nineteenth century; in the West they were not. Thus cultural Jewish nationalism was much more at home in czarist Russia and Poland than in Germany, France, or England. To the degree that it existed in the West, it had to be veiled as religious difference, the only kind of difference that was politically acceptable. In the East, Jews could abandon religious belief (e.g., as Simon Dubnow and Ahad Ha-Am did), and still regard themselves—and be regarded by others—as fully Jews. In the West, Jews could (and felt they should) do the same with Jewish national ties, but they could not, without bucking the cultural context, declare themselves both atheists and Jews. The United States represents a much less clear-cut case. Not only did its Jewry only gradually amalgamate from the ethnically diverse Jewries of East and West, but American public opinion has been inconsistent with regard to the long-term role of ethnic traditions within American public life. American Jews could never be certain about the nature of their ethnicity and which forms of identity were acceptable in their country and which were not.

Of course, the casting out had its counterpart in the affirmation of the remaining elements. These were often deemed the "essence" of Judaism and, as such, served as the basis for Jewish identity. Collectively, they became its historical component. But Jews differed, not only along the religion versus nation axis, but also within each category. For the religionists the divisive questions were theological: Does the Jewish religion require belief in revelation at Mount Sinai or only in a divine illumination reflected in human documents and progressively better understood? Does Jewish law continue to have binding force? Is it subject to human alteration? For the nationalists, the principal question was: Does Jewish tradition impose upon Jewish nationality some secular, if not religious form of chosenness or is it compatible with the quest for national normalcy? If the former, then the Jewish past bequeaths a content that sets the people of Israel apart. If the latter, then difference is limited mostly to forms, especially language. Thus the Jewish past remained crucial for Jewish identity, but it now consisted of selective readings, selective affirmations. Jewish scholarship militated against distortion of the past, but it did not prevent—indeed it facilitated—the combination of its materials into varying and even conflicting "usable" pasts.

A similar narrowing of identification occurred with regard to Jewish life in the present. To be sure, the sense of *kelal yisrael* (Jewish peoplehood) had always been modulated by internal differences, between Sephardim and Ashkenazim, for example, but in the modern world these distinctions became sharper and took on various forms. When some Jews began to refer to themselves as "Israelites" or "Mosaites," they meant thereby to indicate both a break with the past and a separation between themselves and those of their coreligionists who still embodied the characteristics associated with the term *Jew* in the public mind. This name change phenomenon, usually associated with the early nineteenth-century Jews of France and Germany, was, of course, not limited to them. The Zionists, too, wanted a new self-designation, and some of them alighted upon the same term, Hebrew (*ivri*), which had become especially popular among pre-Zionist or non-Zionist Jews in the United States. "To be or not to be!" wrote Berdichevski: "To be the last Jews or the first Hebrews."

The modern age is characterized by a proliferation of Jewish subidentities that sometimes weigh more heavily than the larger category of which they supposedly represent a branch. For German Jews, for example, their Germanness made them a clearly different sort of Jew and they wanted to emphasize that difference vis-à-vis *Ostjuden* (East European Jews), whether the ones still in the East or those who had joined them in Germany or America. For some Reform Jews, only the adjective "Reform" made possible the identity of "Jew."

This narrowed identity was reflected most clearly—as identity shifts usually are—in Jewish education. The redefinition of Jewishness purely in terms of Jewish belief called for the use of the catechism as the most appropriate vehicle of instruction. To be a religious Jew in the nineteenth century required knowing the principles of the faith. Thus it became common in Orthodox as in Reform circles to teach "theology to little tots of seven or eight," as the educator Emanuel Gamoran once called it derisively. National Jewish identity, on the other hand, required attention to the historical experience of the Jewish people, and hence the textbook was a simplified and inspirational version of Jewish history. Gradually the two came together as Jewish nationalism penetrated the synagogue.

Justification

Once Jewish identity had become less than total, it seemed the more imperative to argue for the significance of what remained. Paradoxically, sometimes the grandeur of the claims made for it increased proportionately as its scope declined. Convinced that being a Jew in the modern world meant maintaining a religious tradition but not an ethnic one, Abraham Geiger declared that the Jews were nothing less than "the people of revelation." It was not that they had prophets among them that entitled them to the designation, but that they possessed a collective religious genius. Zacharias Frankel went still further when he declared that revelation continued within contemporary Israel, a revelation, he insisted, of no less authority than that at Sinai. And Samson Raphael Hirsch, in refusing every theological concession to modernity, made Judaism as absolute as its supernatural source.

Although it is a novelty of the modern period, the concept of the "mission of Israel" among the Gentiles has very little to do with religious reform. Rather it is the consequence of non-Jews and Jews calling Jewish viability into question. In order to sustain loyalty to Judaism, it was felt necessary to show that Jews as Jews could contribute something to the modern world that it did not yet fully possess. For those who reduced Judaism to a religion, the contribution had to be religious; for national Jews it had to be cast in terms of political or social institutions.

Thus the mission of Israel appears already in the writings of Moses Mendelssohn and in all three of the modern religious currents that developed in Germany and that were later transplanted to the United States. During the period that Jews lived ghettoized, the "chosen people" concept had shored them up in times of persecution: in the long run, God would not neglect the people God had chosen. The mission of Israel concept played a similar role. At a time when it was not Israel's suffering and threatened physical survival that raised theological questions, but Israel's prosperity and assimilation, the notion that Jews still had an important contribution to make as religious Jews saved them from despairing of the significance of their faith and of its survival in a more hospitable environment. The mission of Israel is no less ethnocentric an idea than Israel's chosenness. This was the more so when the argument was made that not only was Israel called upon to teach a more lofty religious and moral truth to the Gentiles, but in the end the Gentiles would leave their own tradition behind and adopt a universalized form of Judaism itself. Before the nineteenth century would close, the American religious reformer Isaac Mayer Wise was convinced, "Judaism will be THE religion of the great majority of intelligent men in this country." It is not surprising that anti-Semites picked on the mission of Israel as prima facie evidence of Jewish arrogance.

The counterpart of the mission of Israel doctrine in Zionism is the notion that the Jews will build a model society in Zion. Indeed, ideological reconciliation between Western Judaism and Zionism became possible in no small measure because some Zionists, Ben-Gurion among them, wanted a state that would embody prophetic values and exemplify them for the world. On the other hand, the Zionism of secular normalcy was viewed with ambivalence even by American religious leaders like Solomon Schechter, who were more sympathetic to those thinkers—Ahad Ha-Am, for example—that at least stressed its unique moral foundations.

But raising the significance of the selected elements or interpretation of the Jewish past and future was only part of what Jewish viability seemed to require. Jewish identity had not only become selective with regard to its own totality, it had also been forced to make room for competing identities that had their own historical traditions and their own vision of the future. The relation between Jewish identity and these other identities ranged from incompatibility to compartmentalization, harmonization, and finally to complete identification. Let me describe each of these alternatives.

Incompatibility

The most radical position on the one extreme was that which attempted to keep the premodern, encompassing Jewish identity intact by seeking to exclude competing influences altogether. That was possible only if Jewish education remained unchanged, limited to the sacred texts of Judaism. There could be no room for secular subjects except insofar as they were required for practical purposes like business or medical care. The obvious example of this approach is Rabbi Moses Sofer of Pressburg, who still in the 1830s tried to hold out against every intrusion of modern thought or values into the sacred sphere of Judaism. He and his disciples were determined to remain Jews without conjunction: Jews and only Jews, not Jews and anything else. Sofer's position stands out because he was the first to fully recognize the dangers of modernization for the traditional life and tried to raise the barrier as high as possible. But it was not an isolated position. It became characteristic for Jewish Orthodoxy in Eastern Europe and has its advocates among the ultra-Orthodox today. It is a strategy of maximal exclusion for the sake of containing the identity of Jews as completely as possible within the Jewish sphere.

For the rest of the Jewish spectrum in modern times the category of incompatibility was less inclusive but no less important. Those Jews who were ready to make peace with the segmentation of Jewish identity nonetheless had to erect their own barriers. Given that some elements of non-Jewish culture were compatible with Judaism, that did not mean all were. The converse of affirming a segmental Jewish identity was the negation of non-Jewish identity elements that were seen to conflict with it. Not every possibility was permissible on the other side of the conjunction.

As one reads the theologians, ideologists, and scholars of German Jewry in the nineteenth century one is struck by the recurrence of a particular identity that in their eyes stood in irreconcilable contradiction with Judaism. One could not be a Jew, they held, and at the same time a pagan. In eighteenth- and nineteenth-century Europe, paganism experienced a lively revival. One can easily draw the line from Voltaire to Nietzsche. But Jewish writers did not restrict themselves to obvious examples. They found paganism—the very antithesis of Judaism, they believed—as an essential element in both German philosophy and Christianity. The Jewish theologian Solomon Ludwig Steinheim declared Judaism the religion of revelation and paganism the epitome of its denial. "You can be only one or the other," he wrote, "either a heathen and a philosopher or a believer in revelation." One had to camp either with the Jews on Mount Gerizim or with the pagans on Mount Ebal. His contemporary Solomon Formstecher presents the same dichotomy, but in terms of his particular theology: paganism represents the religion of nature; Judaism that of spirit. Perhaps the most vehement of the German theologians on the question was Samuel Hirsch who, in struggling with the then dominant Hegelian philosophy, could not brand it with a more damning epithet than to call it a "sublimated paganism."

Both contemporary manifestations of paganism, philosophy and Christianity, were seen as threats to Jewish survival. The first gave intellectual and moral sanction to a secularism that could and did frequently displace a Jewish identity which, as mentioned earlier, in the Central and West European context had to be expressed in terms of religion. The second, as the majority faith, tempted its prospective proselytes with all manner of political, professional, and social advantages. Not surprisingly, Heinrich Graetz's *History of the Jews*, written more to strengthen Jewish identity than to contribute to knowledge, is harsh on pagans, Christians, and certain contemporary philosophers. He knows that their principles undermine Judaism. When, at the end of the nineteenth century, paganism did penetrate Jewish thought, it occurred among Eastern European Jews. The Hebrew poet Saul Tchernichovski, writing in veneration of the pagan god Apollo, could prostrate himself before "life, strength, and beauty." For Jews in the West, whether or not they were Orthodox, such adulation meant the negation of Jewish identity as they had defined it. Indeed, the revolutionary thrust of Tchernichovski's poetry, like Berdichevski's essays, could be contained only within the framework of a national identity for which the religious tradition was not an essential component.

Were there also political ideologies that were deemed incompatible? I must admit that I know of none save those that posed a direct threat to Jews because they openly espoused anti-Semitism. Jews in Europe and the United States tended to be concentrated in certain segments of the political spectrum but they were not absent from any portion of it that was not hostile to their interests as Jews. In the twentieth century some Italian Jews became fascists; and a few German Jews were sympathetic to Nazi political philosophy on every point save its anti-Semitism. Rabbis did preach against communism, but mainly on account of its atheism. It, too, was a form of paganism.

Finally, for some religious Jews, historical criticism was a product of modernity they judged incompatible with Judaism. Samson Raphael Hirsch may have differed from Moses Sofer in allowing for *derekh erets* alongside Torah, but, unlike the spokespersons for a non-Orthodox Judaism, he had to reject historical Wissenschaft (scientific analysis) when applied to Judaism. Jewish identity was based on belief in the divine origins of both the Written and the Oral Law. To hold, on the basis of research, that the law was of human origin, even in part, meant to undermine what was fundamental to being a Jew. The Jewish religious conservatives in Germany drew the line between Torah and Talmud; the reformers denied the very possibility of incompatibility and hence gave history precedence over text. For some of the critical scholars themselves, their study—ironically perhaps—itself became an expression of their identity as Jews.

Compartmentalization

A second possible way of relating a narrowed Jewish identity to competing external identities was to set the Jewish and non-Jewish apart without dwelling too much on their relation. Moses Mendelssohn pioneered this solution, though he did not stick with it. Early in his career, Mendelssohn lived, as it were, in two worlds, that of Judaism and that of the German Enlightenment. He was at once a man of the Aufklerung (Enlightenment) and an observant Jew. It was only when non-Jews began to question whether that dichotomy did not represent a contradiction that Mendelssohn was forced to confront the issue and move from the position of compartmentalization to that of harmonization.

Yet even though Mendelssohn abandoned his first position, it did live on. Perhaps the best contemporary example is within the modern Orthodox community where scientific training is acceptable and even desirable, but where the question of whether its implications may be incompatible with the traditional theology of Judaism is seldom explored. The contemporary position is best characterized as the practical appropriation of elements external to Judaism with the firm intent of not allowing the consequences of such appropriation to affect the Jewish segment of identity. One is both scientist and Orthodox Jew, but the former identity is not integrated, except superficially, with the latter.

Harmonization

More common than compartmentalization is harmonization. This is a process whereby certain non-Jewish elements with which Jews come to identify are seen as not conflicting with the Jewish ones, but rather complementing or enhancing them. This has been the path taken by modern Jews almost invariably with regard to the literary and artistic cultures of the nations into whose midst they were thrust by Emancipation. Beginning as outsiders, they became enthusiasts and soon also active participants. One need only read Samson Raphael Hirsch's rapturous exaltation of the poet Friedrich Schiller or Hermann Cohen's encomiums on Kant to appreciate how deeply German Jews across the religious spectrum had come to identify with the host culture. In the writings of most, if not all of its leading figures, they discerned cultural values that they believed were fully compatible with the religious ones that defined them as Jews. They frequently noted the affinities. Recently scholars have emphasized the creation and persistence of Jewish subcultures in the age of Emancipation. The notion is valid in that even Central and West European Jews maintained ties that were broader than the officially sanctioned ones of religion. But the intellectual and aesthetic culture of Jews in the West was dominantly German or French or English or American. That was true for Zionists almost to the same degree as it was for non-Zionists. Only in the East, where the Haskalah and then the Zionist revival were able to use Yiddish and Hebrew could one speak meaningfully of a primary Jewish culture. Except for very limited circles, Jewish cultural creativity in the West was secondary to the non-Jewish national culture. Thus most Jews there were Jewish by religion and European by culture, each selectively, each complementing, and enhancing the other—but each also competing for attention in a competition that the Jewish sector gradually lost.

The harmonization mode has been as common in politics as in culture. Perhaps the best example here is *liberalism*. The term itself is equivocal, referring both to a political philosophy and to a religious one. German Jews toward the end of the nineteenth century frequently called themselves inclusively "liberals," designating thereby their religious affiliation as well as their place on the political spectrum. For them, liberalism had moved to the center of individual identity and become its chief determinant. As a generalized governing principle, it manifested itself concurrently in their political and religious lives. As liberals, they could be neither conservative in politics nor orthodox in religion. Their Judaism had to meet the test of a more fundamental Weltanschauung (world outlook).

Although locating liberalism at the center of identity was especially characteristic for German Jews, it has also been common in the United States. Rabbi Stephen S. Wise presents a good example. His preference for the noninstitutional designation "Liberal Judaism" not only reflected his distaste for denomination and division, it was also a way to bring together his own religious and political commitments. Devotion to the one reinforced devotion to the other. What was true for Wise remains true for Jewish liberals in the United States today. Still, a majority of American Jews remained loyal to liberalism even in political climates where the designation had become unpopular. Liberalism for them continues to serve as a connector between Jewish and non-Jewish identifications.

Further to the left on the political spectrum, the linguistic identity no longer obtains. To be a socialist Jew does not designate a particular approach to the Jewish religion. But those Jews who became socialists (except for extremists like Leon Trotsky and Rosa Luxemburg) did attempt to find common ground between their Judaism and their socialism. A good example here is the utopian socialist and Zionist Nahman Syrkin. For Syrkin, Jewish history was "nothing else than the unending struggle of the prophetic ideal for realization," which meant the attainment of economic equality. He urged the creation of "a truly Jewish socialism." For Syrkin and many others among the non-Marxist socialists both inside and outside the camp of Zionism, a selective reading of Judaism, focusing upon the message of social justice enunciated by the biblical prophets together with a socialism stripped of historical determinism, yielded a single foundation of values and therefore the basis for an integrated identity, at once Jewish and socialist.

Equivalency

At the furthest remove from declaring all or some external values or traditions incompatible with Judaism was finding them identical with it. Declarations that give evidence of such equivalency cannot be dismissed as mere hyperbole, even if they do tend to occur in rhetorical contexts. Rather, they are born of a single fundamental commitment that cannot be split in two, not even into parts that could be recognized as fully harmonious. My example here is the famous statement of Justice Louis Brandeis made to a gathering of Reform rabbis. "The Jewish spirit, the product of our religion and experiences," Brandeis insisted, "is essentially modern and essentially American." The Jewish pioneers in Palestine, as Brandeis saw them, were nothing less than "Jewish pilgrim fathers." The anti-Zionist rabbi, David Philipson, may have thoroughly differed with Brandeis on whether Zionism was either Jewish or American, but not on the essential identity of the latter two. His bookplate illustrates his position clearly: an American flag and a flag emblazoned with the Ten Commandments overlap each other in the foreground with George Washington and (Michelangelo's) Moses looking on benignly from behind. Here, at least ideally, a single encompassing identity has been created anew, but this time welded together from two independent historical traditions, their diversity minimized for the sake of oneness.

All of these modern permutations of Jewish identity still exist today. Of the first and last—the utter rejection of competing identifications that characterizes contemporary ultra-Orthodoxy and the refusal to contrast Americanism and Judaism that especially marks the perpetuators of classical Reform Judaism—we may note that they require no conjunction. But they represent only a small minority of Diaspora Jews today. Most live with the necessity of selecting and reselecting whatever lies historically within the Jewish sphere that is still worth affirming, of locating the boundaries between that sphere and other loyalties, and of determining the relationship between the territories on each side of the division. How we use Jewish education to instill Jewish identity depends largely on how we deal with these issues.

Educational Implications

Diaspora Jewry lives in an environment where the social barriers that preserved its biologic continuity even in the absence of salient shared religious or Jewish nationalist commitments are falling with a rapidity that is at the same time morally admirable and existentially disastrous for Jewish continuity. How is Jewish education, once the dispensable support of social segregation, to become its functional substitute?

In trying to answer this question we confront a dilemma that has been fundamental for Jewish education throughout modern times. Phrased in terms of my analysis, the dilemma is this: If the educator takes a position toward the incompatibility end of the spectrum, emphasizing how different Jews and Judaism are (or should be) from non-Jews and non-Judaism, he or she runs the risk of not being heard. If, on the other hand, the teacher's stance is closer to the other extreme, where Judaism's relevance is clearly apparent, that relevance is likely to be purchased at the price of its individuality and hence of the Jews' survival as a distinctive entity.

Given the realities of Diaspora Jewish life, it is totally unrealistic to believe that Jewish education can begin from within the sphere of Judaism. Outside of cloistered circles, the issue is no longer "Being Jewish and. . . ." It is the other way around: "My child is assuming many identities; I'd like her or him also to become Jewish." While ideally we would want the Jewish identity to come first in the process of identity formation, that can occur only in the home, not in the school. Educators have no choice but to begin with what is already there. As Franz Rosenzweig already realized with regard to adults when he created his *Freies Jüdisches Lehrhaus* (Free Jewish Study Center) in Frankfurt after World War I, Jews whose locus of identity lies so far beyond the boundary marker with Judaism can only gradually, step-by-step, be led across it.

A philosophy of Jewish education whose goal is to create separation through dissonance (a technique among some recruiters for Orthodox institutions) will only create disaffection. To be successful, Jewish education must begin with harmonization, interrelating the Jewish values that are taught with those that have equivalents in the contemporary world outside Judaism. Examples would be the moral values underlying environmentalism, nondiscrimination, or reverence for all of life. But not to go beyond this approach means to depict Judaism simply as a yea-sayer to the Zeitgeist and hence as entirely dispensable. Pointing out how much Judaism shares with contemporary culture, except as an opening gambit, is a luxury we may have been able to afford earlier in our social history but cannot any longer.

Our contemporary social and demographic situation demands that the ultimate stress be on disjunction and difference, not on similarity. The task is to delineate more clearly the boundary between the Jewish self and the non-Jewish one and to show how the two spheres, while they may in some respects be similar or complementary, contain elements that cannot be reconciled. That means the process of selection (a process as essential for Jewish education as it is for Jewish identity formation) will come to focus on those elements in Judaism that make it unique. Showing the Jewish child

"Where Judaism Differed" (the title of a book written by Rabbi Abba Hillel Silver more than forty years ago) would be a useful way of defining the objective of the Jewish history curriculum. Pointing out where Judaism differs *today* is perhaps even more important.

Of course, the intellectual component is only part of the educational enterprise and when one is educating for identity perhaps less consequential than nurturing emotional attachment. The latter, however, depends on experiences, not knowledge. Ideally, such experiences are recurrent, in the nature of ritual acts rather than in one-time life-cycle events or personal confrontations with Holocaust sites or with the State of Israel. But the common element in these is their particularity. Jews and only Jews observe the Sabbath in this manner, have undergone an unparalleled disaster, and have re-created a national culture in a land that for millennia was not theirs.

It is time also to emphasize the negative: "To be a Jew is not to be. . . ."—especially not a Christian, but also not a pagan and not a syncretist. The lines of incompatibility need to be redrawn for our time and conveyed to our children. I fully realize how difficult this is in an age of families that are multiply diverse. But there can be no effective yea without an unabashed nay.

Obviously, Jewish education should not end in negation. The positive task is to increase the territory lying within the segmented sphere of personal identity that is recognized as Jewish and to make it fundamental for identity as a whole, both in its separation and uniqueness and as the integrator of a larger totality. Within the specifically Jewish realm, Jewish education needs to shape patterns of thought and action in ways that render them most impervious to dissolution. Beyond the Jewish sphere, its goal is well expressed in a phrase already employed by Judah Leon Magnes that has recently gained popularity: to enable Jewish children to see their entire world "through Jewish eyes." The two spheres together—the enhanced and sharply differentiated specifically Jewish one along with its non-Jewish counterpart penetrated by Jewish vision and purpose—can constitute a viable Jewish identity, even today.

Chapter 2

✺

Jewish Religious, Ethnic, and National Identities: Convergences and Conflicts

---

Daniel J. Elazar

It hardly needs to be said that the concept of "identity" as a (perhaps *the*) touchstone of Jewish life is an entirely modern and postmodern one, indeed, mostly the latter. Throughout all previous epochs of Jewish history from the beginning through the modern epoch, Jews knew who was a Jew and how. Of course there were questions around the peripheries. In Hellenistic times many Jews assimilated and other non-Jews became Jews or Judaizers and distinctions had to be made between who was who. Problems arose with Marranos in various periods in Jewish history, but for the vast majority of Jews, not only was their identity clear but the issue never came up and the concept was foreign to them. In many cases, for non-Jews, who was a Jew was even more clear in the sense that they often defined even Jews who had converted to other religions as Jews for their own reasons. The question of identity, then, is at most a modern question and, with perhaps the exception of a few Western European countries, has received attention as such by Jews only since World War II.

Efforts at Jewish Polity Building and the Emergence
of the Pattern of "Jewish Identity"

Prior to the modern epoch, it was not possible to separate Jewish religious, ethnic, and national identities. Nor would the possibility have occurred either to Jews or to non-Jews of the time. Every period that might be characterized as a time of crisis in identity was directly connected with some issue confronting the Jewish people as a collectivity, either constitutional, national or political, and usually involving all three elements. Although we have little concrete information other than the biblical account, the Bible clearly suggests that this was the case with regard to the Exodus from Egypt and to the establishment of the monarchy a few centuries later. The division of Israel into two kingdoms could have separated Jewish religious and political identities but in fact did not. Indeed, the Bible describes the establishment of a new common framework to unite the citizens of the two kingdoms, which is referred to as *aheinu bnai yisrael*, which can be translated as "our brother Israelites," recognizing kinship as the basis.

The next crisis that we might refer to as involving issues of identity was at the end of the eighth century B.C.E. after the destruction of the northern kingdom by Assyria when Judah under the rule of King Hezekiah extended its control over much of the territory of the destroyed kingdom. Judah welcomed many refugees from the north, and thereby included all of those Jews who remained identified as Jews in Eretz Israel. However, it could not reach out to those Jews exiled by the Assyrians who became known in the collective Jewish memory as the ten lost tribes. Although the latter disappeared as political entities, some families among them, maybe even quite a few, survived as Jews and later rejoined the Jewish exiles from Judah after Nebuchadnezzar destroyed the southern kingdom early in the sixth century B.C.E.

The destruction of Judah in 586 B.C.E. undoubtedly provoked another crisis as Jews had to find a way to preserve their identity outside of a territorial state. It was in the wake of that crisis that the Jewish Diaspora came into being and began to develop its own communal institutions to preserve Diaspora Jewries. That initiated a new era in Jewish history, one in which it was no longer possible to preserve Jewish identity primarily through territorially based political entities.

New political arrangements were found at the time of Ezra and Nehemiah during the second Jewish return from Babylon or, more accurately, from the empire of the Medes and the Persians in the middle of the fifth century B.C.E. Only a minority of the Jews in the world actually settled or resettled in Judea (or the Persian province of Yahud). Accordingly, the Anshe Knesset Hagedolah, constituted as their governing body, made provision for symbolic representation from the Jewish Diaspora, consisting of a few men who would come to Judea for a few years to represent their Diaspora communities. This device, the conjunction with the rebuilding of the Temple and the half-shekel Temple tax throughout the Diaspora, provided a formal linkage among all Jews. In point of fact, the problems of transportation and communication—in other words, insufficient technology—kept this linkage more symbolic than real. It disappeared by the end of the Bar Kochba revolt.

Another kind of arrangement came during the ascendancy of the Resh Galuta and the *yeshivot* of Babylonia during the initial period of Arab Muslim ascendancy in West Asia and a good part of the Mediterranean littoral. When the Arab empire was at its height by the end of the eighth or the early ninth centuries C.E., a majority of the Jews of the world were living within it and subject to the authority of those great Jewish institutions in Babylonia. The very grave problems of transportation and communication were sufficiently overcome to keep the Jewish communities in the Islamic world within the common Jewish polity and within the leadership of its institutions. This situation lasted until the Arab empire began to break up and local rulers wanted to detach "their" Jews from loyalties to Babylonia for purposes of their own empire-building. The system began to collapse in the tenth century and by the middle of the eleventh was totally disrupted.

After that, the Jews scattered throughout the world, often in small local communities, especially in Europe that increasingly held an ever-larger share of the Jewish population as Jews migrated to the Ashkenazic lands and as Spain was reconquered by Christian rulers who set up a number of small kingdoms in place of al-Andalus, the Iberian Arab empire. Jews were able to maintain only a semblance of unity through the responsa of *posekim* (Halakic decisors), carried by Jewish merchants and other travelers to far-flung Jewish communities. While this system of responsa correspondence was more or less worldwide, it was never able to develop beyond a system of authoritative correspondence. On one hand, it was successful in keeping virtually all Jews within a common Halakic tradition; but, on the other, it could not provide them with the executive institutions needed to enable their polity to function as such.

The Jewish situation in this respect worsened in the modern epoch, beginning in the seventeenth century and decisively spreading in the eighteenth. The autonomous Jewish communities were destroyed by the non-Jewish rulers in country after country even before the individual Jews were emancipated. Thus it was no longer necessary for increasing numbers of Jews even to be bound by Halakic decisions as interpreted by their *posekim*, thereby disrupting even the limited but still effective constitutional framework of the Jewish polity in favor of the new Jewish condition of modernity.

Only after the modern epoch was well advanced and even moving toward its conclusion, when perhaps half of the Jews in the world had been emancipated and most of the others had lost their communal autonomy even if they were still restricted in their rights of citizenship by the governments of their host countries, was world Jewry able to begin to develop modern alternatives for the by then well-nigh destroyed traditional polity. Chief among them and the most successful was the Zionist alternative that offered all Jews, no matter what their religious, cultural, and political understanding of Judaism was like, a chance to actively identify as Jews. The Zionist alternative also established a set of institutions through which Jews could manifest that identity and in turn that could undertake collective Jewish action, particularly in connection with the reestablishment of a Jewish national home in Eretz Israel that was intended by the Zionists to fully restore the Jewish polity and that it has done, albeit in a way quite different from that which the Zionist theoreticians of those days then envisaged, however they envisaged it (Hertzberg 1970).

At first Zionism had competition from other proposed solutions to "the Jewish problem" including emancipation, assimilation, socialism, Diaspora nationalism, and traditional religious Orthodoxy. All of the others proved wanting in pursuing the Jewish goal of Jewish survival and maintaining Jewish identity, yet joining the modern world, each for reasons of its own. In the end, only Zionism succeeded in finding a way to achieve its goals while pursuing both objectives as a result of the Holocaust, the heavy hand of Stalinist communism, and the reestablishment of the State of Israel (Laqueur 1977; Sachar 1976–87 & 1980; Vital 1990, 1987, & 1982).

The reestablishment of the Jewish state came fortuitously at the same time that rapid, nay, revolutionary strides were made in transportation and communication technology. The Zionist enterprise had, in many respects, been a product of the first stages of that revolution. The revolutionary changes that took place after

1948 not only made it easier for the Zionist enterprise to bring Jews to Israel, but also made possible rapid, then instantaneous, connection between Jews in all parts of the world, in turn allowing them to undertake common activities insofar as they wished to do so or were not restrained from doing so by the governments of their host countries. That restraint also diminished after 1948, and especially after the fall of the Communist bloc from 1989 onward.

These changes came during an epoch of great migrations that led millions of Jews to move not only to the reborn State of Israel but even earlier to the other new worlds of the great European frontier. Western Europe had been substantially *judenrein* (free of Jews) from the fifteenth century until the Jews' return in the eighteenth century. By that time Jews were moving then to the New Worlds of North and South America, southern Africa, and Australia for Ashkenazim and Sephardim alike, although mostly the former, and South and East Asia, first for Sephardim and only later for Ashkenazim in smaller numbers for purposes of business rather than settlement.

Thus by the end of the 1940s, after the great migrations, the Holocaust, and the establishment of the State of Israel, the earlier Muslim and Christian heartlands of Jewish settlement had been almost emptied of Jewish communities, while new communities had developed, at times into powerful ones, beyond that old core area, west and east, and to a lesser extent south and north.

There may well be a direct connection between these massive migrations and the increased voluntary character of Jewish identification in Jewish life. In continental Europe and in the Muslim world where Jews had lived for centuries, even after full communal autonomy was eliminated, strong vestiges of autonomy remained. Jews who wished to be Jews had to be members; governments collected taxes for the communities, or enforced by law taxes collected by the Jews themselves. Communal religious establishments had control over Jewish law and religion. In most cases, only Jews who wanted to give up all connection with Judaism and Jewish life— which often meant converting to another religion or at the very least walking away from all economic, social, religious, educational, or cultural benefits that their communities and the Jewish people as a whole might provide—could refuse to accept basic communal discipline.

In the New World no such basic communal discipline existed. The communities were entirely or virtually entirely voluntary. Their institutions were private bodies in state law and adherence to them was strictly voluntary. Moreover, in some cases, the United States, for example, efforts to give Jewish communal institutions any kind of monopoly were illegal under state antimonopoly legislation.[1]

As a result, key questions for Jewishness began to revolve around "identity" rather than birth, affiliation, or conformity to some kind of standard. Identity was subjective and voluntary, as distinct from the objective and communal if not compulsory association of an earlier time. Moreover, as the world continued to open up for Jews, even the social pressures that might have led Jews to identify voluntarily against their basic desires as individuals fell away, making the matter of identity increasingly a matter of individual choice. Not surprisingly, this meant that Jewish institutions and practices had to readapt themselves, even transform themselves, to this new kind of voluntary Jewishness and Judaism, something that was totally or almost totally absent from Jewish life in earlier times (Goldscheider & Zuckerman 1984; Cohen 1983).

A person who saw herself as Jewish could make any claims, adopt any practices, or maintain any affiliations and get away with them. At first, those kinds of Jews were no more than "Jews at heart," but remained ethnically and thus Halakically Jews. Then Jews began to intermarry at substantial rates, often raising their children as non-Jews. More recently, some Jews have declared themselves Jews even as they accepted a belief in Jesus as messiah. Moreover, people born non-Jews began to declare themselves Jews if it suited their purposes to do so without undergoing any formal conversion. The 1990 American National Jewish Population Study revealed that up to a third of those who considered themselves Jewish by conversion had not undergone any kind of formal conversion, even a non-Halakic one.

Jewish institutions readapted themselves to attract people who identified as Jews without asking too many questions as to how they were Jewish. Jewish education was shifted to build upon the need to foster or strengthen Jewish identity rather than the need to equip Jews whose identity was taken for granted with the tools necessary to live a Jewish life, whether traditionally defined or otherwise.

Regional Varieties of Jewish Identification: The Territorial Dimension

While all of the foregoing is generally true for Jews in the Diaspora, it is only partly true for the Jews in Israel. Israeli Jews live within a sovereign Jewish state where elements of the old order of

Jewish communal authority have been adapted and the powers of state sovereignty are used not only to support them but also to support other coercive measures which, with or without their common Israeli element included, serve Jewish ends. The differences between Israel and the Diaspora, that is, between having political sovereignty and not, are the most dramatic of differences in the Jewish world today. Furthermore, that Israel now has approximately 4.5 million Jews—a number that is growing—while the world's largest Jewish community, the United States, has about 5.8 million—a number that is either static or declining—suggests how important Israel is even though it is the only one of its kind. But differences between the various Diaspora communities also should be taken into consideration when planning Jewish policy.

A Jewishness based on identity rather than on an assumed way of life complicates matters for Jewish survival, but, at the same time, seems to be the only way to achieve Jewish survival in our times. The question remains as to whether even that is enough. First, identity must be built or established and then ways must be developed to translate that identity into concrete and continuing manifestations. That, indeed, has been the modern Jewish project and it looks as if it will be the postmodern one as well. Speaking social scientifically, it does not seem likely that it will be a successful project. It requires too much voluntary effort on the part of a population that essentially is becoming more ignorant of what being Jewish is all about, generation by generation if not even more quickly. In addition, it must be achieved in the face of horrendous competition which, precisely because it seems so open and welcoming, is so dangerous to the success of the project, imposing its norms and ways on the Jewish people in the name of freedom, choice, and democracy, very real values in their own right. At the same time, however, Jews have confounded social scientists or their predecessors for many centuries. Hence, as long as the effort is made, no final verdict can be registered.

How that effort is made is based upon many factors, one of which, at least, must be the starting point from which people born Jews—or identified as such—begin. While there was always less uniformity about that than the Jewish romanticists of the day might have liked to suppose, even in the times when Jews saw themselves as all bound by Halakha and living under the authority of the Jewish community unless they chose to change their religion, still today the diversity in ways is almost immeasurably greater. Moreover, that diversity is far more the result of choice, either ideological or territorial, neither of which were very likely matters of conscious choice in the past. This chapter focuses on the territorial dimensions of choice rather than on the ideological.

Most of those who seek to understand contemporary Jewry are aware of the ideological dimensions and have greater or lesser understanding of them; but many Jews, even in the highest leadership positions, are unaware or insufficiently aware of the territorial dimensions. Jews who look the same, dress the same, speak the same language, and are engaged in the same pursuits, Jewish and general, may not be perceived by their peers to be as different from one another as they are in matters of Jewish identity and their Jewishness.

We can identify seven basic regional divisions in the Jewish world today.

1. The State of Israel or perhaps more correctly, Eretz Israel.

2. The Jewish community of the United States.

3. The Jewish communities of the rest of the English-speaking world, all of which are essentially products of Britain and the British empire.

4. The Jewries of Latin America.

5. The Jewries of continental Europe west of the former Iron Curtain.

6. The Jewries of the ex-Communist bloc.

7. The Jewish communities and outposts of Africa and Asia.

Let us look at each of these in turn from the perspective of their Jewish identity and perspectives on that identity.

In the first place, they differ significantly with regard to their bedrock perception of what Jews are. For the Jews of Eretz Israel the key concept is that the Jews are a nation. There are variations on this concept. Most Jews in Israel probably consider the Jews to be a nation that includes certain religious dimensions. For religious Zionists, Jews are a nation in which the religious dimension is critical. For the *haredim*, Jews are a nation by virtue of their religion or, more accurately, by virtue of the Torah in which they include the written and oral law; the definition that very much approximates that provided by Saadia Gaon over a thousand years ago. Finally, for a growing number of Israeli Jews, Israel is the focal point of their national identity, but the vast majority of those "Israelis" are of Jewish descent. Hence the two identities are intertwined.

For the Jews of the United States, Jews are principally Jews by religion. Many American Jews, having assimilated so totally into American culture, see Jews as hardly more than a religion. Others see the Jews as a people, albeit formed and held together by their religion. They more or less follow Mordecai Kaplan's definition of Judaism as the religious civilization of the Jewish people, without all that much civilization consciously surviving today. With the exception of a small handful, even American Jews who are strongly committed to Jewish peoplehood understand that peoplehood primarily in religious terms.

In the rest of the English-speaking world, Jews are an ethnic group sustained by their religion. In Latin America and continental Europe, Jews see Jewishness as primarily a function of ethnicity, that is, the Jews are an ethnic group.

In Latin America, Jews are an ethnic group sustained by family, language, or other aspects of culture, and concern for the Jewish state. Religion is an almost nonexistent factor for most Latin American Jews. Exceptions include those who have turned to ultra-Orthodoxy, or converts to Judaism, or Jews who feel a need to identify in some measure with Jewish religion in order to separate themselves from the Catholicism of their societies.

In Western Europe Jews are an ethnic group perhaps most sustained by anti-Semitism—real or perceived, manifest or latent—in consequence of which Jews perceive themselves as different from French or Germans or Norwegians, even though they may be very much integrated into their country's civic life and culture. Jewish religion is residual and its institutions are more overtly ethnic anchors than they are in other parts of the contemporary Diaspora. Thus they are more likely to prefer a formal communal Orthodoxy regardless of their personal beliefs and practices because of the association of traditional Jewish religion with Jewish ethnic identity. Since they are located in countries where there are principal churches or religions, even if they are no longer established, they preserve older traditions in their institutions regardless of the behavior of their people. It is easy for Jews to fall into the same pattern, just as for American Jews, the great diversity and competition of churches and sects has made it easy for them to experiment with institutionalizing different paths to Judaism.

In all three regions, but especially in Latin America and continental Europe, Jews feel less "at home" in their host countries than do either Israeli or American Jews. They see themselves bound by some kind of mystic cord to the State of Israel regardless of whether they ever intend to settle there. Latin America has a phrase for it: *madre patria* (mother fatherland), that is to say, the fatherland prior to the new one in countries of immigration. Even if the term or an equivalent is not used and if the migration took place centuries ago, that phrase describes the feelings of Jews in all three regions.

Perhaps the most radical new senses of Jewish identity are to be found among the Jews of the ex-Communist bloc. Jews elsewhere, however much they are engaged in redefining who is a Jew, begin with those who are defined as Jews Halakically and expand from there. Even if they include self-identified and "self-converted" Jews, they have not abandoned traditional definitions to the extent that is apparently the case in the ex-Communist bloc.

In a small meeting with fifteen of us sitting around the table a few years ago, I asked Mikhail Chlenov, the head of the Vaad—then the umbrella organization for Soviet Jewry and now rather in limbo since the demise of the Soviet Union—how many Jews there were in the USSR. He prefaced his response by giving me the Soviet Jewish definition of who is a Jew. There were three categories:

a. Jews who were Jews by virtue of being identified as such on their Soviet internal passports;

b. People whom everybody knew were Jewish even though they had managed to secure a different national identification on those passports; and

c. "Those who identify with the fate of the Jewish people," namely non-Jews who became connected with the Jewish people through marriage and the family relationships it established.

Not only was there nothing Halakic about this, but the definition was certainly not religious in any form and was only partly (and not very formally) ethnic. In a sense it could be described as national since at least in theory "national" can be multiethnic. But most important is that it was a subjective product of certain objective conditions, not exactly voluntary but not necessarily authoritative either.

A look at the ex-Soviet republics and at the rest of the Communist bloc suggests that this definition exists well-nigh universally within them. This is a thoroughly modern or contemporary definition. Theoretically, it poses serious new problems for the Jewish people and for their accepted definition or definitions of Jewish identity. In practice, at this stage, because the State of Israel more or less implicitly accepts that definition under the Law of Return, it has become a working one for many purposes, many of them very important.

In theory, that definition would cease to have effect when people have to be identified on their Israeli identity cards according to the Halakic definition of who is Jewish. It is quite surprising that there have been so few cases in which problems have arisen publicly. In part this has been due to a generous conversion policy on the part of the Israeli chief rabbinate, now being challenged by at least one of the new chief rabbis, which has prevented problems of this nature from reaching the stage of public exposure. In the two, three, or four cases that have, it is usually when somebody has died unexpectedly and thus a decision has to be made as to whether or not he or she was Jewish. All of these cases have either been dealt with or swept under the rug.

Those confrontations that have taken place have exposed the difference between those Jews whose sensibilities about Jewish identification rest on contemporary criteria, and those whose sensibilities rest on traditional ones. For the former, for example, an Israeli soldier of dubious Jewish ancestry was to be considered Jewish because he had identified with the Jewish state to the point of serving in the Israeli army and even giving up his life for Israel. In their eyes that should be enough or more than enough. For those whose sensibilities are more traditional, when push comes to shove, they must rely on traditional Halakic definitions, although in most cases they would prefer that the matter not be raised at all. Within the ex-Communist bloc itself, only now, as a result of the presence of Jews from other countries, are Halakic questions even being asked and in general it can be said that the Chlenov definition prevails.

In the case of the final grouping, we are essentially dealing with Jewish outposts, either because they are minuscule survivors of older communities now emigrated or destroyed, or because they are minuscule settlements of Jews from elsewhere for whom business and professional interests bring them to Jewishly out-of-the-way places. Theirs is a Judaism of self-identification based on either religious or ethnic grounds or on some combination of both. With the exception of those who are religious and who need to find other Jews in order to properly carry out religious commandments, they are Jews who seek Jewish companionship in strange lands. In an anthropological sense, they are Jews by culture but only in the most basic sense. In other words, they bear with them certain kinds of Jewish cultural traits, even if they know very little about Jewish civilization. One might best refer to them as tribal Jews. Inter alia, they serve to remind us that underneath, Jewish identity for most of those born Jews is tribal, however it is filtered through other definitions. Indeed, the great problem with contemporary changes in Jewish identification is that most of them require abandonment or minimization of the tribal dimension and hence even Jews who accept them fully in theory are often uncomfortable with them in practice, except to the extent that their own tribal identification has been diluted or modified.

This may be a latent reason why emancipated Jews have so emphasized universalism as a cornerstone of Jewish identity and self-definition. Obviously, it is in the self-interest of those Jews who seek to become part of the larger world, however defined, to emphasize universalism and its corollary, openness, because as a minority, universality justifies their acceptance into the larger world of which they seek to be part. This is as true of Israeli Jews active in the left-wing Meretz party as it is of American Jews active in the politically liberal American Jewish Congress. Being Jews, it is not enough for them to say that it suits their interests to promote universalism. Rather, they must make it an ideological principle, sacred and inviable; and so they have, introducing it as such into the very structure of Jewish identity as they see it even though, in fact, it often works counter to all those elements that we know are necessary to Jewish identity.

The simplest and perhaps most vulgar demonstration of this phenomenon is found in the case of intermarrying children of "modern" Jewish families. The Jewish child comes to his or her parents with a non-Jewish partner. The parents will often indicate their disapproval for what are essentially tribalist reasons and the child will retort that he or she was raised to be universalist in outlook so why now should this next step be inappropriate? The parents, despite their feelings, are stuck. So with that problem and the desire not to alienate their children, they acquiesce. But the story is not yet over. After the marriage takes place and the Jewish parents come to know the non-Jewish spouse and his or her family, they often discover that they are very nice people. At first they are even surprised by that since their tribal instincts had told them that all non-Jews are at least latently hostile or uncivilized, that Jews are special, and here these are human beings like all other human beings. This is even more pronounced when there are few overt religious and cultural differences between them because of assimilation. So the devil is not so bad. They are then at a loss as to what to base their Jewish identity on.

Implications for Jewish Education

The implications of this situation for Jewish education are several. First and foremost, we can now see throughout the Jewish world, including Israel, that it takes almost no time for a civilization to be disrupted by lack of proper education of its new generations. Ten years is probably enough to do the deed. Considering that a demographic cohort is about five years in length, if two cohorts do not receive proper education in their heritage, that heritage is radically disrupted, its continuity lost, and it can only be revived by a conscious effort by later cohorts with all the problematics attendant upon rediscovering what was once living and "natural" (i.e., so deeply rooted in one's culture that it was second nature) through conscious learning and deliberate design, which has no basis in a continuing culture.

The phenomenon of a disrupted culture is visible in every Jewish community in the world including Israel. In the Diaspora, communities seeking modernization or assimilation into what were for them new societies either rejected or neglected proper Jewish education of their children, both at home and in the schools. In Israel, many of the early Zionist pioneers rejected traditional Judaism and deliberately refrained from passing it onto their children at home or in more formal educational frameworks. By now the results are apparent. For the vast majority of world Jewry, all we have left is a kind of communicated tribalism, certain universalizable elements of general culture compatible with tradition transformed to conform with the new environments in which Jews found themselves, and certain patterns of political culture and behavior that are not even recognized for what they are but are deemed by their bearers to be universal (e.g., Jewish humanitarianism and aspirations for communal solidarity). The second part of the equation is exemplified by the *hozer b'tshuva* ("newly religious") phenomenon. Here we see people raised without Jewish tradition finding their way back to it but having to acquire it painfully on their own and thus often unable to discriminate between its essential elements and peripheral expressions.

Education must take place both in the home and in other settings. The home experiences are often so subtle that children are unaware that they are being taught. That is what makes them so vital. There is very little basis for assuming that a formal substantive education can replace home experiences or that substance can be provided by informal education trying to foster certain kinds of actions based upon commitment without the appropriate knowledge base. In the past two generations, Jewish educators thought that perhaps schools or less formal educational settings could substitute for the home in this respect. It cannot be said that they never succeeded. There were always those few who were thirsting for something they might have gotten in those settings instead of at home, at least for a while. For the most part, however, they failed to provide an alternative for something for which there is no alternative.

Partly in response to the first points, we find that there are today two conflicting views in Jewish education: the substantivists and the experientialists. The former are committed to teaching substantive knowledge and information and expect that those who come to learn with them or their parents accept a system of learning that rests on substantive study. The latter are convinced that their students do not devote enough time to Jewish education for that purpose and do not have enough interest in it, so they strive to make Jewish education experiential, in part to replace what the home used to provide, in part to give people a good feeling about feeling Jewish since they cannot give them much else. The former expect relatively long hours and serious commitment to Jewish education, but, perhaps paradoxically, have also had more success with those students who have come into their framework without that commitment than have the experientialists who have recognized the reality in which they find themselves and are willing to try to work within it.

By and large, experientialism has failed to achieve what it was designed to achieve, demonstrating willy-nilly that only in rare cases can there be even a partial substitute for home-acquired experience, and that the minimal time available for attempted substitutes is clearly inadequate. By the same token, the substantivists have failed to attract a sufficient percentage of Jewish students, whether they seek to introduce them to traditional religious Judaism or to modern national-cultural Jewishness, and even many of their efforts to provide the requisite time through non-Orthodox day schools, for example, have become "watered down" to deal with the populations that they serve. It is too easy to conclude that what we need is a combination of both substance and experiences, but that would be so facile as to be worthless. Of course it is true, but it is not a truth that we can operationalize outside of a few places and in a few cases because the major transformations in Jewish society fail to make operationalization a reality.

The variety of basic forms of Jewish identification requires that there be a variety of curriculum designs to meet different sensibilities. This means that there can be no centralized curriculum design as many Israelis have proposed from time to time. In an adaption of the principle: *ki mitzion tetsei torah* ("Out of Zion come the Torah"), some body in Israel will attempt to provide a curriculum for Jewish education throughout the world. We know that empirically it does not work for many reasons that one might consider to be extraneous to education per se, that is, politics, but we also know empirically that it does not work qua curriculum.

An analysis of the varieties of Jewish identification may add another dimension to our understanding. Jews are not only different ideologically, but also territorially where they might assume a priori that there might be no significant differences.

At one time we could speak of a common tribalism underlying those differences and indeed there are still echoes of that in many quarters. During this past generation we have discovered that common tribalism has either disappeared or so lost compelling force for most Jews that it remains merely a vestigial sentiment for the vast majority of those who identify with it.

Not only that but holding onto the other forms of identification taken alone involves reliance on a weak reed. American Jews, recognizing the reality of—and hence the strength of—(non-Orthodox) religious identification in the United States sought in the first postwar generation to rebuild Jewish education strictly or overwhelmingly along (non-Orthodox) religious lines. In the end, the vast majority of the now-dominant synagogue supplementary schools were reduced to an emphasis on "synagogue skills" for the young which, as the young people got older, proved to be woefully inadequate to give them reasons to be seriously Jewish in the very attractive face of American society. The end result is well-known.

Nor was ethnicity any better though there has never been a proper curriculum emphasizing ethnicity alone. Either it slides over into religious education or into national-cultural education or into some combination of both. Ethnicity by itself has no content beyond the experiential and would essentially involve cooking classes. Even Jewish folk dancing, a relatively new product of the Zionist movement, would not do. Besides, in most of the New World countries the ethnicity movements have been an effort on the part of newer ethnic groups to stake claims to social legitimacy prior to their massive assimilation into the general society. What they seek is massive assimilation as equals. For that they have to claim the worth and legitimacy of their ethnicity for a brief period.

Ideology could, perhaps, have provided Jewish education with a better route, but all the secular ideologies that Jews embraced or with which they flirted over the past two hundred years have come to an end, at least as compelling forces. Zionism, the most successful, could compete in the education marketplace only where Jews found it in their self-interest to learn about it and Israel, its product, usually so that they could be rescued from their places of exile; thus their education became part of their approach to Israel.

National-cultural education required too much time and often went against the grain of learning how to be absorbed in the majority host cultures. The Hebrew language, and to a lesser extent Yiddish, was for a while successful in some places where Jews did not yet see themselves as assimilating into the host cultures and did still consider the possibility of resettling in the Jewish state. Just as those two feelings diminished, thus too have Jewish languages declined as a successful tool for maintaining Jewishness.

The recent exception to this general rule was in the ex-Soviet Union where more than a handful of Jews worked very energetically, even desperately, to learn Hebrew because they planned to get out and Israel was their destination. In the English-speaking countries where Jews rapidly acquired the language difficulties associated with English-speakers, language education as the anchor for Jewish education rapidly proved to be counterproductive, even where attempts were made and the population seemed willing, as, for example, in Hebrew-speaking summer camps.

So, on the basis of our analysis, we are left with no positive recommendations in which we have confidence. Education is successful only when it is part of a total life experience. Accordingly, we need either to restore or to find new forms of total life experiences for Jews that will attract them. Some are attracted even now as a result of conditions quite external to the Jewish people, perceived to involve the social demoralization generated by contemporary society leading to a return to other ways of life and is outside of the purview of this chapter. We see, on the contrary, a growing gap between the small minority of Jews who are prepared to invest in substantive Jewish education, and the vast majority who are not, who at best want some minimal palliative experientially based efforts. In the Diaspora, actually it is easier to get those in the latter category to think that "Jewish education" has some value since in their own ambivalent ways most Jewish parents seen to want to pass on their Jewishness to their children. Survey after survey shows the results.

I refer not to the substantive results of the questionnaires but to the categories that the questionnaires provide. All of the questions are based upon the kind of minimal experiential educational time that is the norm. They almost never have any data about the few who pursue more substantive education because there are just too few of them in the minds of the surveyors or the surveyed. In the general field of education, we have long since come to conclude that just four or five years of full-time education usually produces functional illiterates. In social scientific surveys of Jews, a Jewish education of that intensity would be off the upper end of the scale and for good reason. This should give us real pause.

Conclusion

So we make no recommendations because we have none to make that have legs to stand on. On the other hand, we know that our Jewish commitments and concerns demand that we continue working to improve the situation. No doubt we should and no doubt we will. We will continue to do more of the same in one form or another, implicitly relying on a few inspired teachers who will continue to have a significant effect. Perhaps that is all we can expect at this point in our history.

Note

1. Arthur A. Goren provides an excellent case study example of this in his discussion of the New York Kehilla's failure to sustain its regulation of kosher meat (Goren 1970).

References

Cohen, Steven Martin. (1983) *American Modernity and Jewish Identity*. New York: Tavistock Publications.

Goldscheider, Calvin, and Alan S. Zuckerman. (1984) *The Transformation of the Jews*. Chicago: University of Chicago Press.

Goren, Arthur A. (1970) *New York Jews and the Quest for Community; The Kehilla Experiment, 1908–1922.* New York: Columbia University Press.

Hertzberg, Arthur, (ed. (1970) *The Zionist Idea.* Westport, Conn.: Greenwood.

Laqueur, Walter Ze'ev. (1977) *A History of Zionism.* London: Weidenfeld and Nicolson.

Sachar, Howard Morley. (1976–87) *A History of Israel.* New York: Knopf.

———. (1990) *The Course of Modern Jewish History.* New York: Vintage Books.

Vital, David. (1982) *Zionism, the Formative Years.* New York: Oxford University Press.

———. (1987) *The Origins of Zionism.* New York: Oxford University Press.

———. (1990) *The Future of the Jews.* Cambridge, Mass.: Harvard University Press.

54

Ar ⌣.
The Jews

Sergio DellaPergola

"The structure of Judaism, once so solid, is crumbling away before our very eyes. Conversion and intermarriage are thinning the
ranks of Jews in every direction, and the loss is the heavier to bear,
in that the great decrease in the Jewish birth-rate makes it more
and more difficult to fill the gaps in the natural way." To many a
reader, these words will probably sound familiar. They would seem,
indeed, to have been picked up from the debate that in recent years
has unfolded between two camps of supposedly "optimists" and
"pessimists" over the present and future of American Jewish demography and identification, and more generally of the future of
Jewish population worldwide. While the English style of the prose
just quoted, in spite of the translator's efforts, would fit the widely
known notion that some of the leading pessimist analysts of contemporary Jewish society are European-born Israeli intellectuals
with a special predilection for the German (or maybe Italian) language, these words come out of another epoch. They are the opening
paragraph of the first version of Arthur Ruppin's major sociological
work (Ruppin 1913: 3).

Ruppin's *Die Juden der Gegenwart* first appeared in 1904 in
Berlin. Two revised editions, published respectively in 1911 and 1920,
were translated into English as *The Jews of To-day* (1913) and into
other languages (e.g., Ruppin 1922). *The Jews of Today* carried the

re, scientific approach, and initial data base out
rge Ruppin's major work *Die Soziologie der Juden*
s later elaboration *The Jewish Fate and Future*
arefully researched analysis of the sociodemographic
nditions of the Jews a hundred years after emancipa-
attention to the endangered continuity of a Jewish peo-
he first time in modern history was facing the challenges
le assimilation, and provided scientific foundations to the
d programs of the Zionist movement that had just emerged
a new solution to the Jewish people's problems.

his chapter has no pretension of providing an even superficial
le of the life and work of Arthur Ruppin. Very interesting ele-
nts can be drawn from his own *Memoirs, Diaries, Letters* (pub-
shed in English in 1971), which provide fascinating background to
his many other publications. Rather, the main purpose of this chapter is to provide some historical-sociological perspective to the present discussion of Jewish identity. Some of the major structural
characteristics of world Jewry will be examined at a distance of
ninety years through a comparatively similar approach. By looking
in social scientific perspective at the *Jews of Today*, then and now,
we may draw some comparisons about the sociodemographic profile
of world Jewry at the beginning and the close of the twentieth century. We may also contribute to the initial development of a history
of the study of Jewish sociology and demography (see Bachi 1993).
Perhaps more importantly, we may help evaluate whether and how
a certain basic view of the world—in our case, the main paradigm of
Jewish sociology and demography—is still actual and relevant, or
perhaps has become superseded by new facts and by new ways of
understanding those facts.

In the process, we may be able to review, validate, or reject, the
analytic work of our predecessors, thus gaining added insights on
the strengths and weaknesses of the sociodemographic approach;
and, enriched by a perspective from the past, we may be able to improve our current understanding of the complexities and implications of changing Jewish identity patterns.

The Man and His Work

Arthur Ruppin was born in 1876 in Posen, a province perched
geographically and culturally between Poland and Germany, in a
moderately traditional Jewish family. His family, although rooted in

German society and culture, displayed relatively recent Eastern European origins. Thus Ruppin, while tending himself to a quite enlightened and rationalistic approach to Judaism, also was conversant with traditional Jewish culture. His principal professional training was in the legal field, and as such he filled in his young adulthood some positions with the Prussian administration. At the same time, he developed a major interest in economics, particularly the agricultural aspects in which he managed to acquire an early practical experience. To the field of sociology and demography he basically arrived as an autodidact, first through the very process of writing his first major book, and soon later by joining Alfred Nossig (who had founded in 1902 an Association for Jewish Statistics) and by becoming instrumental in the development of the *Bureau fur Demographie und Statistik der Juden* and of its periodical publication, the *Zeitschrift fur Demographie und Statistik der Juden* in Berlin (1905).

While the quantity and quality of Ruppin's work are remarkable, the statistical methods he employed were neither very innovative nor technically very sophisticated. Nor do his published works display massive doses of conventional scholarship, through the use of heavy footnoting and systematic bibliographic references. Indeed, Ruppin did not particularly insist on incorporating his analyses into a body of supposedly universal social-scientific theory, unlike contemporaneous European scholars who were also devoting attention to Judaism and Jewish society—such as E. Durkheim, M. Weber, and W. Sombart—or the later mature sociological elaboration in which American social scientists—notably the Chicago school—were to play the leading role. It was the special case of the Jews that polarized Ruppin's attention; the examination of such a special case from all possible relevant angles fulfilled the unique, very solid, and relevant product of his work.

Ruppin's main contribution to an innovative layer of scholarship is, on the one hand, a massive and systematic effort of documentation, based on large-scale multinational compilations from the many sources of statistical data on Jewish population and society; and on the other hand, his fresh, insightful, well-reasoned, and coherent interpretations of those data. The one central assumption, which represents a general theoretical postulate that not all general scholarship would take for granted, is that *there exists one Jewish people*. Hence the different data, characteristics, and trends observable about Jews in different geographic places and historical times can be meaningfully incorporated into a unified analysis and interpretation. As such, the descriptive data that abound in Ruppin's work transcend the local and the particularistic and add up to a picture of far greater analytic significance. The development of conceptualizations intended to apply to a wide range of different environments creates a far more exciting and challenging sociology than would be the case if we accepted the widespread assumption that local situations are unique, do not bear comparisons, and have to be dealt with on a case-by-case basis.

Furthermore, Ruppin usually tied his analytic conclusions to a further body of action- or policy-oriented considerations and suggestions. Indeed, a central aspect of Ruppin's work concerns his simultaneous involvement with scientific-analytic work, on the one hand, and with practical-political work, on the other. Throughout the entire course of his professional life, Ruppin played a central role in the development of Palestine, as the chief emissary of the World Zionist Organization between his arrival in 1907 and the end of World War I, and as an influential member of the Zionist directorate during long portions of the interwar period, until his death in 1943. By his explicit admission, Ruppin never believed that only one of the two worlds, the scientific and the practical, deserved his exclusive devotion. During different periods of his life either type of interest absorbed most of his time, but never was the other totally neglected.

Ruppin, the strategically located participant-observer, was highly praised during his time. The kind of integrated scholarly practical approach to contemporary societal issues that Ruppin impersonified would later become the object of some questioning within that very Hebrew University that he had so much contributed to promote (and much of the land of whose campus, incidentally, he had managed to purchase). Eventually, another pivotal figure in the development of contemporary Jewish sociology, Marshall Sklare, would recognize that Ruppin's pioneering work was being continued by the scholars of the Hebrew University's Institute of Contemporary Jewry (Sklare 1993: 189).

The Question and the Answer

At the very core of Ruppin's concern stand two key and complementary aspects. On the one hand stands what is normatively perceived as a dangerous transformation of the Jews: the emerging process of *assimilation* into the surrounding non-Jewish society. On the other, stands the answer to be provided through a movement of *national revival*: Zionism. These are the two major parts in the volume *The Jews of Today*, and the same basic twofold approach will coherently continue to constitute the backbone and trademark of Ruppin's later work in the field of Jewish sociology. It does not change fundamentally throughout the nearly forty years of its analytic elaboration, although numerous revisions naturally emerge out of his developing a more mature understanding of the topic, in response to the very dynamic trends of his time, and out of a sincere effort to come to terms with some of the more complex issues. Among the latter—one should stress at this particular time—the most elusive appeared to him the question of the emerging relationship between Jews and Arabs in Palestine.

Ruppin's Zionism never departed from a fundamentally practical path. Based on his acute sociological conceptualization of Jewish societal needs, the major strategy would be one of radically changing the actual existential conditions of the Jews. This would include three fundamental elements: (a) the creation of an autonomous and self-supporting economy of Jewish producers and consumers, the cornerstone of which would be the return to Jewish agricultural work in Palestine; (b) revival of the Jews' own national language, Hebrew; and (c) territorial segregation of the Jews (Ruppin 1913: 238). A fourth crucial condition for the furtherance of Jewish culture, the establishment of a Jewish school system, would naturally develop once the three first conditions are met.

There seems to be in this analysis an analogy with the idea of Ruppin's contemporaneous and fellow compatriot, Martin Buber, that "culture is not a matter of will; it did not come into the world as a preconceived act, but has always . . . fed parasitically on the flow of life" (Buber 1929, quoted in Shapira 1993). While Buber—also deeply interested in Jewish sociology—was referring to a deeper layer of religious experience, it was in Ruppin's more pragmatic sense, too, that the more profound aspects of social life really mattered, rather than the intellectual constructs that could be built upon them. Success in achieving the major structural transformations in the current situation of the Jews would then be instrumental in making the *yishuv* in Palestine viable and attractive for further immigration; and it would eventually bring the *yishuv* to a position and level where it could serve as a major cultural center and source of inspiration for world Jewry.

Creating these new real facts appeared to Ruppin far more relevant and feasible than pursuing recognition within the international political community, or focusing on the internal political institutions of the Jewish *yishuv* (society in the Land of Israel) to be, which characterized the efforts of most of his contemporaneous Zionist leaders. Ruppin's Zionism was practical, sociological, and in a sense apolitical—more in line with Ahad Ha'am than with Herzl; but Ruppin was acutely aware that the very essence of Zionism meant politics.

One of the most intriguing conclusions reached in rereading Ruppin is that he did not seem to fully appreciate the short-term feasibility of the creation of an independent Jewish state. Until very shortly before his death, he expressed doubt—definitely a scholar's more than a politician's trait—about the amount of success that would crown his lifelong efforts with promoting a sounder Jewish future, through vision, action, and scholarship. The sociological and demographic implications emerging from the new existential situation of Jews growing to form the majority of population in a sovereign State of Israel would eventually provide an illuminating test of the relevance of Ruppin's Jewish sociology.

Jewish Assimilation: The Basic Typology

Ruppin sought to provide a concise typology of the major processes shaping the current transformation of the Jews. Along with specifying the major variables at work, Ruppin tried to provide a quantification of the composition of the Jewish population worldwide according to its relationship to these main processes (see table 1). The main variables involved in such typology concern socioeconomic aspects (economic condition, educational attainment, and urbanization), religious attitudes, demographic behaviors (birthrate), and identificational correlates of demographic trends (rates of intermarriage and conversion). By collating the relevant indicators for Jews in different countries, Ruppin suggested a fourfold partition, clearly implying a sequential-chronological evolution from the more traditional to the more assimilated types of Jewry. Each section, or stage, was typically represented by Jews in a particular geographic area or social class within geographic partition.

In general, a typology offers a parsimonious descriptive as well as a predictive tool aimed at understanding some central feature in society. A synthetic presentation of the kind shown in table 1 tends to reflect the obvious trade-off of depth and complexity for the advantage of compression within limited space. Ruppin's typology may be interpreted as an attempt to assess the chances of Jewish continuity in a later generation in relation to the observed circumstances in the

Table 1
The Four Sections of World Jewry According to Ruppin

Variable Number	1st Section 6 million	2nd Section 3 million	3rd Section 2 million	4th Section 1 million
Typical Representatives	The great mass of Jews in Russia and Galicia	Settlers in England and America, and Roumanian Jews	The mass of German Jews	Rich Jews and Jews of university education in all the big towns
Economic Condition	Workers, artisans, and shopkeepers without means and of uncertain livelihood	Artisans and merchants with modest but settled income	Well-to-do bourgeoisie	Wealthy bourgeoisie
Religious Outlook	Orthodox	Liberal	Freethinking	Agnostic
Education	Cheder	Jewish elementary schools	Christian elementary and secondary schools	Public school and university
Birthrate per 1,000 souls	30–40	25–30	20–25	15–20
Percentage of Mixed Marriages*	0–2	2–10	10–30	30–50
Conversions per 10,000 souls	0–2	2–5	5–15	15–40

Source: Adapted from Ruppin (1913: 15).

*As originally published. Ruppin's *percentages of mixed marriages* were in reality *percent ratios between the number of mixed marriages and the number of endogamous marriages*. Based on his method, frequencies are higher, and become greater than 100% once there are more mixed than endogamous marriages, which in the usual notation is described as over 50% of mixed marriages. Ruppin's percentages are easily converted into conventional percentages through the following simple arithmetic:

$$f_c = f_R/(100 + f_R)$$

where f_c are conventional percentages and f_R are Ruppin's percentages.

present generation. Belonging to each section in the typology implies different probabilities of Jewishness at a later time—both for the population involved and regarding transmission to a next generation—evidently not on a case-by-case basis but on the aggregate.

Besides its substantive interest, Ruppin's model represents a significant statement of the unidirectional and fundamentally irreversible nature of assimilation. His position does not basically differ, in fact anticipates other sociological formulations of assimilation theory, prominently among which stands Milton M. Gordon's influential work (1964). Ruppin sees all major demographic, socioeconomic, and identificational characteristics to be forming one cluster in which change in one major aspect tends to be synchronized with changes in each other aspect. Geographic mobility, particularly movement from Eastern Europe to Western societies and from smaller settlements to larger urban places, appears to go hand in hand with general socioeconomic embetterment, secularization, educational promotion, declining birthrates, and increasing rates of intermarriage and of conversion from Judaism. A gradual transition is involved from the one extreme of an ecologically segregated, poorly trained, and economically marginal, religiously observant, and universally inbreeding Jewish community with high rates of demographic growth, to the opposite extreme of a wealthy, highly educated, geographically dispersed, agnostic, and assimilated group with low or negative population growth.

The main Jewish identificational parameter chosen by Ruppin to evaluate the Jewish quality of a community is *religious outlook*. Of the several different dimensions that might be taken to define the overall nature of Jewish identity (Herman 1977), religion is taken as the more powerful and comprehensive one, consistent with the leading role of religion in the historical evolution of Jewish society and its interplay with the non-Jewish societal environment. Sociologically, the Jewish religion is not only a matter of creed; it also inseparably involves a set of individual practices and community institutions. At least as an ideal type, Judaism as a religion does provide a highly intense and multiform basis for Jewish collective life. Some of the alternatives for primary identification between Jews as individuals and as a collective, such as ethnicity, community, or culture can be chronologically and functionally derived from a paradigmatic model of Jewish religion. Ruppin sees the Jewish involvement with religion to evolve from orthodox practice through a more liberal and selective religious stance, toward freethinking and agnosticism. The ultimate station of this possible chain is conversion out of Judaism.

Ruppin's typology of world Jewry at the beginning of the century leads to the quantification shown in table 1. Of the twelve million Jews at that time, about half (six million, mostly in Eastern Europe) belonged to the first and most traditional sector; about one in four (three million, including the new immigrants in England and America) had reached the second transitional stage; and about one in four belonged to the more modernized sectors, of which two million (typically represented by German Jews) still displayed some attachment to Jewish culture, while one million (mostly associated with upper urban social strata, regardless of country of residence) appeared on the verge of loosing contact with any sense of Jewish identification. In Ruppin's view, left to its own internal dynamics, the whole Jewish population would undergo the whole four stages of his assimilation cycle, down to complete disappearing. Besides a major reversal in the world societal conditions, which Ruppin considered unlikely, the major force able to reverse such a process would be Zionism.

Ruppin did not or could not launch a full-scale discussion of the status and characteristics of American Jewry. At the time of his early writings, America was still in the process of absorbing its mass immigration, and therefore Jews in America still carried many of the traits of the respective communities of origin in Eastern Europe. Yet, Ruppin included Jewish immigrants in America (and England) in the *second* and incipiently modernizing section of his basic typology, thus implying that by the very process of geographic mobility and environmental change something becomes irreversibly modified in the original sociodemographic and cultural patterns of migrants. Ruppin was well aware of the importance of the new centers of Jewish life in the United States and made a point in visiting them in the early 1920s. Writing in the early 1930s (Ruppin 1931: chap. 38), he grasped some of the distinctive organizational and identificational traits of what then already was the largest Jewish community in the world. While recognizing the elements of diversity between the experience of American and European Jewish communities—most significantly German Jewry that constituted the fundamental platform of his analyses—Ruppin did not reserve to America a fundamentally different path in his assessment of the expected sociological evolution of Diaspora Jewries. By that he was taking an analytic stance that would become the object of a lively and still continuing debate.

Notably, all of the examples in Ruppin's early typology refer to European Jews and to their descendants overseas. Lack of reference to Jews in Asia and Africa, most of whom would easily fit the first of Ruppin's four sections, possibly reflects their comparatively lesser numerical weight at the beginning of the century, and Ruppin's naturally better acquaintance with the situation of European Jewries. Ruppin appeared to be much affected by the nineteenth-century school of thought that had postulated a connection between physical traits, or race, and human character. Ruppin's thinking in this direction is characteristically reflected in his quite sanguine statements about the commercial predisposition of the Jews, and probably a similar frame of mind would apply to his understanding of the causes for the much underdeveloped social status of Jewish communities in Muslim lands. To be true, he argued that "Heredity determines what may become of a human being; the environment determines what *does* become of him" (Ruppin 1971: 261). But he obviously undervalued the fact that North African and Asian Jews—allowing for time lags in transitional processes—were essentially affected by the same large-scale sociohistorical processes that applied to the numerically more important branches of European Jewry.

Ninety years since its first formulation, past the Shoah and the independence of the State of Israel, Ruppin's Jewish sociology may well serve as a baseline for assessing what has become of the contemporary Jewish people along the continuum he outlined, between identification and assimilation.

Jewish Assimilation: Structural and Cultural Variables

Definitions and Data

Any attempt to develop a contemporary typology of world Jewish population similar to the one originally conceived by Ruppin is bound to meet significant challenges. The first fact to be noted is the radical change in the available data base. Whereas Ruppin could count on a nearly complete coverage of world Jewry's main sociodemographic characteristics through national population censuses and vital statistics, today's documentation has to come primarily from a sustained effort by Jewish organizations. The 1990 NJPS (National Jewish Population Survey) in the United States provides a case in point of the respective advantages and disadvantages, involving high costs and tremendous technical problems in the definition, identification, and actual coverage of the target population.

Research on Jewish communities in numerous countries is problematic if existent at all, and comparability of data tends to be far from ideal because of the different definitions and techniques implemented in each effort of data collection. On the other hand, one conspicuous advantage over Ruppin's data base has emerged whenever new sources of data have incorporated a selection of Jewish identificational variables together with general sociodemographic variables. The complex interplay between social-structural and sociocultural aspects in Jewish population can thus be better appreciated than by mere juxtaposition, as was the case in the past.

Problems involved with the accumulation of empirical evidence add up with the growingly complex and elusive character of Jewish identity. The deepening process of assimilation, becomes increasingly manifest in the development of what Herbert J. Gans (1979) has called "symbolic ethnicity" and what Peter Y. Medding (1987) has called "segmented ethnicity." The ethno-religious group's formerly cohesive and multifaceted identificational complex tends to break down into several different components, parts of which can be freely and selectively picked up and recombined with elements taken from other traditions and cultures. A greater variety of eminently customized, individual identities are thus created, in contrast with the more standardized identificational norms of the past. Consequently, the sharp hiatus that once prevailed between Jews and "non-Jews"—with the possible intermediate category of the religiously disaffiliated—has now turned into a near-continuum. In this new context of an increasing "subjectivization" or even "flux" of ethnicity (Lieberson & Waters 1988; Waters 1990), a growing number of individuals will have experienced more than one religious or ethnic identification in the course of their lifetimes, or even at any given point in time. Decisions on where to put the cutting points between groups have become increasingly arbitrary.

To clarify matters, if not to overcome the issue, a new terminology has been developed to cover the range of alternative statistical definitions of a Jewish population (Kosmin et al. 1991; Goldstein 1992; DellaPergola 1991). Thus, in the recent practice, the concept of *core Jewish population* refers to all those who currently (at the time of a given survey) define themselves as Jewish, including persons who were not born Jewish and Jews who do not identify their religion as Jewish. The *extension* consists of former Jews or immediate descendants of Jews who currently identify with another religion. Together, the core and extension form what we define the *extended Jewish population*. The latter, together with any other members of the respective households that never were Jewish or of recent Jewish origin, form the *enlarged Jewish population*. Jewish population figures that will be mentioned in the following section consistently refer to the *core* definition.

Matters are more complicated with regard to individual patterns of Jewishness. Cases of the total lack of any Jewish identification among members of a core Jewish population may be found along with cases of partially Jewish behaviors and attitudes among persons who belong to the extended or enlarged population but not to its core. Studying the Jews does not coincide anymore, as it once did, with studying those who display any interest in Judaism.

Social-Structural and Cultural Variables

One immediately apparent fact concerning the Jewish Diaspora is that some of the evolutionary trends devised by Ruppin do seem to have run their full course. The near totality of contemporary Jewish populations now live in urban places. Levels of secular education have greatly improved, leading to academization of well above one-half, and in some countries over 80 percent of the present young Jewish adult generation. Most of the Jewish labor force has been gradually—but massively—moving from crafts and commerce, to management and the liberal professions. One of the most significant changes over the last century concerns the widespread improvement in health conditions and longevity. A further diffused transformation concerns the declining universality of the nuclear family, and has resulted in a generalized decline in birthrates. Jewish populations have consequently become markedly aging. By and large, world Jewry (at least in the Diaspora) has become rather homogeneous with regard to its demographic patterns and socioeconomic characteristics.

The relationship between socioeconomic and ideational characteristics is a central aspect of the whole development of Jewish societies, and can involve significant mutual feedbacks. While the contemporary sociodemographic characteristics of Jews basically conform the third and fourth stage of Ruppin's typology, the amount of ideational-cultural differentiation within the Jewish population of the 1990s is still substantial. The deep and diffused transformation of Jewish social structure does not always or necessarily imply a parallel transformation in Jewish identification. Patterns of social mobility have exerted visible effects on Jewish identification over time, but the relationship has worked the other way around, too. As noted, many sociodemographic characteristics of Jews worldwide have undergone a considerable homogenization, which has prompted the expectation that social-structural similarity should enhance other forms of communal cohesiveness among the Jewish population (Goldscheider 1986). This tends to be true regarding Jewish social class concentration and a persisting distinctiveness in Jewish occupational distributions. However, for the purpose of the present discussion of Jewish societies in the perspective of an assimilation typology, social class is not an efficient variable, precisely because of its substantial lack of internal differentiation.

A considerable amount of diversity still persists in the *Jewish ecological density* of the proximate residential environment. Throughout Jewish populations, the full range of situations can be observed, from virtually complete segregation to complete dispersal among non-Jews. Jewish ecological density influences the frequency and quality of social interaction, hence directly or indirectly affects a variety of other processes, from availability of Jewish community services to choice of spouse. It is true that in contemporary societies, sophisticated communication systems make possible interaction at a distance. Nevertheless, no real substitute can be reasonably assumed for the range of opportunities and experiences created by physical proximity and community density. While Jewish ecological density has probably declined in the course of time, in conformity with Ruppin's expectations, Jewishness of the environment is not an irreversible property, being sensitive to manipulation by concerned individuals or communities. In different places and under changing circumstances the density of Jewish environment has declined or increased (Della-Pergola 1989). Therefore, the quest for an efficient, sufficiently diverse indicator of the Jew's *social-structural* distinctiveness versus assimilation can be effectively served by a measure of ecological density reflecting Jewish residential patterns.

Turning now to the assessment of the *cultural* dimension of Jewish assimilation, we earlier mentioned religion as Ruppin's fundamental criterion for defining and measuring the intensity of Jewish identification. The sociocultural transformations that have occurred since Ruppin's early writings demand that we move beyond the concept of one variable displaying different amounts of intensity, from highest to lowest. In the context of widespread modernization and secularization, Jewish identification might possibly have evolved from one pattern, religion, to other patterns of a more secular nature, yet of no lesser intensity and significance for Jewish individual and collective continuity. Therefore secularization—in

Ruppin's view the typical correlate of Jewish assimilation—should not be automatically assumed to exert that effect.

It seems essential to consider that a person's Jewish identification can be expressed through *individual* beliefs, attitudes, and behaviors, as well as by being part of a *collective* or community. Taking this into account, we define the two major alternatives to *religion* that have emerged for a positive and meaningful Jewish identification as *ethnicity/community*, and *cultural residue*, each of which deserves a brief review.

Attachment to Judaism mainly defined through *religion* implies holding a complex of particular beliefs, norms, and values as well as the consistent performing of ritual practices that are in a sense unnatural—a burden one takes upon oneself not immediately and functionally related to some materially defined (or economic) benefit. Judaism involves complying with relatively rigorous behavioral rules coupled with submitting oneself to possible sanction by a recognized authority or by the whole community. Numerous Jewish ritual acts require the presence of a quorum of other Jews. Active Jewish identification through religion necessarily involves the simultaneous presence of a unique complex of values, norms, and behaviors, and by belonging to an exclusive community.

Attachment to Judaism through a sense of shared *ethnicity,* typically consists of maintaining patterns of association that include a far greater amount of spontaneous and nonspecific contents than would be the case with religion. Such an involvement with a Jewish community, while expressing empathy for Judaism, does not necessarily involve peculiar beliefs and behaviors, nor clearly defined sanctions in case of a lack of compliance with such normative standards. A case in point is affiliating with a given Jewish Landsmanshaft (immigrants' association), or in a more recent context, the Jewish Community Center. While participants will tend to be exclusively or mostly Jewish, the contents of that participation will often incorporate a vast amount—if not a majority—of nonuniquely Jewish symbols and information. Jewish ethnic/communal identification may often involve the persistence of some element of religiosity, as shown by the diffuse though inconsistent presence of traditional observances among Jewish populations that on many accounts one would define as secular. This is why it seems justifiable to include in the *ethnicity/community* type of identification many Jews whose main attachment to Judaism is through a religious congregation. When the contents of the Jewish congregation's collective interaction have been transformed to incorporate large amounts of symbols and concepts taken from the outside, nondistinctively Jewish world, the sense of community has been preserved, but the element of religious, or in broader terms, cultural *exclusiveness* has been lost.

Attachment to Judaism may still persist independently of a clearly recognizable pattern of personal behavior or functional involvement in the collective life of a Jewish community. A person may display interest and some knowledge in one's own Jewish historical past, tradition, and culture. Knowledge of a Jewish language, extensive interest in Jewish scholarship, or even a sense of "home" nostalgia—which once acquired may be indelible—may be cases in point. We define this further main mode of Jewish identification as a *cultural residue*. Viewed in this particular context, culture is a looser and subaltern concept, especially when considering that most of those who display this mode of Jewish identification actually are illiterate in Jewish philosophy, Jewish literature, and out of Israel, the Hebrew language. A *cultural residue* therefore provides a more ambiguous and less binding parameter for defining Jewish identification—typically to the communally unaffiliated. It does not provide a mutually exclusive bond with regard to outsiders, as may be the case with *religion* and *ethnic community*, and can be more easily acquired, shared, or lost. In this case too, sporadic elements of religion and of ethnicity/community involvement may accompany the *cultural residue* mode of Jewish identification which, however, is mostly expressed through individual intellectual attachment—no matter how intense.

Each of the three major modes of Jewish identification (*religion, ethnicity/community,* and *cultural residue*) may be manifested through the whole gamut from most to least intensive. Therefore, in terms of the typical weakening inherent in the assimilation process, each could theoretically be rated as a parallel, equally significant pattern. Passages of Jews from one mode to another, which have occurred to a large extent in the course of the process of modernization and secularization, might be equated with a mere transformation of formal contents without impact on overall intensity. We shall nevertheless posit here that the different major patterns of Jewish identification can be arrayed on a hierarchical ranking. Identification according to *religion*, involving an exclusively Jewish individual practice *and* an exclusively Jewish community of orientation, appears to be a stronger mode of Jewishness than *ethnicity/community*, which involves a (largely) exclusive community but no particular individual practice; the latter, in turn, overpowers a Jewish identification that is manifested through a *cultural residue*, where neither element of particularistic individual practice or community of orientation is present.

The preceding discussion yields the following tabular classification of the major modes of Jewish identification:

Exclusively Jewish Individual Beliefs and Practices	Exclusively Jewish Community of Orientation	
	Yes	No
Yes	*Religion*	
No	*Ethnicity / Community*	*Cultural Residue*

In this scheme, an active expression of exclusively Jewish beliefs and practices at the individual level is not considered a realistic possibility in the absence of an exclusively Jewish community of orientation.

To these three major positive categories of Jewish identification, a fourth and weakest one should be added to take account of those Jews for whom *none* of the preceding modes and patterns of Jewish identification consistently apply. Some remnants of either three major modes may be present among Jews who belong to this fourth group. In practice, declining intensities of Jewish identification often tend to be compensated for by increasing identifications with alternative religious, ethnic, communal, or cultural frames of reference; otherwise, a weakened Jewish identification may simply be an indicator of a weaker overall sense of group identification among the relevant individuals. Many, indeed, while still formally belonging to a core Jewish population, display weak or no attachment to Judaism coupled with a substantial presence of distinctively non-Jewish ritual behaviors and/or attitudes. The latter may reflect a person's increasingly non-Jewish proximate relational networks, or the active attempt to create a syncretic identificational solution. The existence of such *dual Jewish-non-Jewish* identities has been clearly documented in America through the 1990 NJPS (Della-Pergola 1991). It has its counterpart among those non-Jewish members of an extended or enlarged Jewish population who display some traits of Jewishness. The latter, however, are beyond the concerns of the present chapter.

While our discussion so far, with several but after all not crucial modifications, replicates and extends Ruppin's own conceptualization, one macroscopic development makes the contemporary global picture significantly different from Ruppin's time: it is the emergence of Israeli society alongside the Jewish Diaspora as a new component of world Jewry. How can we typologically reconcile the substantially different parameters of a Jewish majority in a sovereign state with those of relatively small and dispersed Jewish minorities?

Interestingly, the major change introduced by Israel's presence in the sociology of the Jews seems to operate via the social-structural rather than via the cultural side. In fact, each of the four different modes of Jewish identification we have recognized, may and if fact does exist in Israeli society. While specific elements of the identificational and cultural experience of Jews in Israel and elsewhere may be different (Liebman & Cohen 1990), the main typological distinctions just discussed equally apply in Israel and in the Diaspora. Differences, as we shall see, may concern the relative weight of each identificational type rather than the existence in Israel of an entirely innovative type of identity that could not be deduced from the previous Diaspora's Jewish experience. What appears to be decisively innovative and mutually exclusive toward situations known from the Diaspora's experience is an entirely new level of what we have called "ecological density." Jews in Israel not only have achieved a status of majority at the local level, which can be observed as well in several Diaspora communities in the past and present, but they add to it the fundamental dimension of political sovereignty. For the purpose of our discussion, the critical manifestation of statehood is an all-inclusive, integrated, pluralistic, competitive political system that provides the sole existing opportunity whereby a mode of active interaction is achieved among the whole Jewish population in a given country or locale. Such a measure of total participation in an activity of specifically Jewish or generally civic relevance cannot be ever achieved in the partial, sectorial, and voluntaristic Jewish community's organizational structure that prevails in the contemporary Diaspora setting. In fact, the overwhelming diversity of existing Jewish organizations to a large extent reflects the different modes of identification (religious, ethnic/communal, or cultural-residual) that were just described, and the separate needs of the respective Jewish constituencies.

An Updated Typology

Before turning to descriptive data on the variation of contemporary Jewish populations according to the criteria of identification or assimilation now outlined, a cautionary statement is in order.

The attempt to compare past and present on one dimension of Jewish society cannot ignore the contextual differences on other dimensions. When using certain definitions of Jewish identification, there will be no pretension that the intensity of those identifications is the same today as it once was, rather that the current *significance* of those definitions fairly corresponds to what it was at another historical time. Moreover, the essentially *continuous* nature of distributions along the two assimilation-identification ranges discussed here should be emphasized. While the attempt to create discrete categories may be justifiable for the sake of presentation and comparisons, it clearly constitutes a simplification of an actually more complex and very fluid reality, which might equally well be described through alternative categorizations.

Frequencies of Mixed Marriage

A first attempt to compare the changing levels of Jewish assimilation in the course of the twentieth century is illustrated in table 2. Estimated frequencies of mixed marriage—one of the key indicators in Ruppin's typology—are shown together with estimates of the combined Jewish populations in all countries where the respective levels of heterogamy were observed. A mixed marriage in this analysis is a current, new union in which the non-Jewish-born partner keeps his or her original religious identification after marriage. For the earlier date, the estimates are Ruppin's (adjusted for some necessary data manipulation; see the notes to tables 1 and 2). Estimates for the mid-1930s and late 1980s are our own, based on as systematic as possible a scan of the available evidence (DellaPergola 1993).

The process of assimilation, as operationalized through mixed marriage, appears to have greatly advanced nearly without exception in most countries. At the beginning of the century, the largest segment of world Jewish population was located in countries where the rate of intermarriage was less than 2%. By the mid-1930s, the largest segment included Jews in countries with a rate between 2% and 9%, and the second largest was in countries with a rate of 9% to 23%. By the late 1980s the situation had radically changed, with over one-half of the total world Jewish population living in countries where the rate of mixed marriage was estimated at between 45% and 55%. This category included the two largest Jewish populations in the Diaspora: the United States and the former USSR. The second largest group, dominated by the Jewish population in Israel, was the one displaying extremely low rates of mixed marriages.

Table 2
World Jewish Population Distribution, by Estimated
Frequencies of Mixed Marriages, 1900s–1980s

Percentage of Mixed Marriages	1900s[a]	Mid-1930s[b]	Late-1980s[b]	Late-1980s revised[c]
Total	12,000,000	16,600,000	12,979,000	12,979,000
0–2	6,000,000	4,130,000	3,659,000	3,659,000
2–9	3,000,000	6,700,000	54,000	54,000
9–23	2,000,000	5,725,000	161,000	761,000
23–33	1,000,000	45,000	944,000	994,000
33–45			818,000	2,743,000
45–55			7,186,000	686,000
55–75			156,000	4,081,000
75–95			1,000	1,000

Sources: 1900s, adapted from Ruppin (1913) (see table 1); 1930s and 1980s, adapted from Della-Pergola (1993).

[a]The Jewish population distribution reflects Ruppin's four sections in table 1. The data refer to a combination of geographic locations and social strata within the Jewish population. Mixed marriage frequencies differ from those reported in table 1, because of the reasons explained in note a to table 1. We recalculated Ruppin's percentages of mixed marriages to make them compatible with the conventional use in the literature.

[b]Our estimates are based on countrywide or regional total frequencies of mixed marriages. Specifically, countrywide averages were used for the frequencies of mixed marriages in the United States and in the (former) USSR.

[c]Revised estimates of Jewish population distribution, were obtained by allocating the respective frequencies of mixed marriages to four different strata of Jewish population in the United States, by denomination (Orthodox, Conservative, Reform, or none), and to the (former) USSR.

Actually, the data reported in table 2 are not fully comparable because of the different calculation methods. Ruppin tried to construct homogeneous strata by combining geographic locations and social strata within the Jewish population of different countries, while our estimates for the 1930s and 1980s are based on country-by-country total frequencies of mixed marriage, thus loosing the internal diversity that exists between different Jewish subgroups within each country. This may explain why in the estimates for the 1930s the stratum with highest frequencies of mixed marriage (23%–33%) has such a smaller Jewish population than at the beginning of the century. Another reason may be that Ruppin overestimated the size of his fourth section (the most assimilated). In an effort to improve the comparability of more recent estimates with earlier data, we disaggregated the two largest Diaspora populations—the United States and the former USSR. Jewish population was redistributed according to the frequencies of mixed marriages within four Jewish denominational groups in the United States—Orthodox, Conservative, Reform, and none (Kosmin et al. 1991)—and within the fifteen former Soviet republics (Tolts 1993). The revised estimates show that the prevailing 45%–55% mixed marriage frequency in the late 1980s resulted from averaging quite different behaviors within U.S. and former USSR Jewries. In the revised estimates (see the last column of table 2), the Jewish population characterized by comparatively lower frequencies of mixed marriages is substantially larger than in the original version. At the same time, however, the largest Jewish population group worldwide shifts from the 45%–55% to the 55%–75% mixed marriage category, thus pointing to an even stronger progression of the assimilation process.

Quite interestingly, by the late 1980s, over half of the world's Jewish population, and nearly 80% of Diaspora Jews were intermarrying at a rate substantially above the highest value in Ruppin's original range. Yet, at least in the short term, the Jewishness of such Jewish population would not be discounted. On the other hand, by the early 1990s Israel's Jewish population had increased to over 4.3 million—mostly due to immigration from Eastern Europe. At this point, the section of world Jewish population with the *lowest* rates of mixed marriage had also become the longest, partially recreating the global situation that prevailed at the beginning of the century. Israel's influence had effected a true quantum leap in the history of Jewish assimilation.

Jewish Ecological Densities and Modes of Identification

A more complex, and sociologically sounder, attempt to evaluate the progress of Jewish assimilation is presented in table 3. A bivariate typology is developed that tries to give account of the simultaneous but not necessarily identical changes that have occurred in the social-structural aspect of *Jewish ecological density* and in the sociocultural aspect of the *main mode of identification with Judaism*. Recalling our previous discussion, four levels of Jewishness of the immediate residential environment are defined: *Israel*, where Jews are the majority nationally and typically form the near totality of inhabitants at the neighborhood level; and three types of neighborhoods in Diaspora communities where Jews constitute dense, medium, or thin minorities, or respectively, *more than 35%, 5% to 35%,* and *less than 5%* of the total inhabitants. While the densities selected are clearly arbitrary, the inherent continuum

Table 3
A Structural-Cultural Typology of World Jewish Population, 1900s–1990s—Tentative Evaluations (Core Jews)

Jewish Ecological Density[a]	Main Mode of Jewish Identification				
	Religion	Ethnicity/ Community	Cultural Residue	Dual Jewish- Non-Jewish	Total
1900s					
Total	6,000,000	3,000,000	2,000,000	1,000,000	12,000,000
Israel	0	0	0	0	0
Dense (>35%)	4,500,000	1,500,000	500,000	0	6,500,000
Medium (5%–35%)	1,000,000	1,000,000	1,000,000	500,000	3,500,000
Thin (<5%)	500,000	500,000	500,000	500,000	2,000,000
1990s					
Total	2,000,000	5,900,000	4,100,000	900,000	12,900,000
Israel	1,000,000	2,700,000	500,000	100,000	4,300,000
Dense (>35%)	500,000	100,000	100,000	0	700,000
Medium (5%–35%)	300,000	1,700,000	1,700,000	300,000	4,000,000
Thin (<5%)	200,000	1,400,000	1,800,000	500,000	3,900,000
Difference 1900s–1990s					
Total	−4,000,000	+2,900,000	+2,100,000	−100,000	+900,000
Israel	+1,000,000	+2,700,000	+500,000	+100,000	+4,300,000
Dense (>35%)	−4,000,000	−1,400,000	−400,000	0	−5,800,000
Medium (5%–35%)	−700,000	+700,000	+700,000	−200,000	+500,000
Thin (<5%)	−300,000	+900,000	+1,300,000	0	+1,900,000

Sources: 1900s, adapted from Ruppin (1913), see table 1; 1990s, adapted from Schmelz and DellaPergola (1994). Cell distributions are our estimates.
[a]Percent of Jews among total population residing in immediate surrounding area.

involves passing from an environment that is predominantly Jewish, or where at least Jews constitute a highly visible component of the total social environment, to a thin Jewish presence in an overwhelmingly non-Jewish environment. On the cultural side, the four main modes of identification with Judaism, just defined as *religion*, *ethnicity / community*, *cultural residue*, and *dual Jewish-non-Jewish*, are suggested to express a ranking of intensities from strongest to weakest. Each combination of ecological density and mode of identification being possible, the result in Table 3 and in the attached graphs is a 4 × 4 classification in which persons may be found in consistently strong or weak Jewish structural and cultural modalities, or in inconsistent combinations of the two.

The upper part of table 3 refers once again to Ruppin's original typology, which we modified in an attempt to account for both structural and cultural aspects. The four categories of Jewish identification repeat Ruppin's four sections, adapting—or possibly forcing—them into our Jewish identificational classification. Keeping in mind that when Ruppin wrote *The Jews of Today*, Palestine's Jewish population barely reached fifty thousand persons; the three categories of residential density in the Diaspora at the beginning of the century were estimated from detailed listings of Jewish population distributions by localities that are available for the relevant years (a processing for Eastern European localities first appeared in DellaPergola 1983). The single largest group reported in table 3 for the 1900s is formed by Jews combining a religious mode of identification with living in neighborhoods with high Jewish densities. In fact at that time not only did Jews constitute large minorities, but often constituted the absolute majority in the respective residential environments, reflecting past limitations on the Jews' residential opportunities, or even the persistence of such constraints.

In the central panel of table 3 a similar bivariate classification is attempted for the early 1990s. The data on residential density in the Diaspora are based on a careful scan of available Jewish population distributions by small areas—such as postal codes in the United States—or inference based on the total number and percent of Jews in different cities where such more detailed data were not available. In this respect, it is interesting to note that in the United States such detailed inspection of residential characteristics provides an overall distribution that strictly matches the perceived Jewishness of residential neighborhoods of NJPS respondents. Notably, more respondents consider Jewish residential concentration to be important than actually live in a densely Jewish environment.

This indicates that residential diffusion, or more generally structural assimilation, does not necessarily reflect a deliberate choice to move away from a Jewish environment, but rather is the product of socioeconomic and other practical constraints. The fact remains that, although the residential characteristics of Jews are still remote from indifferent diffusion among the non-Jewish population, a clear tendency toward declining Jewish ecological densities can be detected in the more recent data. We grossly estimated that around 1990 about the same numbers of Jews in the Diaspora (4 million) lived in moderately Jewish neighborhoods (5% to 35% of Jews among total inhabitants) and in thinly Jewish environments (less than 5% Jewish). Some 700,000 were estimated to live in densely Jewish neighborhoods (above 35% Jewish).

With regard to estimating the distribution of contemporary Jewish populations by modes of identification, data for Jews in the Diaspora were obtained by compiling the recent evidence from NJPS in the United States, from a variety of other similar surveys in other countries, and from Jewish institutional sources. Special attention was paid to the substantial range of variation that prevails between Jewish communities worldwide. Our typology is based primarily on the frequencies reported in such sources regarding a variety of *actual Jewish behaviors*, especially observance of religious traditions and membership in Jewish organizations. Evidence on Jewish attitudes served as a complementary source for assessing the overall variation in modes of Jewish identification among the Jewish public. Available data on ritual and on other religious observance provide useful information to evaluate the number of the religiously identified. Significant country-by-country differences appear, although the ranking of Jewish rituals by observance frequencies tends to be quite similar in the various countries. Clearly the presence of organized religion in Jewish community life tends to be greater in the United States than in the majority of other Diaspora communities, although this does not necessarily imply a particularly high frequency of religious behaviors (Liebman & Cohen 1990; Kosmin & Lachman 1993). The presence of religion also tends to be greater in Great Britain than in France or in most Latin American communities, with Eastern Europe at the lowest end of the continuum. Concerning formal community affiliation—an important element in evaluating the number of Jews who mostly identify through an ethnic/communal mode—the percentages affiliated may be as high as 90% in Mexico, about 70% in England, less than 40% in France, between less than 20%, and more than 70% in different cities in the United States, and—until recently—close to nil in the former USSR.

Our analysis tried to assess the presence of different combinations of religious observance, community affiliation, and other cognitive or attitudinal aspects of Jewishness among each major contemporary Jewish population. In the case of the United States, which numerically dominates the Diaspora totals, preference for, and affiliation with, the major denominational movements was carefully considered in relation to actual religious practices and to other aspects of Jewish identification. The respective estimates were obtained by carving out of each denomination the subpopulation that appeared to fit better with each mode of identification according to our typology (Rebhun 1993). Thus, for example, our estimate of the religiously identified in the United States includes persons who identify with the Orthodox, Conservative, or Reform denominations, but with different and declining proportions of each group. Interestingly, our overall classification of the modes of Jewish identification in the United States conforms—ex post facto— with the 1990 NJPS finding that American Jews believe they are, in descending order, a cultural, ethnic, and religious group (DellaPergola 1991).

Recent evidence on the modes of Jewish identification in Israel was provided by a national survey of family formation and fertility (Peritz & Adler 1993) and by a national survey on beliefs, observances, and social interaction among Israeli Jews (Levy, Levinsohn, & Katz 1993). Additional evidence was gathered through data on enrollment in the different religious and lay sectors of the Israeli educational system, and by analyzing the returns at recent Israeli political elections in conjunction with the stance of each party concerning religious and national issues (Schmelz, DellaPergola, & Avner 1991). The dual Jewish-non-Jewish category in Israel is meant to reflect the presence of the more marginally identified sections among recent immigrants from the former USSR.

By the 1990s, based on these admittedly tentative evaluations, the largest number of Jews globally appeared to identify through a mode of ethnicity/community, as just defined. Within this subtotal, possibly approaching six million Jews worldwide, the largest section is represented by the mainstream Jewish population in the State of Israel which, while tendentially secular, has maintained some traditional practices and has incorporated them into a predominantly ethnic/national mode of Jewish identification. We may evaluate at about another two million the number of Jews whose main mode of identification is through active religious participation—half of which in Israel; over four million those—mostly communally unaffiliated Jews in the Diaspora—who appear to keep at least some residual elements of a cultural attachment to Judaism; and close to one million those Jews whom we have defined as carriers of a dual Jewish-non-Jewish identity.

By comparing the estimates for the beginning of the century and the 1990s in table 3 and in figures 1 and 2, it becomes clear how greatly the religious mode of Jewish identification coupled with dense Jewish residential environments has declined in the Diaspora. Conversely, both the intermediate and weaker modes of Jewish identification *and* the thinner Jewish ecological environments have become substantially more typical. The Shoah, with its disastrous Jewish population cuts, accounts for most of these changes. Further significant changes are related to gradual transformations in the Jewish identification of contemporary communities. The emergence of Israel's presence in the contemporary world is felt through the distinctive Jewish environmental conditions it has created, and through the reinforcement of an essentially ethnic/national/communal mode of Jewish identification, rather than by enhancing the religious mode of Jewish identification that predominated in the past.

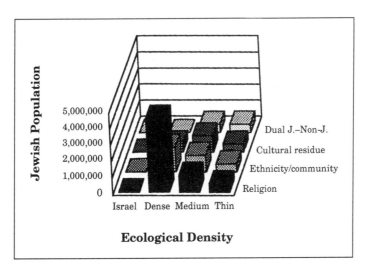

Fig. 1
Structural-Cultural Typology of World Jewry, 1900s

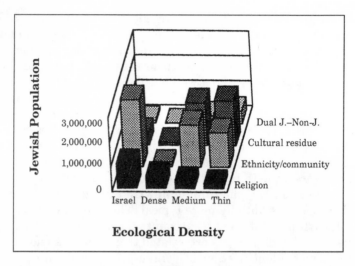

Fig. 2
Structural-Cultural Typology of World Jewry, 1990s

Summarizing the major changes between the 1900s and the 1990s, on balance world Jewry lost 4 million people belonging to the densely settled religious type, and another 1.3 million densely settled ethnic/communal Jews; it acquired 2.7 million ethnic/communal Israelis, and 1.3 million thinly settled Jews of the cultural residue type. The comparatively modest change in the estimated size of the Jewish population in the dual Jewish-non-Jewish identificational mode may be explained by the inherent instability of what constitutes for many a stage of passage toward ceasing from being part of the Jewish population altogether. Finally, world Jewry in the 1900s could be described in the form of an inner core of the more strongly identified and less socially mobile, surrounded by a gradually less Jewishly identified and more socially mobile semiperiphery and periphery. In the 1990s, the global picture pointed to growing polarization between the Israeli main (ethnic/communal) mode of Jewish identification, and the Jewishly thinned, culturally residual peripheries among Diaspora communities.

It is quite obvious that taxonomic exercises like the one attempted here cannot pretend at any degree of precision and only can be suggestive of very broad trends. Moreover we have emphasized, and we reiterate here, that Jewish society is not separated into discrete categories, bur rather constitutes a very fluid continuum. Passages from any category to another may be easy and frequent, occur in any direction, and in fact may be repeatedly experienced by the same individual over a life cycle. Different ways of handling the concepts and data we tried to muster may certainly produce somewhat different results (see, e.g., Cohen 1991). It is unlikely, though, that the overall estimates obtained would result in a picture substantially different from the one suggested here.

Looking at the Future

Arthur Ruppin, while proposing a powerful theory of Jewish societal evolution, was rather cautious with regard to anticipating the future course of Jewish history. In the preface to the second edition of *Die Juden der Gegenwart* (Ruppin 1904) he wrote, "I make no claim to being a prophet, but the signs of the time demand an interpretation and I have given mine." Later, in 1932, Ruppin wrote in his diaries that "The history of the world knows no laws, not even of probability. It is therefore senseless to prophesy about it" (Ruppin 1971: 261).

These words sound a healthy warning signal to those—like ourselves—who have been interested in developing and analyzing Jewish population projections. Indeed, the typical initial assumption of those who elaborate such computational exercises is that the basic conditions in the system will supposedly remain more or less as they are known to be at the time of the elaboration of such projections. The assumption of a gradual progression of a given process, such as assimilation, is tantamount to forecasting a linear evolution of history and society. But the last decades of Jewish history illustrate a strikingly nonlinear experience: the destruction of European Jewry, Israel's independence, and the continuing large-scale geographic redistribution of Jews through mass international migration, all constitute major exceptions to the linearity hypothesis.

What in fact should be centrally considered in any prognosis of the future development of Jewish society, whether at the beginning or the end of the twentieth century, is the Jews' belonging in, and to a significant extent dependence on a complex and integrated political/socioeconomic world system. The latter's capacity for change and sometimes revolution has consistently defied the best analytic minds and systematization efforts. Predicting the Jewish future amounts first of all to predicting the world system's future—an objective definitely beyond the scope of a reasonable agenda for a sociology of the Jews.

Looking back, Ruppin will have been proven wrong on several important accounts. In spite of his assumption that beyond certain levels of modernization and secularization there would be no Jewish existence, large, modern, and sophisticated Jewish populations and communities continue to persist today. Some of his assumptions about the relationship between race and character would be dismissed by a contemporary scholarship which, nevertheless, was able to carefully assess the genetic similarities and dissimilarities among Jews of disparate geographic origins (Bonné-Tamir & Adam 1992). And he could not foresee that only five years past his death stood the realization of Zionism's capital goal: a large, politically sovereign, Jewish settlement in Palestine.

But, consistently with Ruppin's expectations, assimilation, measured through the frequency of mixed marriages, Jewish ecological density, and the main mode of identification with Judaism, would continue its progression. The new highs reached would raise new questions about the contents, viability, and transmissibility of an increasingly stretched Jewish identity in the longer term. Zionism, through the independent State of Israel, would exert a deep effect in slowing down or even reversing the assimilation of the Jews. Interestingly, in the new Israeli context, Jewish assimilation would be at least partially set back by way of a structural process—the creation of an entirely new dimension of ecological density able to significantly reduce the interaction between Jews and non-Jews—more than by radically changing the mode and quality of Jewish identification. The effect of adding the new Israel category in a typological classification of world Jews would be felt through an expanded set of *social-structural opportunities*, rather than through a different range of *cultural choices*. Such a result sounds like a vindication of Ruppin's views about the role of Zionism in creating the essential facts to enhance continuity of the Jewish people.

All things considered, ninety years after his first *Jews of Today*, Arthur Ruppin is alive and well. The complexities of an ever-evolving Jewish identification are not over. Nor are the challenges confronting those who try to elaborate a viable sociology of the Jews.

Acknowledgments

The author heads the Division of Jewish Demography and Statistics (DJDS) at the A. Harman Institute of Contemporary Jewry, the Hebrew University of Jerusalem. I wrote this chapter while on sabbatical leave at the Von Grunebaum Center for Near

Eastern Studies and Department of Sociology, University of California Los Angeles (UCLA), and at the University of Judaism, Los Angeles. I thank the host institutions, and especially Profs. Georges Sabagh of UCLA and the Hanan Alexander of University of Judaism, for granting a stimulating environment for research. Some of the materials discussed in this chapter reflect research carried on at the DJDS by Dr. Mark Tolts and Mr. Uzi Rebhun. Useful critical remarks to a first draft were provided by Deborah Dash Moore, Riv-Ellen Prell, Serge Moscovici, Mehdi Bozorgmehr, and David N. Myers. Finally, I wish to express fond and longing thoughts to my senior colleagues of many years and predecessors as DJDS directors: the late prof. Roberto Bachi, who as a young immigrant-academic in late 1930s Palestine enjoyed Ruppin's encouragement; and the late prof. Uziel O. Schmelz, who was one of Ruppin's students.

References

Bachi, R. (1993) "Personal Recollections on the History of Research in Jewish Demography." Paper presented at the Eleventh World Congress of Jewish Studies, Jerusalem: Hebrew University.

Bonné-Tamir, B., and A. Adam. (1992) *Genetic Diversity among Jews: Diseases and Markers at the DNA Level*. New York: Oxford University Press.

Buber, M. (1929) "Three Stations." In M. Buber. (1961) *Nation and World*. Jerusalem (Hebrew).

Cohen, S. M. (1991) *Content or Continuity? Alternative Bases for Commitment. The 1989 National Survey of American Jews*. New York: American Jewish Committee.

DellaPergola, S. (1983) *La trasformazione demografica della diaspora ebraica*. Torino: Loescher.

———. (1989) "Jewish Urban Ecology in European Cities: A Comparative Approach." In *Papers in Jewish Demography*, edited by U. O. Schmelz and S. DellaPergola. Jerusalem: Hebrew University, Jewish Population Studies, no. 19: 303–36.

———. (1991) "New Data on Demography and Identification among Jews in the U.S.: Trends Inconsistencies and Disagreements." *Contemporary Jewry* 12: 67–97.

———. (1993) "Israel and World Jewish Population: A Core-Periphery Perspective." In *Population and Social Change in Israel*, edited by C. Goldscheider. Boulder: Westview Press, 39–63.

Gans, H. J. (1979) "Symbolic Ethnicity: The Future of Ethnic Groups and Cultures in America." *Ethnic and Racial Studies* 2, no. 1: 1–19.

Goldscheider, C. (1986) *Jewish Continuity and Change: Emerging Patterns in America*. Bloomington: Indiana University Press.

Goldstein, S. (1992) "Profile of American Jewry: Insights from the 1990 National Jewish Population Survey." *American Jewish Year Book* 92: 77–173.

Gordon, M. M. (1964) *Assimilation in American Life: The Role of Race, Religion and National Origins*. New York: Oxford University Press.

Herman, S. (1977) *Jewish Identity*. Beverly Hills: Sage Publications.

Kosmin, B., S. Goldstein, J. Waksberg, N. Lerer, A. Keysar, and J. Scheckner. (1991) *Highlights of the CJF 1990 National Jewish Population Survey*. New York: Council of Jewish Federations.

Kosmin, B. A., and Lachman. (1993) *One Nation under God; Religion in Contemporary America*. New York: Harmony Books.

Levy, S., H. Levinsohn, and E. Katz. (1993) *Beliefs, Observances and Social Interaction among Israeli Jews*. Jerusalem: Louis Guttman Israel Institute of Applied Social Research.

Liebman, C. S., and S. M. Cohen. (1990) *Two Worlds of Judaism: The Israeli and American Experiences*. New Haven: Yale University Press.

Lieberson, S., and M. C. Waters. (1988) *From Many Strands: Ethnic and Racial Groups in Contemporary America*. New York: Russell Sage Foundation.

Medding, P. Y. (1987) "Segmented Ethnicity and the New Jewish Politics." In *Studies in Contemporary Jewry*, edited by E. Mendelsohn. Vol. 3: 26–45.

Peritz, E., and I. Adler. (1993) "Religiosity Patterns in Israel." Paper presented at the Eleventh World Congress of Jewish Studies, Jerusalem: Hebrew University.

Rebhun, U. (1993) "Trends in the Size of American Jewish Denominations: A Renewed Evaluation." *CCAR Journal: A Reform Jewish Quarterly* (winter): 1–11.

Ruppin, A. (1904) *Die Juden der Gegenwart*. Berlin: Calvary.

———. (1913) *The Jews of To-day*. Translated by M. Bentwich. New York: Henry Holt.

———. (1922) *Gli Ebrei d'oggi dall'aspetto sociale*. Translated by D. Lattes and M. Beilinson. Torino: Fratelli Bocca.

————. (1930–31) *Die Soziologie der Juden*. Berlin: Juedische Verlag.

————. (1931–33) *Hasoziologia shel hayehudim*. Tel Aviv: Shtibel (Hebrew).

————. (1940) *The Jewish Fate and Future*. London: Macmillan.

————. (1971) *Memoirs, Diaries, Letters*. Edited by A. Bein. London: Weidenfeld and Nicholson.

Schmelz, U. O., and DellaPergola, S. (1994) "World Jewish Population, 1992." *American Jewish Year Book*. 94: 465–89.

————., and U. Avner. (1991) *Ethnic Differences among Israeli Jews: A New Look*. Jerusalem: Hebrew University and American Jewish Committee, Jewish Population Studies, no. 22.

Shapira, A. (1993) "Buber, Herder, and German 'Volkism.' " *Studies in Zionism, A Journal of Israel Studies* 14, no. 1 (spring): 1–30.

Sklare, M. (1993) "The Sociology of Contemporary Jewish Studies." In M. Sklare, *Observing America's Jews*, edited by J. D. Sarna. Hanover: N.H., Brandeis University Press, 181–202.

Tolts, M. (1993) "Some Basic Trends in Soviet Jewish Demography." In *Papers in Jewish Demography 1989*, edited by U. O. Schmelz and S. DellaPergola. Jerusalem: Hebrew University, Jewish Population Studies, no. 25: 237–43.

Waters, M. C. (1990) *Ethnic Options: Choosing Identities in America*. Berkeley: University of California Press.

Sergio DellaPergola

Appendix
Data and Assumptions for Table 3

A. Jewish Ecological Densities: Estimated Percentage Distributions, Early 1990s

Country[a]	Jewish Population	Total	Dense (>35%)[b]	Medium (5%-35%)[b]	Thin (<5%)[b]
United States	5,620,000	100	7	51	42
France	530,000	100	6	32	62
Russia	415,000	100	9	29	62
Canada	356,000	100	9	49	42
United Kingdom	298,000	100	14	49	37
Ukraine	276,000	100	14	44	42
Argentina	211,000	100	9	39	52
Brazil	100,000	100	9	49	42
South Africa	100,000	100	19	49	32
Australia	90,000	100	19	49	32
Hungary	56,000	100	9	9	52
Germany	50,000	100	4	24	72
Belarus	47,000	100	14	44	42
Uzbekistan	45,000	100	4	44	42
Mexico	40,000	100	24	49	27
Rest of Diaspora	366,000	100	6	22	72

[a]Fifteen largest Jewish populations in the Diaspora, ranked by size. Jewish populations as in Schmelz and DellaPergola (1994).
[b]Percent of Jews among total population residing in immediate surrounding area.

B. Jewish Identification Modes: Estimated Percentage Distributions, early 1990s

Country	Total	Religion	Ethnicity/ Community	Cultural Residue	Dual Jewish-Non-Jewish
Israel	100	23	63	12	2
United States	100	10	35	45	10
France	100	15	25	55	5
Russia	100	1	36	50	13
Canada	100	20	50	20	10
United Kingdom	100	27	44	27	2
Ukraine	100	3	52	35	10
Argentina	100	10	57	28	5
Brazil	100	15	60	20	5
South Africa	100	15	65	20	–
Australia	100	15	60	25	–
Hungary	100	12	33	45	10
Germany	100	10	40	30	20
Belarus	100	5	40	45	10
Uzbekistan	100	33	33	33	1
Mexico	100	38	50	12	–
Rest of Diaspora	100	16	30	39	15

A Traditi
Educe
Contem

Harvey E. Goldberg

And he shall turn the heart of the fathers to the children, and the heart of the children to their fathers.

—Malachi 3:24

Introduction

One central feature of Jewry's contact with modernity has been the movement of children into schools run by the state, or conforming to basic rules and goals established by the state. This shift challenged the traditional arrangements in which family, community, and school reinforced one another in a relatively consistent manner. The exact pattern has varied greatly from country to country. Often, the state has permitted the establishment of Jewish private schools in order to inculcate Jewish knowledge, skills, and commitments. These, too, partake of modernity, in that each school reflects a particular view of Judaism emerging in the nineteenth or twentieth centuries—a blending, or patching together, of attachment to Jewish tradition and life in a contemporary society. Such schools, rather than being spontaneous expressions of communal values, often seek

olds that are at variance with the way in
nd practices have been worked into the lives

contradictions like these frequently are over-
research. Field workers tend to seek out a neatly
or community, focusing on its particular content and
he functional specificity of modern life encourages the
he school" or "the family," but less commonly the complex
s between them. But Jewish life, despite its heterogeneity, is
ot completely segmented and compartmentalized. Diverse ide-
ical currents and groups touch upon one another, particularly
ithin the setting of schools. The general "mobility" of modern life
often means that parents are not able to send their children to
schools that precisely reflect their notions and patterns of contemporary Jewish living. They often select schools that represent outlooks that are close, but not identical, to their own. The "marginal"
but, I will argue, extremely dynamic area thus created deserves
exploration.

This chapter will begin such an exploration in an autobiograph-
ical mode. The "autobiography" is more that of a family than of an
individual. By examining an account of one family and its relation
to Jewish education across generations, and in different settings of
modern Jewish life, some features and dilemmas of contemporary
Jewish primary education are brought to the fore. It also reveals the
family to be a critical unit within which orientations to Jewish education and culture are formed and reformulated. The second part
of the chapter will expand upon several questions raised in the family story.

* * *

My paternal grandfather emigrated to the United States from
Eastern Europe (I believe from Galicia). My father (an eldest son)
spoke sparingly about his family, but related that my grandfather
made a living as a butcher, moving to various Brooklyn neighborhoods in the wake of constant competition. When recalling his
mother who died in 1932, my father marveled at her ability to
quickly and accurately compute sums in her husband's shop without
knowing how to read or write.

My father's Jewish education took place in the years preceding,
and during World War I. I know little about his Hebrew training except that it probably involved hiring a *melamed* (tutor) to give him
lessons aimed primarily at preparing him for his Bar Mitzvah. Cer-

tainly there was no attempt to link his religious studies to other educational traditions.

For whatever reason, my father grew up attached to books. One story he told concerns his French studies in Boys' High School. The class was reading a French novel out of a bowdlerized textbook edition. In a used bookstore, my father acquired the original novel, without realizing how his classmates' books differed from his own. This difference emerged unexpectedly one day when he was asked to read aloud, causing much embarrassment to the teacher, and, I suspect, glee to the class.

At the age of fifteen my father finished high school. With his inquisitive mind, he had entertained thoughts of attending Columbia University. This did not prove to be financially feasible; he enrolled instead in Brooklyn Law School as soon as he was old enough to be admitted. He thus was launched early into the world of earning a living, but this did not quench his literary thirst. His interests were somewhat avant-garde for someone of his milieu. A two-volume edition of Frazer's *Golden Bough* and Havelock Ellis's multivolume study of human sexuality were books that adorned our bookshelves ever since I can remember.

During nights when I could not fall asleep, my father sometimes sat in my room telling me stories from Greek mythology. He often put himself to sleep reading mystery novels. But about the time that my parents transferred me to a Jewish day school from the local public school and afternoon Hebrew school (Goldberg 1985: 100), my father evinced a more systematic interest in Jewish studies.

Books on Judaica began to replace the "whodunits" at his bedside. He undertook to systematically review the whole Bible, first relying on English translations and commentaries, but later reviving and improving the Hebrew he had learned in his childhood. One topic that deeply grabbed his interest was the story of the newly discovered Dead Sea Scrolls and he closely followed Edmund Wilson's account of their discovery and meaning in *The New Yorker* (see Wilson 1955). As the years went on, almost all his free time became devoted to this end: to learn—and to teach—as he became active in various programs of adult Jewish education.

The culmination of this process was his early retirement and enrollment as a rabbinical student in the Jewish Theological Seminary of America (JTS) in the mid-1960s. Over half a century had passed since he first entered law school. In his studies, he often drew upon his legal expertise, comparing rabbinic law with American or Roman law.[1] The ability to "return" to a world in which his ethnic origins and intellectual horizons mingled comfortably provided the last decades of his life with purposeful activity, satisfaction, and a sense of closure.

The impact of my father's evolving orientation to Judaism must be placed in the context of the influences from my mother, and from my maternal grandmother who lived with us until she passed away. While I surmise that my father came from a Galitzianer (from Galicia) family, my mother clearly was "Lithuanian." Her father had died in Beylorussia when she was an infant, and my grandmother came to America with her only child when my mother was two years old. My grandmother earned a living as a peddler, and on at least one occasion attempted to open a small store which, however, did not succeed. While cast in the role of a poor peddler, partially dependent on relatives, she retained a sense of pride based on Jewish learning.

The details of briefly recollected stories are not clear, but my grandmother came from the area in White Russia in which the HaBaD movement (of the Lubovitcher hasidim) flourished, pitting itself against Haskala (enlightenment) influences that surrounded them. My grandfather, as he appeared in brief family narratives, was steeped in rabbinic learning at a young age, but also was exposed to secular knowledge. Stories portrayed him as the youngest and most outstanding of five brothers of a respected family.[2] This was the image retained and perpetuated by my grandmother, his wife for a very short time before his early death.

My mother also portrayed my grandmother as devoted to learning, telling stories of her demands, as a young girl, that she be given the chance to study in the *kheyder* (Jewish school) just as boys did. She certainly knew how to read from the prayer book and was literate in Yiddish. It was the practice in our family that my father's father (who lived in an old-age home in Brooklyn) would come to our home each Passover to lead the Seder. Much later it was explained to me that my mother's mother resented him; she was a *Litvakh* with pride in her family's heritage of learning, looking down on a simple Galitzianer who only knew how to read prayers in a rote manner.

I had no sense of such tension at the time: both grandparents died within about a year of one another around the time of my Bar Mitzvah. What is clear is that my grandmother was a dominant figure in our family with regard to my Jewish education, teaching me to recite *krishma* (*qriat shma`*) and blessings when I was young, and taking pride in my accomplishments after I began Hebrew school. In those years, my father's most obvious concerns did not revolve around Jewish culture and education. He still worked in his law office on Shabbat mornings, but concurred in encouraging my Hebrew and religious training.

Elsewhere (H. E. Goldberg 1985: 100–102), I have described the main elements of my Hebrew education in a suburban section of the borough of Queens. Beginning in a local Hebrew school that was part of a Conservative synagogue, it later involved both an Orthodox day school and high school on the one hand, and informal educational frameworks within the context of the Conservative movement on the other. This combination placed me in a position of shifting through the knowledge and the disparate worldviews presented to me in these diverse settings, and there is no doubt that my overall outlook was shaped by my experience within the Conservative movement. While an undergraduate student at Columbia University, I took courses at the Jewish Theological Seminary of America (JTS) that continued to reinforce that outlook. While never formally finishing a degree at the JTS, the training I received there has oriented me both in my academic career and nonacademic Jewish life.

Classes at the JTS were not only an intellectual experience. For those Jewish youths studying there while attending college in New York City, the school provided a social setting and an arena of courtship. It was there that I met my wife, Judy. Judy had grown up in New Britain, an industrial town in central Connecticut. Like myself, her mother had been born abroad (in the area south of Riga) and her father in the United States, and they were part of the town's Jewish community. It required a special effort to maintain the integrity of a Jewish community in a town like New Britain. Judy attributes her attachment to Jewish studies to the rabbi of her synagogue who sought in every way possible to hold the interest of Jewish youngsters after the age of Bar or Bat Mitzvah. This rabbi, Harry Zwelling, convinced her to pursue her B.A. degree in New York where she enrolled in the "Joint Program" of the JTS and in the Columbia University School of General Studies.

I met Judy during her first year in New York, when I was in my third year in college, after spending a year in Israel. She energetically improved her knowledge of Hebrew, but equally became part of the JTS community. Within a short period of time she became a sought-after baby-sitter for members of the faculty with young children. As part of our courtship, I was mobilized to participate in the task of baby-sitting and thereby began to become acquainted with some of our teachers on a more personal level. In this manner we came to know the family of David and Tzipora Weiss-Halivni, and

Judy also lived for a while in the home of Abraham and Sylvia Heschel. Together we developed some sense of how masters of Jewish learning, each in a unique style, put together Jewish tradition and the contemporary world in their lives, and transmitted their commitments to their children.

These experiences provided the cultural materials from which we fashioned our own family ways after leaving New York. When completing graduate studies, on the basis of a field study in Israel (H. E. Goldberg 1985: 108–9), I accepted a job in the Department of Sociology and Anthropology at the University of Iowa in Iowa City. Taking up residence in a small midwestern town was not a usual move for our circle of Jewishly conscious friends. A number of them cited a survey that recently has gained some notoriety among rabbis and Jewish educators that revealed an intermarriage rate of 40 percent in the state of Iowa (a figure that is no longer unusual on the landscape of American Jewry). All of Iowa had a Jewish population of about seven thousand, and we arrived in Iowa City in the fall of 1966 as the parents of a boy and a girl, aged three and two, respectively. Iowa proved to be a very pleasant setting to live and work, but it always was apparent to us that it was not a place within which one could transmit a Jewish heritage with any degree of intensity or certainty.

By 1971 we were the parents of four children, the elder ones then in the third and second grades. When our youngest son was born in 1969 we had paid the plane fare of a *mohel* (circumcisor) from Chicago to come to our home to perform the *brit milah* (circumcision) (one of many instances of modern technology serving traditional values). This was somewhat of a special occasion for the small community in Iowa City, which usually made do with the services of a Jewish urologist in the university hospital. In one instance, I was asked to help guide such a medico-ritual event by directing the reading of the *berakhot* and other passages.

This was not the only time that I was called on to be a quasi-rabbi in Iowa: twice, when a rabbi was not in town, I found myself reciting *tsidduq ha-din* and delivering a eulogy at a funeral. While I did my best to help these families in need, I never wanted to be cast in a rabbinic role. I found it challenging enough to struggle with socializing our own children as Jews, and was never comfortable pretending to assume responsibility for the spiritual life of an entire community.

It was always clear to Judy and myself that the Jewish future of our children would take us away from Iowa City, to which we were attached in many other ways. One potential option was a metropolis in "the East," which would entail paying high fees for Jewish day schools while hassling with all the other pressures of big city life that Iowa City had spared us. The other option was Israel. When the opportunity to join Hebrew University arose we, after deliberation and debate, embarked for Jerusalem in the fall of 1972.

We knew of course of the split between secular (*mamlakhti*) and religious (*mamlakhti dati*) national religious education in Israel, but somehow assumed that this problem would sort itself out—that "Jewish education" in the Jewish state would not be a major concern. This turned out to be a very mistaken assumption.

When first arriving in Jerusalem we lived in a neighborhood of an established and highly recommended *mamlakhti* school, where we decided to enroll our two older children. We were concerned about the totally secular atmosphere of the school but also were so involved in getting settled that we did not fully relate to the matter at the time. It should be appreciated, of course, that even "secular" life in Israel touches upon Jewish tradition in many ways. That spring, our daughter's third-grade class prepared a model Seder to which parents were invited. It was gratifying to observe our daughter read easily from the text, and I also was pleased that a traditional Haggadah was chosen, and not a Haggadah adapted for "modern" educational purposes.

This was not the case with regard to all of the texts our children used. During the course of the year I perused a "Bible for Students" that presented "selected" parts of the book of Bereshit (Genesis). It very much annoyed me to find the biblical text chopped up in this manner. I recalled that in my first year in a day school in New York I was placed in a third-grade class that was studying Bereshit (Genesis). The book we were using was a standard *humash* with Rashi. We proceeded chapter by chapter, but when we came to the story of Yehudah and Tamar, we were told, without any explanation, to skip to chapter 39. Having been enrolled in the day school late in my elementary school career, I was older than the other students in the class and proceeded to read through the ignored story, as far as I could understand it. Whatever one may think of this educational approach, there was no attempt to tamper with the text itself that ultimately was left open for examination. I find this to be far more integrous than deleting a segment of a classic text deemed inappropriate by some committee. Neither my father nor I could easily live with bowdlerization.

This mini-incident encapsulates major dilemmas of education and culture in Israel. Orthodox groups feel the need to fiercely defend their positions and do so by claiming that Judaism has never changed in the past, so there is no need to change it now. Nonorthodox Israelis who define themselves as *lo dati* (not religious) feel that Israeli youths must have some connection to the treasured literature of the past but, having excised "religion" from "Jewish culture" have often moved clumsily in attempting to form a modern secularized but also Jewish culture. Since the formal establishment of the two trends in education in 1953, the cultures of two school systems have grown further apart. Parents educated in *mamlakhti dati* schools in the 1950s were sending their children to very different institutions in the 1980s even though they were known by the same name. This holds true for the Jewish content of *mamlakhti* schools as well. Neither of the existing systems expressed the approach to Judaism within which we had been brought up.

A year after our immigration we moved into a new neighborhood of Jerusalem close to the Mt. Scopus campus of the university. That was an area in which many people we had known from our pasts in Connecticut and New York, who had moved to Israel after the Six-Day War, also settled. Most of these people had decided to send their children to the local *mamlakhti dati* school. Although not in agreement with the overall philosophy of Orthodoxy, they felt that an exposure to some religious approach was better than none at all. In addition, the concentration of families from a Conservative background in the area provided a framework for the children that helped cushion the discrepancy between the version of Judaism presented to them at school and that which they experienced at home. We decided to join this trend feeling that it was important for our children to have some exposure to traditional religion. I half-seriously and half-jokingly mused that I would rather have teenage rebels becoming secular with some solid grounding in Jewish sources than rebels who became ultra-Orthodox on the basis of little knowledge. As our younger children reached school age, we also enrolled them in the local religious schools.

After a few years in this neighborhood a number of the parents from our background got together to see if it were possible to set up a school that reflected a nonorthodox religious orientation. This first took the form of a series of classes that operated within the framework of the local *mamlakhti* school, but was designated as the *masorti* or "traditional" trend. The program was set up with only the first three grades. Our two younger children, then entering the third and second grades, were participants in this experiment on the Israeli educational scene.

Since then the *masorti* trend has developed in various ways. Today, known by the acronym TaLI (Ackerman & Showstack 1987; Goldring & Zisenwine 1989), it has the support of the Ministry of Education, as a way of increasing the presence of Judaism in *mamlakhti* schools. The very first *masorti* class, in which our second daughter participated, disbanded after the seventh grade. Our (youngest) son decided to leave the school after the sixth grade in order to enroll in the local *mamlakhti dati* school that his two eldest siblings had attended.

Each of our children has followed a somewhat different course through the Israeli school system in the search for an education reasonably consonant with our own sense of Jewish culture and tradition. Our eldest son, subsequent to our move to the new neighborhood, studied only in standard religious schools. After elementary and junior high schools (*hativat beinayim*) near our home, he attended one of the few religious high schools in the city that was not considered a yeshiva. This, needless to say, was an all-boys' school. When our first daughter reached high school age, she was accepted to a girls' religious high school recently designated as an experimental school by the Ministry of Education. This experiment took place under the leadership of Alice Shalvi, at that time a professor of English literature at the Hebrew University who served as headmistress of the school on a volunteer basis—convinced that it was possible to combine orthodoxy with a broad humanistic education.[3] This school, named Pelech, continues to exist but is still very much a singular experiment and constantly has been under pressure from diverse directions because of the thin line it attempts to walk. Our third child (daughter) also enrolled in Pelech after her *masorti* class had disbanded and after she had spent one year in a nearby *mamlakhti* junior high school.

When our youngest son left the *masorti* program, he studied in the same religious junior high school and then high school in which his older brother had been a student. He was extremely unhappy in this setting, being unable to accept the authoritarian and unsatisfactory answers to his questions. One teacher challenged his inquisitiveness by referring to him gratuitously as a "philosopher." He decided to leave that school and his third and fourth years were spent in a newly formed boy's high school established by David Hartman that sought to cultivate an orthodoxy capable of encompassing general culture (Friedman 1989: 313–21). Within ten years of his short life, this son had participated in the founding of two separate schools seeking to blaze new trails in Israeli education.

* * *

A Tradition of Invention

The details of the foregoing account are highly idiosyncratic but they also condense a patterned theme. Both my children and I attended schools that provided a rich Judaic environment but that differed from the orientations of our homes, challenging us to seek a satisfactory integration in our own individual lives. My father, too, while following the familiar trajectory of jettisoning many of the intense traditions of Eastern Europe when he was young, eventually devoted much of his energy to seeking a synthesis between Jewish and general culture and passing what he had learned onto other adults. If I read the bits of stories about by mother's parents correctly, they also reflect a generation fiercely committed to Jewish life that simultaneously had become aware of the necessity of accommodation to the wider world within the context of Jewish society.

This family history constitutes a record of rapid change, but also one of continuity-in-flux whose specific form is unpredictable from one generation to the next. It undoubtedly parallels stories that could be told of many Jewish families who have not become secularized on the one hand nor absorbed in ultra-Orthodoxy on the other (e.g., see Dershowitz 1991: 23–34). Moreover, this active search for a staunchly Jewish middle ground may itself constitute a kind of "tradition" or perhaps metatradition within the kaleidoscope of modern forms of Jewish commitment.

Such a metatradition is not confined to any one segment of Jewry but appears most vividly at the interstices among them. These "traditions" clearly are invented anew in each situation, but I suggest that focusing on the family indicates that the commitment to, and skills required in, such invention may be transmitted across generations. One aspect of a "tradition of invention" is the readiness to experiment with, and be exposed to, various, and inherently unstable, educational ventures. The pages that follow will continue to cite personal experiences and assorted observations, but will emphasize some general social dynamics associated with educational efforts that seek to steer a Jewish course in the uncharted seas of modernity. Most of these efforts are small in scale when viewed one at a time, but together they constitute a significant moment in the transmission of Jewish culture in the contemporary world.

The Search for Balance among Modern Jews

My own story is closely linked to educational enterprises of the Conservative movement in the United States, and to people from that movement who settled in Israel. The search for a committed but nonself-segregating approach to Judaism is more general, however. My Orthodox high school was located in Far Rockaway, Queens. One of the large synagogues in that area was known as Sha'arei Tefillah and represented an approach that today would be called "modern Orthodox," although I do not think that the precise phrase existed at the time. The rabbi of the synagogue was Emanuel Rackman, later to become the chancellor of Bar-Ilan University in Israel. While I did not live in Far Rockaway, many of my friends from school attended that synagogue.

Several years ago, I spent a semester at Brown University and taught a course called "Anthropological Perspectives on Jewish Culture." One student wrote a paper on his childhood synagogue in North Miami Beach, Sha'arei Tefillah. Its founders were members of the synagogue of the same name in Far Rockaway who felt that they could not find a synagogue in Florida that precisely replicated the open but Orthodox atmosphere they had known in the North. It was curious and pleasing for me to come upon the continuation of the tradition of my high school friends, and for this student to discover someone who had known the original Sha'arei Tefillah.

The search for a persuasive approach to Judaism embracing the contemporary world may be found in approaches to the "left" of Conservative Judaism, as well as in modern Orthodoxy. One of the monographs assigned in the aforementioned course analyzed a Reform synagogue in the Los Angeles area (Furman 1987). Within this synagogue was a *havurah* (prayer group) that sought to forge for itself a more traditional style of prayer than that adhered to by classical Reform Judaism. The *havurah* is a social and religious form that developed in the United States in the late 1960s. One of the signal characteristics of the *havurah* movement was that it sought to escape from the conventional denominational boundaries within American Jewry and to rediscover a more authentic Judaism (Prell 1989; Reimer 1993).

These various specific developments—in New York, Florida, California, and elsewhere—must be placed against the broad backdrop of modern Jewish history, including patterns of migration. Ismar Schorsch, current chancellor of the JTS, once pointed out to me that modern rabbinic seminaries in Central Europe and the United States have arisen in locales constituting the geographic and social borders between Westernized Jewry and traditional Jewry to the East. This certainly applied to the JTS in New York. The educational roots of the faculty members who gave this institution its reputation for several generations were mainly European, but taught students whose childhood experiences were in the United States. By definition, education in such a situation is cross-cultural and potentially cross-ideological as well as cross-generational, a situation creating dynamic tension and requiring the constant exercise of choice. Similar situations characterized many of the Jewish elementary and high schools in modern times seeking to inculcate their own versions of contemporary loyalty to Judaism.

Students Navigating among Worlds

When I transferred, at about the age of eleven, from a public school near my home to a Jewish day school far away, it implied moving from a setting where I represented one of the more traditional families within the community into a milieu in which I was in daily contact with those who were more observant than me. This involved pretending that I was familiar with, and committed to, practices that were new and demanding. It was only much later that I came to realize that a significant number of students in the school were children of Conservative rabbis whose parents felt that an elementary education in an Orthodox institution gave them a basis in Jewish study and living that could not be duplicated in the afternoon Hebrew schools attached to Conservative synagogues. Very few of these (then unknown to me) Conservative elementary school colleagues continued onto Orthodox high schools.

I did make the choice to continue onto such a high school (in Far Rockaway). I was part of the second high school class of that institution, an established day school which, during the year before, had begun to expand its program beyond the eighth grade. Here, the discrepancy between my religious orientation and that of my friends was even greater. I was able to handle the tension because the school was in another neighborhood, and my own synagogue and community remote from that of my classmates. As discussed elsewhere (H. E. Goldberg 1985: 100–101), I learned a great deal of material in that school, while absorbing broader perspectives to Judaism in the context of Conservative youth programs. In the latter settings, I became attached to spoken Hebrew, a subject that was not at all valued in my yeshiva high school milieu. Girls studied some Hebrew literature, but the boys' program stressed Talmud. One copy of a literature textbook found its way into our classroom, and I remember enjoying the short stories in it while hiding the book underneath the Talmud. Little did I know at the time that I was reinventing the methods of acquiring "forbidden knowledge" developed in Eastern Europe the century before.

Even though I was the only closet Conservative Jew in the school, there was nevertheless a gap between the school's administration and staff, on the one hand, and the students on the other. The policy of the school was to teach boys the Talmud, according to traditional methods, to the detriment of other Judaic subjects. The students were asked to group themselves in *hevrusa* (study pairs) each morning to try to penetrate the text by themselves before hearing the teacher's explanation. In fact, more time in *hevrusa* was spent discussing our school's basketball team, which played in a league of other yeshiva high schools, than was devoted to the Talmud. For my friends who came from Orthodox families, this was probably perceived as a normal "generation gap" that did not cloud the atmosphere of taken-for-granted religious norms within which they lived. Charles Liebman has described modern Orthodoxy as making "a virtue of their inconsistency" (Liebman 1979: 23).[4] For me, it drove home the disparity of norms and actual behavior within which I found myself. It probably also endowed me with insights, skills, and biases later expressed with regard to my children who found themselves in similar situations in Israeli schools.

Some Sociological Dilemmas of Modern Jewish Schools

In addition to the internal reactions of youngsters in such complex situations (to which we shall return shortly), a disjuncture in experience between home and school creates the desire and demand for new educational frameworks in tune with the worldviews and educational outlooks of parents. This is one factor leading to the ongoing proliferation of Jewish schools—some moving to the "right" and others to the "left"— both in the Diaspora and in Israel. When I attended day school and high school in the early mid-1950s, the Solomon Schechter day schools, later set up by the Conservative movement, did not exist. Today, my Far Rockaway school has been disbanded. Its continuation within the modern Orthodox community

is represented by several schools in the general area, each with a
slightly different orientation.[5] Problems created by this continuing
proliferation are a matter of explicit concern to Orthodox educators
in the United States (Simins 1992).[6]

Trends toward ideological fractionalization may be discerned in
Israel as well. About twenty years ago a group of Orthodox parents
in Jerusalem, dissatisfied with the lack of religious intensity and
study in the state religious schools, set up a special school calling itself "Noam." In the opposite ideological direction, the creation of the
masorti framework within the state school system, just discussed,
was mostly the initiative of immigrants from the United States. It
did merit the commitment of a few native-born Israelis, however,
who felt that this trend was restoring to Israeli education a Jewish
element that had been part of the general education when they
were young, but that had since been greatly diluted.

While the focus of this discussion is on schools as expressions of
ideology, the link between the formation and expansion of these
schools and of other social concerns cannot be ignored. The growth in
the number of students studying at day schools[7] in the United States
in the 1960s is not only an outcome of a commitment to specific religious ideologies. These institutions were also private schools, attended by children from (upper) middle-class backgrounds, and often
served as a refuge for families seeking alternatives to the deteriorat-
ing public education in urban areas. One yeshiva high school on
Manhattan's Upper East Side has an established reputation for
sending its graduates to the top colleges in the United States.

While the overall educational setting in Israel is different, these
factors are not absent there. The *masorti* trend in our neighborhood
rapidly became an independent school. It developed a reputation as
a good school (and may have had some "snob appeal" because it was
associated with Americans), thereby attracting families who were
not mainly concerned with its special religious orientation. The experimental Pelech School that our daughters attended, and the new
school of our younger son, both demanded supplementary payments
from parents to underwrite their enriched programs (a general phenomenon in middle-class Israeli life, designated "gray education").
Both these high schools have been accused of catering to Western
immigrants. However one evaluates these special cases, it is well-
known that elite yeshiva high schools within the broader Israeli religious education system evolved into mechanisms reinforcing the
separation between youngsters of European and Middle Eastern
origins. All of these trends assume a broadening financial base from

which to develop new educational projects: in the Diaspora such a base is largely voluntary while, in Israel, government budgets play a crucial role.

Both the rapid creation of new shades of tradition-oriented schools and the fact that new schools attract students for reasons other than their declared ideological content mean that these schools are often more internally heterogeneous than originally envisioned by their founders. While they were set up in order to reduce ideological stress by providing a setting in which parents, teachers, and children all were operating on the same religious wavelength, this rarely takes place in so smooth a fashion. One source of difficulty is that economies of size require bringing in students who are cut out of different ideological cloth from those in charge of a given new school.

Another factor creating ideological heterogeneity is the lack of teachers who neatly match the ideological job description for a recently formulated pedagogical ideal. Such schools often have to rely on a staff that is only partially committed to the aims of the institution, or on teachers reflecting an alternative ideology. This was a major problem facing the new *masorti* program in Israel. One of the principle teachers during the early years of that program is now the headmistress of the Pelech school, an Orthodox institution. This kind of tension exists in settings based on other orientations. For example, one sensitive issue in *mamlakhti dati* education has been the prominence of teachers educated in ultra-Orthodox *beis yaakov* schools. In ordinary synagogue schools in the United States, on the other hand, David Schoem has documented the gap between children and teachers in his poignantly titled article: "Learning to Be a Part-time Jew" (Schoem 1988). In the former case there is concern that teachers may have undue influence on children, while in the latter, the perceived problem lies in the fact that the pupils and their homes dictate the tone of (afternoon) school life, and not the teachers. The basic point is that despite the attempts to provide an internally consistent socialization framework, Jewish educational institutions in the modern world frequently re-create, often in a transfigured manner, the gaps that they seek to overcome.

Viewed as a general pattern, the desire for a homogeneous educational environment often leads parents and communal leaders to establish "their own kind" of school. Usually, they cannot do this without taking in ideological outsiders, as students and as teachers. The result is a series of overlapping cycles that characterize educational efforts of varying hues: the formulation of "new" educational

philosophies and frameworks, the limited success in actualizing these
philosophies and plans in a manner protected from neighboring influences and internal discord, and the subsequent creation of new efforts
to find the ever-elusive correct path in the next generation.

Centrist Ideologies and Individual Commitments

Successive splintering and endemic instability are well-known
phenomena among and within radical political groups. One notable
feature of the religious scene in contemporary Israel is that this dynamic of sequential fissioning is found among those small circles
seeking to keep astride a golden mean of Judaism-plus-modernity.
In Israel, religious centrists are the radicals! It also should be underlined, however, that this "cyclic" process cannot be viewed in
terms of a timeless model. As time goes on, new efforts in this direction are not identical to those of the previous generation. Each attempt takes place in new historical circumstances.

One thrust of historical change within which these searches
and experiments arise is the heightened prominence of extreme religious groups and the widening gap between them and Jews to
whom Judaism, as a religion, has become increasingly foreign.
From this point of view the creation of a religious center waxes ever
more problematic. A corollary of this trend is the growing diversity
in formulations of Jewish religious identity and institutional life between the poles. While two generations ago one could comfortably
divide religiously organized American Jewry into Reform, Conservative, and Orthodox (ultra-Orthodoxy was still seen as a marginal
phenomenon), today there are rabbinic schools representing a Reconstructionist ideology ("between" Conservative and Reform)
as well as a Metivta of Traditional Judaism that originated within
the Conservative world but that has moved toward Orthodoxy
(Wertheimer 1989). In Israel, the splintering of Orthodoxy has become increasingly evident, including developments that blur the
distinction between it and ultra-Orthodoxy. A small segment of modern Israeli Orthodox views the nascent *masorti* efforts positively,
while the majority are quite distanced from it.

This rapidly growing diversity, and educational instability of
each group, may create and maintain a significant number of individuals who have had experience in a variety of religious frameworks and who are in a constant search for the shifting ground of
optimal balance in their Jewish lives. Such individuals have a par-

tial knowledge of paths other than their own, as well as familiarity with some of the people who walk them. Despite the repetitiveness of the pattern from a sociological point of view, however, these centrist trends remain distinct from one another and their overall impact is thereby diluted.[8]

In order to fathom the fractionalized nature of these mean-seeking efforts, attention should be given to the implications for the individual of the social processes discussed. Common sense posits that contact with diverse orientations that are close to one another should lead to the appreciation of a range of approaches and a sense of solidarity with them, but casual observation and sociological intuition suggest that the opposite tendency is often evident. Individuals who have invested much thought and affect to achieve a finely tuned personal worldview tenaciously hold onto the ideological and behavioral combinations they have found meaningful, with little willingness to look sympathetically at their close ideological neighbors.[9] In addition, they often shore up their hard-earned stances by intensive and extensive involvement with a relatively small circle of like-minded associates.

One must appreciate the power of dilemmas created by dissonant socialization experiences in one's childhood and young adulthood. Divergent influences and their entailed contradictions, even when resolved within specific life histories, often leave the individual with few internal resources to look beyond the solution that he or she has forged. The depth of struggle to overcome dissonance in childhood and young adulthood contributes to the persuasiveness of myths and ideologies in adulthood that appear to banish earlier disharmonies. One of the puzzling recollections of my student year in Israel (1958–59) was that members of the religious kibbutz on which I spent three months would typically begin telling the story of their settlement by referring to the preparatory camp (*hakhshara*) in Europe where they worked together as youngsters before coming to Palestine. I now better understand the centrality of such an experience that can perhaps be compared to the pivotal place of the Conservative movement's Ramah summer camps in the United States. More than one of my acquaintances from that background links Camp Ramah to his or her personal Jewish revelation. In the Israeli setting, once more, Aran's study of Gush Emunim points to the problematics of ideology faced by Israeli teenage yeshiva students and Benei Akiva youth movement members in the 1950s who later were in the forefront of a political movement seeking to overcome the perceived contradictions between "Zionism" and "Judaism" (Aran 1986).

The Elusive Middle Road

Not all those who have experienced a complex and self-contradic-
tory ideological education become fervent believers in a well-defined
path. Some turn their back on ideological concerns altogether, while
others may continue to seek, with greater or lesser energy, a reasonable position linking competing ideals in a pragmatic, livable manner.
Within a field of options, the choice of a particular life-position and
pattern of practice often stems from orientations and praxis within
the family. When individuals who were exposed to a Judaicly complex
background have to shape the future of their own children, the labil-
ity of, and choice among, Jewish educational frameworks make the
family a crucial factor in the process of selection. The anecdotes and
studies cited herein may thus constitute a picture of middle-of-the-
road Jewish continuity, composed of many discontinuities, where one
source of consistency, insofar as it is evident, is to be found in family
commitments and resources.

If such a continuity does exist, it would be naive to liken it to
continuity in settings in which family, school, and community support one another in a taken-for-granted manner. To the extent that
one can point to "family traditions" that have cultivated the active
re-creation of committed but selective approaches to Judaism, these
families attach themselves to schools and communities through active choice, undoubtedly accompanied by the unconscious transmission of norms and behaviors built into all family life. Our discussion
probably has taken greater note of the ironies of the modern Jewish
condition than the plain continuities; the story Chaim Weizmann
tells of his mother, pulled in one direction by her Communist son
and another by her Zionist child, has been repeated in many versions by contemporary Jewish families. My argument is that such
ironies notwithstanding, seeking to unravel mechanisms of continuity, as well as those of spiritual fracturing is a worthwhile endeavor.

Today, "tradition" is perpetuated with unexpected twists and
turns. A simplistic model would place each generation removed from
the "ghetto" or the *mellah* further down the road to assimilation
than the previous one. In the case of my family, my father's "return"
to intensified Jewish commitment was triggered by my own development in that direction: "transmission," if you wish, from son to father. This is not an isolated instance. A well-known phenomenon
among modern Orthodox today is stricter observance on the part of
children than their parents.[10] "Return" can have multiple outcomes.
Having decided to become immigrants in a new society (as our

grandparents did), Judy and I have also made our children into our teachers. I daresay this is an aspect of modern life in general, even in situations of geographic stability.

Family ties frequently are inimical to ideologies. Moreover, tightly knit ideological communities often seek to co-opt symbols of familial solidarity. Menahem Friedman (1987: 242) indicates how in Lithuanian yeshivot, which cultivated a cadre of students who viewed themselves as ideal norm-bearers vis-à-vis the members of the communities within which they grew up, the head of the yeshiva was perceived as a father-figure. These were the institutions out of which contemporary ultra-Orthodoxy developed.

Middle-of-the-Judaic-road families, by contrast, gingerly but purposefully, seek to cut out a path among competing (but sometimes overlapping) ideologies, communities, and schools. They expose their children to these influences, but also work at modulating the impact of these educational structures on their daughters and sons. This undoubtedly took place within some families of Middle Eastern backgrounds who sent their children to *dati* (religious) schools in Israel. What are the orientations and resources that enable families to accomplish this? In addition to questions of family structure (Bunis 1992), the nature of the parents' Jewish education, the forms of their communal involvements, and their strategies of ritual life are undoubtedly crucial. Families that themselves have had sustained exposure to a Jewish heritage, and that have been willing to engage in different forms of Judaic commitment, provide the potential for transmitting Jewish culture in a manner that does not prefer the signs of belonging to a specific group over broader patterns of Jewish identification and general attachment to Jewish culture.

Conclusion

If a brief ideological interjection be permitted, I would like to believe that broadly sketching these phenomena might encourage the willingness of diverse small groups seeking the center to look both to their "left" and their "right," and that such a glance would enhance their willingness to situate their own "optimal" solutions within a broader historical trend. Aside from a commitment to the continuity of Judaism, they all value, explicitly or implicitly, individual choice and autonomy. But the nature of this valorization differs. Among the non-Orthodox, the value implications of Western individualism are taken for granted: people get involved with Judaism to the extent they choose, if at all. Those who assert that Halakha has an a priori claim on them, in contrast, do not provide a general statement of how autonomy fits into their Jewish commitments, even though it is clear from their behavior that they exercise much individual choice in matters Jewish.[11] Their ability to choose is enhanced by the givens of a democratic society, but one facet of Orthodox ideology is to ignore this fact that is now so taken for granted that it is not normally noted. By speaking in terms of God's commandments, the authority of the Torah, and so forth, Orthodox ideologies suppress the fact that in contemporary reality they are the authors of the "authority" to which they submit. They thus succeed in drawing a sharp ideological boundary between themselves and various non-Orthodox approaches, which are similar to them in the desire to incorporate tradition into modern life, but that accept as given that such incorporation stems from the choice of individuals. Neither the traditional nor the orthodox, it seems, have succeeded in formulating a compelling argument, arising from the dialectic of Jewish thought and praxis, which valorizes individualism and applies it, reflexively, to choice within the framework of Jewish life itself. Whether or not pointing to sociological parallels and common challenges can provide a basis of concord among these groups, the cultural dynamics of devoted centrist families, their styles of preservation and innovation, and how they interact with educational institutions are matters worthy of detailed investigation.

Notes

A French version of this chapter appeared in Esther Benbassa, ed. (1997) *Transmission et Passages en Monde Juif* (Paris: Publisud).

1. Among his materials from rabbinic school days is a draft of a paper entitled: "Judicial Immunity for Error: A Study in Comparative Law."

2. This was corroborated by my cousin, the historian Louis Schoffman.

3. Shalvi also has been a prominent figure in the Women's Lobby in Israel.

4. The clash between cultures felt in the life of modern yeshiva students, and the humorous reflection upon them, is deftly portrayed in Elliot Oring (1988).

5. Far Rockaway has, in fact, become the center of ultra-Orthodoxy.

6. One factor favoring the creation of schools that bring together children of committed, but varying, Jewish backgrounds is the movement of Jews into cities with smaller communities. There have been other demographic shifts as well. Most of the students in a well-known yeshiva high school in Brooklyn that mainly served youths of an Eastern European background in the 1950s are of Syrian lineage.

7. On day schools, see Michal Moskow (1990), and the references therein.

8. The diversity of centrist orientations is exemplified in the range of educational approaches seeking to bring together *dati* and non-*dati* youths in Israel (Wollman 1990).

9. This is not the place to discuss factors such as organizational inertia and emphasizing distinction in order to compete for funds.

10. Rabbi Louis Jacobs of London recently told me of a forum in which he participated along with an American Reform and a "modern Orthodox" rabbi born in America and now active in Israel. In the course of their discussion they discovered that both Jacobs, known for his intellectual challenge to established English Orthodoxy, and the Reform rabbi, had been born into Orthodox families, while the Orthodox rabbi grew up in a less observant family.

11. The most basic exercise of choice by Orthodox Jews is, first, to live within an Orthodox framework and, then, to select from a range of options, all falling under the Orthodox rubric.

References

Ackerman, Walter, and Gerald Showstack. (1987) "TALI: A New Alternative in Israeli Education." *Conservative Judaism* 40, no. 1: 67–80.

Aran, Gideon. (1986) "From Religious Zionism to Zionist Religion: The Roots of Gush Emunim." *Studies in Contemporary Jewry* 2: 116–43.

Bunis, Mattat A. (1992) "Kinship and an Urban Community in Israel: The Case of Maaleh Adumim." Ph.D. diss., Hebrew University of Jerusalem.

Dershowitz, Alan. (1991). *Chutzpah*. Boston: Little, Brown.

Friedman, Menahem. (1987) "Life Tradition and Book Tradition in the Development of Ultraorthodox Judaism." In *Judaism Viewed from Within and from Without: Anthropological Studies*, edited by Harvey E. Goldberg. Albany: State University of New York Press, 235–55.

Friedman, Thomas. (1989) *From Beirut to Jerusalem.* New York: Farrar.

Furman, Frida K. (1987) *Beyond Yiddishkeit: The Struggle for Jewish Identity in a Reform Synagogue.* Albany: State University of New York Press.

Goldberg, Harvey E. (1985) "Anthropologie et Etudes Juives: Une Perspective Autobiographique." *Pardes* 2: 99–115.

Goldberg, Michael. (1958) "A Layman's Approach to Adult Jewish Education." *Adult Jewish Education* (New York: United Synagogue of America) (Fall 1958): 17–20.

Goldring, Ellen B., and David Zisenwine. (1989) "Developing Jewish Identity: Parents and the Tali Schools in Israel." *Jewish Education* 57, no. 1: 28–34.

Liebman, Charles. (1979) "Orthodox Judaism Today." *Midstream* 25: 19–26.

Moskow, Michal. (1990) "An Integrated Approach to Judaics and General Studies in a Jewish Day School." *Ethnic Groups* 8: 15–27.

Oring, Elliot. (1988) "Rechnitzer Rejects: A Humor of Modern Orthodoxy." In *Between Two Worlds: Ethnographic Essays on American Jewry*, edited by Jack Kugelmass. Ithaca: Cornell University Press, 148–61.

Prell, Riv-Ellen. (1989) *Prayer and Community: The Havurah in American Judaism.* Detroit: Wayne State University Press.

Reimer, Joseph. (1993) "The Havurah as a Context for Adult Jewish Education." In *The Uses of Tradition: Jewish Continuity in the Modern Era*, edited by Jack Wertheimer. New York: Jewish Theological Seminary of America, 393–410.

Schoem, David. (1988) "Learning to Be a Part-time Jew." In *Persistence and Flexibility: Anthropological Perspectives on the American Jewish Experience*, edited by Walter P. Zenner. Albany: State University of New York Press, 96–116.

Simins, Chana. (1992) "Of Schism and Toleration." *Jewish Action* (New York) 52 (3): 59–64.

Wertheimer, Jack. (1989) "Recent Trends in American Judaism." *American Jewish Yearbook* 89: 63–162.

Wilson, Edmund. (1955) *The Scrolls from the Dead Sea.* London: W. H. Allen.

Wollman, Yisrael. (1990) "A Meeting of the Hearts: Reducing Tensions between the Religious and Non-Religious." In *Religious and Secular: Conflict and Accommodation between Jews in Israel*, edited by Charles Liebman. Jerusalem: Keter, 193–214.

Part II

European and North American Variations

Chapter 5

∞

National Contexts, Eastern European Immigrants, and Jewish Identity: A Comparative Analysis

Paula E. Hyman

Jews living in the various Diaspora societies of the modern West have shared a similar set of challenges that emerged some two centuries ago. The process of emancipation, grounded in Enlightenment thought, made it clear in all countries of the West that Jews were expected to adopt the characteristics of the societies in which they lived and to which they owed civic obligations. Assimilation, however, had a different meaning for Jews and non-Jews in the West. Gentiles who accepted Jews as fellow citizens assumed that they would become virtually indistinguishable from the rest of the population except for their religious faith and style of worship. Many proponents of emancipation confidently assumed that the acculturation of the Jews would lead over time to their complete blending with the host population. Jews, on the other hand, while eager to taste of the economic, political, and cultural fruits of equality, presumed that they would retain group consciousness and some degree of particularity within the larger society. They saw no contradiction between their two goals of assimilating to the mores of the larger society and preserving their identity as Jews.

Although the broad challenge of modern states and societies to Jewish self-definition transcended national boundaries, the precise dimensions of the challenge as well as the ways in which Jews might respond to it have been shaped by the political and cultural contexts of specific Western societies. It is useful, then, to engage in the exercise of comparative history to tease out those factors in different national contexts that have facilitated, or impeded, the development of successful strategies for the transmission of Jewish identity and culture from one generation to the next (Birnbaum & Katznelson 1995; Katz 1987; Frankel & Zipperstein 1992). In the framework of this book concerned with the implications of forms of identity for Jewish education, the cultural differences among Jewish communities, and not only their similarities, are of particular interest. Because of our ideological commitments, even scholars of Jewish history and culture often presume that the religious symbols and memory that Jews share have the same meaning for them despite their living in different polities and societies. Although we are immersed in the specificity of the communities whose development we study in depth, when we deal with contemporary issues we often fall back upon slogans that stress mutual responsibility and common destiny (both past and future) rather than pursue to its conclusion a careful analysis of our distinctive patterns of self-understanding and self-presentation in the various societies in which we live.

As an historian I am fully aware of the fact that Jewish identities in the modern world are not fixed, even in one national setting. The factors, both internal and external, which influence Jewish identity change over time. In any society there is also a range of Jewish identities, and any one individual may bear multiple identities (G. Cohen 1979). Still, however tentatively we speak about "national cultures" and however much we recognize their contingency, contrasts between the space offered to Jews for the expression of their particularist identities in three Western countries—the United States, France, and England—suggest the centrality of national contexts in the formation of modern Jewish identities.

In a comparative historical framework, all three of these countries emancipated their Jews early and with relative ease. The United States and France conferred civic equality upon Jews by the end of the eighteenth century; England worked more gradually, capping economic and partial political rights with full political equality in 1858. In all of these societies Jews have experienced considerable upward economic mobility. By the second half of the nineteenth century Jews also participated in the political life of each nation, with France taking the lead in the integration of Jews into its elite political and military echelons (Birnbaum 1992, 1995). Finally, all three Jewish communities have been built upon successive waves of immigrants, although only in America, where the country's very self-definition is as a nation of immigrants, does this fact stand prominently at the center of the Jewish community's sense of self.

By focusing on a comparison of the experience of Eastern European immigrants in England, France, and the United States I intend to demonstrate that a comparative perspective lays bare the ways in which the host society defined the possibilities of acculturation and integration and destabilizes notions of Jewish identity that presume an irreducible core of Jewish cultural traits. The interwar postimmigrant generations of English, French, and American Jewries, although comprised largely of descendants of Eastern European Jews, differed not only in their native languages but in the nature of their Jewish identities and in the patterns of expression of their cultural values.

The Jews from Eastern Europe who arrived in the United States, Great Britain, and France shared similar socioeconomic and cultural characteristics, although the immigrants to France were somewhat more secularized because their migration en masse occurred later than in the other two countries. The immigrants joined societies and Jewish communities that offered different prospects for the persistence of ethnic or minority identity. Both the similarities and differences in their journeys point to the importance of the process of interaction of the immigrants with the cultural features of the larger society and of the Jewish elites already in place.

The comparative role of education in the culture and achievements of American, French, and British Jews descended from Eastern European immigrants provides perhaps the most striking evidence of the interaction of inherited values with structural and cultural aspects of the societies in which the immigrants settled. It has often been noted that among traditional Eastern European Jews learning was a cultural ideal, at least for males. Many American commentators have similarly commented upon the high educational achievements of American Jews, especially of the third and subsequent generations, and have attributed the disproportionate involvement of Jews with general higher education to the secularization of this cultural ideal for religious learning that characterized Eastern European Ashkenazi society. Yet, the comparative experience in the area of education of immigrant Jews and of their descendants in the three communities I have selected points to the impact of both institutional arrangements and social attitudes of the larger society.

Eastern European Jewish immigrants in the United States took advantage of free public education for their children as a tool of acculturation and as a stepping-stone to upward mobility; the children of Jewish immigrants stayed in school longer than was the case for immigrants of other ethnic origins at the same time (Brumberg 1986). It should be pointed out, though, that the commonly held view of the rapid entry of the children of immigrant Jews to institutions of higher education is overplayed; the Alfred Kazins and Irving Howes and their less famous fellow students at the City College of New York in the 1920s and 1930s accounted for only a small proportion of immigrant sons (Gorelick 1981; Howe 1976). It was only in the third generation that a college education became de rigueur, a marker of the acculturation of American Jews. Most scholars now agree that high educational achievement among American Jews was, in general, a result of economic mobility rather than its cause (Waxman 1983). However, in comparison with the children and grandchildren of other immigrant ethnic groups Jews were highly visible in institutions of American higher education, a phenomenon that led to the imposition of quotas in selective universities as early as the 1920s (Wechsler 1977; Synnott 1979; Oren 1985).

The experience of Eastern European Jewish immigrants in Western Europe was somewhat different, despite their presumed shared values. The masses of Eastern European Jews arrived in France only after 1905, and the majority not until the conclusion of the First World War. It has been estimated that in 1914 there were only forty-four thousand immigrant Jews living in France (Green 1986). As in America, free public education was available, but the economic constraints on new immigrants limited their access. The scanty statistical data that we have suggest that only a minority of children of immigrants born in France between 1910 and 1934 were able to acquire more than a primary school education (Bensimon & DellaPergola, 1984). However, in the post-World War II years there emerged, as in the United States, a prominent cadre of academics and intellectuals of Eastern European immigrant Jewish origin, among them Emanuel Lévinas, Annie Kriegel, Bernard-Henri Lévy, Alain Finkelkraut, and Richard Marienstras. And French Jews are currently better educated than is the general French population (although a proper comparison would control for level of urbanization and class) (Friedlander 1990).

A striking contrast is England, where the children and grandchildren of Eastern European immigrants did not duplicate the patterns of the descendants of immigrant Jews in America or in France. Their educational attainments, particularly in the sphere of university attendance, were unremarkable. Todd Endelman has attributed the comparatively low level of high school study for the children of immigrants and university education for their grandchildren to the nature of the British educational system with which the children of immigrants had to contend. Most English youths left school at the age of fourteen; higher education was considered a luxury, readily available only to the upper-middle and upper classes; and there was no English equivalent of City College. Moreover, British society, and the Jewish communal elites in place upon the arrival of the immigrants, did not value intellectual achievement; status accrued to individuals by virtue of birth or through achievement of wealth in business (Endelman 1990). The Jewish love of learning, then, was qualified by the opportunity structure of the host society and by the social rewards attached to higher education.

Although the level of educational attainment significantly influences the identity formation of contemporary Jews, the dominant factor in the ways in which Diaspora Jewish communities construct their identities and position themselves vis-à-vis their fellow citizens is the prevailing cultural attitudes of the larger societies toward minorities. In the case of France, England, and the United States, all three, to a greater or lesser degree, have rejected the concept of ethnic persistence.

As is well-known, the debate that surrounded the emancipation of the Jews in France during the Revolution included the famous remark of the liberal count Clermont-Tonnerre, "To the Jews as a nation, nothing; to the Jews as individuals, everything. They must become citizens" (*Révolution* 1968). The Napoleonic Sanhedrin made explicit the desired transformation of Jewish identity. In response to the question as to whether the Jews living in France saw the French as their brothers the Jewish spokespersonsmen not only fervently assented but privileged their new civic identity over their ancient attachments. They added to their response the remark that French Jews in England, though among English Jews, would feel as among strangers (Mendes-Flohr & Reinharz 1980; Tama 1807). Despite the statements of Jewish elites, the masses of traditional French Jews living concentrated in the eastern provinces of Alsace and Lorraine clearly preserved an ethnic component to their Jewish consciousness for much of the nineteenth century, and for some into the twentieth. The existence of publicly recognized Jewish primary schools in the villages and towns of Alsace in the middle decades of the nineteenth century acculturated young Jews to French values in a Jewish setting that cushioned the encounter. As one Jewish writer reflected upon a popular reader used in the Jewish schools, ". . . there crept into the minds of its young readers a double sentiment—for which the author must be thanked—a proper pride in race and a great love of the fatherland" (Stauben 1860; Hyman 1991). At the same time the urban elites of French Jewry, increasingly located in Paris, recognized the lack of legitimacy—the lack of acceptable language—for their own feelings of ethnic connectedness whose existence Phyllis Cohen Albert has documented (Albert 1982, 1990). The urbanization of the Jews of Alsace, and particularly their migration to Paris, undermined the social reality of ethnic consciousness. Most urban Jews chose nonsectarian public school for their children, and the laicization of French education under the Third Republic (1870–1940) made any other choice seem unpatriotic to the majority who supported republicanism.

Although France welcomed immigrants, it did so on the condition that they recognize both the superiority and the exclusiveness of French culture and adopt it as their own. Eastern European immigrants to France therefore found that the natural display of the ethnic components of their culture—speaking Yiddish in public, for example—was considered inappropriate in French society and deeply threatening by native Jews. In 1926, well before the onset of the depression, the Paris Consistory warned the city's immigrant Jews that if they persisted in sticking together, "we will not be able to overlook the essentially national character of our association"—a veiled threat to withhold financial assistance from immigrants (Hyman 1979).

French political culture rejected both ethnicity and pluralism and became increasingly xenophobic in the interwar years, when the consequences of the postwar mass immigration were most apparent. Yet at that time the younger generation of French Jews struggled to expand the foundation of Jewish self-definition in France beyond religion. Most significant, it seems to me, was the attempt of the Jewish Scout movement, composed of children of Eastern European immigrants as well as long-established French Jews, to assert a multiplicity of acceptable Jewish tendencies and to enable the members of their generation to recapture their originality as Jews in a society whose history and culture were imbued with Christian symbols. Under the impact of Zionism, whose base of support lay in the immigrant community, and especially of German Jewish refugee scouts who arrived in the 1930s, the young leaders of the Scout movement asserted that the identity of French Jews was analogous to that of French provincials, for example, Corsicans (Hyman 1979). That analogy had no great or lasting resonance in

French sociopolitical culture, but it raises for our own time the question of how Jews can legitimate their particularity in a society that even now pays only lip service to pluralism and is deeply disturbed by the persistence of ethnic markers among its most recent immigrants, Muslims from North Africa.

Despite the presence of several distinct ethnic groups—Scots, Welsh, and Irish—in the British Isles, Jews in England have not looked to ethnicity as the basis of their organization and persistence as a recognizable group. Their political emancipation, which followed the economic and social emancipation of their elites, drew upon the parallels that could be drawn between Jewish disabilities and those of dissenting Christian sects—Nonconformists and Catholics. Moreover, most English Jews were far more interested in economic opportunity than they were in political emancipation; after all, only a minority of male citizens in Great Britain were sufficiently prosperous to participate actively in politics (Alderman 1995). The extension of political rights in Great Britain during the midnineteenth century, to which the emancipation of the Jews was linked, was predicated on the existence of a "united public opinion," according to the liberal theorist John Stuart Mill. Such a public consensus, Mills held, could not exist in a country of diverse nationalities with different historical memories. Representative government depended upon shared cultural and historical bonds. British political toleration, therefore, did not embrace cultural diversity; rather, the superior culture of the English elite would absorb inferior cultures, including the culture of the Jews (Feldman 1994).

The absence of cultural support for ethnic organization in England that flowed from the political definition of the nation was reinforced by the comparatively low levels of immigration in general to that country. Because there were so few foreigners and because ethnic differences in Great Britain derived from groups native to the British Isles, the Anglo-Jewish elites were as hostile to manifestations of immigrant Jewish ethnicity as were their French counterparts. They were mortified at the conspicuousness of Yiddish-speaking, working-class immigrant Jews in London's East End. As the *Jewish Chronicle* editorialized in 1888, in the first period of mass migration, "If poor Jews will persist in appropriating whole streets to themselves in the same district . . . drawing to their peculiarities of dress, of language and of manner, the attention which they might otherwise escape, can there be any wonder that the vulgar prejudices of which they are the objects should be kept alive? . . ." (Alderman 1995). Given the lack

of models for ethnic organization, the relatively small size of the
Anglo-Jewish population, and the general openness of general social institutions to individual Jews, it is not surprising that Jews
in England failed to create a network of nonreligious organizations comparable to what has existed in other countries. Moreover, the propertied elites to whom economically successful Jews
aspired to assimilate may have tolerated Jews within their midst
but saw no need to expand their definition of English culture to
include new, non-Christian elements (Endelman 1990).

The United States has offered its Jewish population the greatest possibilities for what is now called "continuity," that is, group
survival. Joining "a nation of immigrants" enabled Jews to view
themselves as an integral component of the builders of the new land
and of its experiment with democracy. Yet, America, too—despite its
exceptionalism—has an ambivalent attitude toward ethnic particularity that has affected the patterns of Jewish self-definition.

On the one hand, as early as the end of the colonial period, commentators living in North America recognized, and celebrated, the
diversity of colonial society. J. Hector St. John de Crèvecoeur, a
prosperous New York farmer born in France, published his reflections on the nature of Americans:

> [T]hey are a mixture of English, Scotch, Irish, French, Dutch, Ger-
> mans, and Swedes. From this promiscuous breed, that race now
> called Americans have arisen. He is either an European, or the de-
> scendant of an European. . . . *He* is an American, who, leaving be-
> hind him all his ancient prejudices and manners, receives new
> ones from the new mode of life he has embraced, the new govern-
> ment he obeys, and the new rank he holds. (Crèvecoeur 1782)

American culture thus derived from what the various settlers
in the New World together created under the impact of their new
experience of social and economic equality.

On the other hand, Anglo-conformity, the adoption by immigrants of an already formed American culture with roots in English
history and literature, has been the dominant concept of immigrant
adjustment to America for much of the country's history. As late as
1915 President Woodrow Wilson stated, "America does not consist of
groups. A man who thinks of himself as belonging to a particular
national group has not yet become an American" (Sorin 1992).

Jews themselves introduced concepts that challenged the
wholesale assimilation of immigrants to a fixed definition of Ameri-

can culture. It was an English Jewish writer of Eastern European parentage, Israel Zangwill, who coined the term *the melting pot* in his 1908 play of the same name set in the United States that was well received in its Broadway production. That metaphor suggested that immigrants of varied nationalities would contribute to an American culture in formation, but it also demanded the blurring of cultural particularities in the crucible of the American immigrant collective enterprise.

Although the American Jewish elite of the earlier Central European migration felt comfortable with melting pot imagery, Eastern European immigrant Jews and their descendants responded with most enthusiasm not to the concept of the melting pot but to the doctrine of cultural pluralism, also defined and promoted by a Jew, Horace Kallen. Born in Germany in 1882, the son of a rabbi, he came to America at the age of five, graduated from Harvard University, and became a professor of philosophy. His 1924 book, *Culture and Democracy in the United States*, which included an earlier essay entitled "Democracy *versus* the Melting Pot," legitimated ethnic particularity within American society. Kallen envisioned America as an orchestra of different instruments that together played "the symphony of civilization." As he described "the outlines of a possible great and truly democratic commonwealth, . . . [t]he political and economic life of the commonwealth . . . serves as the foundation and background for the realization of a distinctive individuality of each nation that composes it and of the pooling of these in a harmony above them all." Ethnic Americans thus participated in American culture, and ultimately strengthened it, by retaining some aspects of the cultural particularity of their immigrant origins. In Kallen's eyes these became marks of distinction once the immigrant achieved a measure of economic independence and acculturation (Kallen 1924; Konvitz 1987).

In practice the three visions of immigrant adaptation—Anglo-conformity, the melting pot, and cultural pluralism—continue to coexist in America, despite the "reemergence" of ethnicity in the past thirty years, the increased proportion of the foreign-born in American society, and the growing acceptance of bilingual education. Moreover, the recent rise of multiculturalism, as distinct from cultural pluralism, has undermined the claims of Jews, and other white ethnics, to an acknowledged culture. The doctrine of multiculturalism and the development of ethnic studies within the university have tended to conflate ethnicity and race; only "people of color" have recognized cultural space within the multiculturalist's vision of American society. American Jews who seek to ground contemporary Jewish identity in the United States in ethnic as well as religious factors face the challenge of disarticulating Jewish identity from the catchall category of "white" in which it has been subsumed.

The institutions of the larger society that disseminate values and culture more generally interacted with immigrants in only limited venues—of which the public school was the most significant. Often the native Jewish community, with its ethnic social welfare as well as religious institutions, has mediated the messages of the larger society to the newcomers. The impact of the host Jewish community on the immigrant population depended on its structure and on the openness of its leaders to the integration of Jews of different classes and cultures within its ranks. The centralization and rigidity of both the French and English Jewish religious communities limited their influence on immigrants and their children seeking to adapt their Eastern European Jewish legacy to the demands of a new cultural environment. The American Jewish community, in contrast, benefited from the plasticity produced by decentralization and voluntarism.

Napoleon had endowed French Jewry with an officially recognized organizational structure supervised by the Ministry of Religion. Although the separation of church and state in 1905 terminated governmental control, the hierarchical communal structure remained in place. Its power was vested in the Central Consistory located in Paris and in the hands of native Jews until after World War II. French Jewry had become used to a system of a rather homogeneous, modern Orthodox format of religious expression (Albert 1977; Berkovitz 1989). The immigrants were able to establish their own religious institutions, but they were not integrated into the consistorial leadership, which saw the immigrants solely as clients of their philanthropy (Hyman 1979; Green 1985). In England, too, Jewish religious life was centralized, although it was not under governmental patronage. The United Synagogue and the institution of the chief rabbinate dominated the organized expression of Judaism in England, setting limits to deviation and providing a model of the coexistence of religious observance along Orthodox lines with acculturation to the values of the English middle classes (Alderman 1992).

American religious life, on the other hand, was based on congregationalism, and American Judaism followed suit (N. W. Cohen 1984; Diner 1992). In fact, Reform Judaism prospered in America, becoming the most prevalent form of Judaism by 1880, because of the localism of American religion and because of the absence within Jewish life of a unified communal structure. Accepting the model of religious pluralism and denominationalism, native Jewish elites who were themselves Reform Jews recognized the need for an Americanized model of traditional Judaism for the children of immigrant Jews, who would find Reform too distant from their families' patterns of Jewish practice and worship and whose social class made them unacceptable as fellow congregants. These leaders funded the reorganization of the Jewish Theological Seminary, which became the center of Conservative Judaism, the largest denomination of the twentieth-century American Jewish community until the 1990s (Sklare 1972). The more acculturated and economically successful of second-generation Jews affiliated with the Reform movement and infused within the denomination a measure of ethnicity and consciousness of Jewish peoplehood (Meyer 1988).

Aside from the structure of each host society's Jewish community and the strategies of native Jewish elites for dealing with the immigrants, the place of religion within the larger society also played a role in the religious acculturation of the children of the immigrants. In France anticlericalism had a long tradition. Because of the cultural and political power of the Roman Catholic Church in French society, committed Republicans who adhered to the legacy of the Revolution, though respectable members of the bourgeoisie, had no problem affirming themselves as secular. This cultural endorsement of laicism, rigorously communicated in French public schools, reinforced the secularism that many Jews had brought with them from eastern Europe and suppressed the need to develop their own religious forms consonant with their settlement within France. For those who sought a Jewish flavor to such rites of passage as marriage and death—and there was less need to do so in France because of mandatory civil marriage and the popularity of nonreligious funerals—the Orthodox forms of consistorial Judaism sufficed. Although religion was the sole legitimate basis for Jewish particularity in France, social forces inspired most Jews not to take Judaism very seriously (Schnapper 1984).

In both England and the United States, on the other hand, civic rectitude and bourgeois respectability demanded an affirmation of religious affiliation, even if devoid of spiritual passion. Secular Jewish identity, therefore, did not find either structural or cultural support within English-speaking Jewish communities. In America religious institutions, as Will Herberg taught in *Protestant, Catholic, Jew*, became the locus for ethnic identity (Herberg 1955). For the children of the immigrants the synagogue center as pioneered by Mordecai Kaplan provided possibilities for ethnic socializing as well as for religious education and worship (Moore 1980; Liebman

1970; Wertheimer 1987). Moreover, in the past two decades the United States has experienced a religious revival. Although American Jews in general seem to be characterized by religious indifference rather than by enthusiasm, the salience of religiosity within American society has reinforced religious affiliation as the primary expression of Jewish identity, even though most American Jews are not ritually observant. And a minority of American Jews have manifested their own varieties of religious revival, ranging from a return to Orthodoxy, the *havurah* movement, Jewish feminism, and New Age Judaism (Wertheimer 1993; Fishman 1993).

It is now clear that religion provides the only culturally affirmed basis for distinctiveness within white populations in the various societies of the West. An ethnic Jewish identity divorced from religious concerns has shown no basis for survival beyond the immigrant generation in any of the Western Diaspora societies that I have surveyed. The problem confronting Jewish leaders and educators is how to transmit a Jewish identity that melds ethnic and religious characteristics to a Jewish population that is distanced from its ethnic roots and fundamentally secular in its outlook.

References

Albert, Phyllis Cohen. (1977) *The Modernization of French Jewry: Consistory and Community in the Nineteenth Century.* Hanover, N.H.: Brandeis University Press.

————. (1982) "Ethnicity and Solidarity in Nineteenth-Century France." In *Mystics, Philosophers, and Politicians. Essays in Jewish Intellectual History in Honor of Alexander Altmann*, edited by Jehuda Reinharz and Daniel Swetschinski. Durham, N.C.: Duke University Press.

————. (1990) "L'Intégration et la persistence de l'ethnicité chez les juifs dans la France moderne." In *Histoire politique des Juifs en France*, edited by Pierre Birnbaum, Paris: Presses de la Fondation Nationale des Sciences Politiques.

Alderman, Geoffrey. (1992) *Modern British Jewry*. Oxford: Oxford University Press.

————. (1995) "English Jews or Jews of the English Persuasion? Reflections on the Emancipation of Anglo-Jewry." In *Paths of Emancipation*, edited by Pierre Birnbaum and Ira Katznelson.

Bensimon, Doris, and Sergio DellaPergola. (1984) *La population juive de France: Sociodémographie et identité.* Jerusalem: Institute of Contemporary Jewry, Hebrew University of Jerusalem and Paris: Centre National de la Recherche Scientific.

Berkovitz, Jay. (1989) *The Shaping of Jewish Identity in Nineteenth-Century France*. Detroit: Wayne State University Press.

Birnbaum, Pierre. (1992) *Les fous de la République: Histoire politique des Juifs d'Etat de Gambetta à Vichy*. Paris: Fayard.

———. (1995) "Between Social and Political Assimilation: Remarks on the History of Jews in France." In *Paths of Emancipation*, edited by Pierre Birnbaum and Ira Katznelson.

———, and Ira Katznelson. (1995) *Paths of Emancipation: Jews, States, and Citizenship*. Princeton: Princeton University Press.

Brumberg, Stephan F. (1986) *Going to America, Going to School: The Jewish Immigrant Public School Encounter in Turn-of-the-Century New York City*. New York: Praeger.

Cohen, Gary. (1979) "Jews in German Society: Prague, 1860–1914." In *Jews and Germans from 1860 to 1933. The Problematic Symbiosis*, edited by David Bronsen. Heidelberg: Carl Winter.

Cohen, Naomi W. (1984) *Encounter with Emancipation: The German Jews in the United States 1830-1914*. Philadelphia: Jewish Publication Society.

Crèvecoeur, J. Hector St. John de. (1782; reprint, 1957) *Letters from an American Farmer*. New York: Dutton.

Diner, Hasia. (1992) *A Time for Gathering: The Second Migration*. Baltimore: Johns Hopkins.

Endelman, Todd. (1990) *Radical Assimilation in English Jewish History, 1656–1945*. Bloomington: Indiana University Press.

Feldman, David. (1994) *Englishmen and Jews: Social Relations and Political Culture 1840–1914*. New Haven and London: Yale University Press.

Fishman, Sylvia Barack. (1993) *A Breath of Life: Feminism in the American Jewish Community*. New York: Free Press.

Frankel, Jonathan, and Steven Zipperstein. (1992) *Assimilation and Community: The Jews in Nineteenth Century Europe*. Cambridge: Cambridge University Press.

Friedlander, Judith. (1990) *Vilna on the Seine: Jewish Intellectuals in France since 1968*. New Haven: Yale University Press.

Gartner, Lloyd. (1960) *The Jewish Immigrant in England 1870–1914*. Detroit: Wayne State University Press.

Gorelick, Sherry. (1981) *City College and the Jewish Poor: Education in New York 1880–1924*. New Brunswick, N.J.: Rutgers University Press.

Green, Nancy. (1986) *The Pletzl of Paris: Jewish Immigrant Workers in the Belle Epoque*. New York: Holmes and Meier.

——. (1985), "The Contradictions of Acculturation: Immigrant Oratories and Yiddish Union Sections in Paris before World War I." In *The Jews in Modern France*, edited by Frances Malino and Bernard Wasserstein. Hanover and London: Brandeis University Press.

Herberg, Will. (1955) *Protestant, Catholic, Jew: An Essay in American Religious Sociology*. New York: Doubleday.

Howe, Irving. (1976) *World of Our Fathers*. New York: Simon & Schuster.

Hyman, Paula E. (1979) *From Dreyfus to Vichy: The Remaking of French Jewry, 1906-1939*. New York: Columbia University Press.

——. (1991) *The Emancipation of the Jews of Alsace: Acculturation and Tradition in the Nineteenth Century*. New Haven: Yale University Press.

Kallen, Horace. (1924) *Culture and Democracy in the United States*. New York: Boni and Liveright.

Katz, Jacob (1987) *Toward Modernity: The European Jewish Model*. New Brunswick, N.J.: Transaction Books.

Konvitz, Milton (1987) *The Legacy of Horace Kallen*. Rutherford, N.J.: Fairleigh Dickinson University Press.

Liebman, Charles. (1970) "Reconstructionism in American Jewish Life." *American Jewish Yearbook* 71.

Mendes-Flohr, Paul, and Jehuda Reinharz, (1980) *The Jew in the Modern World*. New York: Oxford University Press.

Meyer, Michael A. (1988) *Response to Modernity: A History of the Reform Movement in Judaism*. New York: Oxford University Press.

Moore, Deborah Dash. (1980) *At Home in America: Second Generation New York Jews*. New York: Columbia University Press.

Oren, Dan. (1985) *Joining the Club: A History of Jews and Yale*. New Haven: Yale University Press.

Révolution française et l'émancipation des juifs, La. (1789; reprint, 1968) Paris: Editions d'Histoire Sociale 7.

Schnapper, Dominique. (1984) *Jewish Identities in France: An Analysis of Contemporary French Jewry*. Translated by Arthur Goldhammer. Chicago: University of Chicago Press.

Sklare, Marshall. (1955; reprint, 1972) *Conservative Judaism: An American Religious Movement.* New York: Schocken.

Sorin, Gerald. (1992) *A Time for Building: The Third Migration.* Baltimore: Johns Hopkins.

Stauben, Daniel. (1860) *Scènes de la vie juive en Alsace.* Paris: Michel Lèvy freres.

Synnott, Marcia Graham. (1979) *The Half-Opened Door: Discrimination and Admissions at Harvard, Yale and Princeton, 1900-1970.* Westport, Conn.: Greenwood.

Tama, Diogene. (1807) *Transactions of the Paris Sanhedrim.* Translated by F. D. Kirwan. London.

Waxman, Chaim I. (1983) *America's Jews in Transition.* Philadelphia: Temple University Press.

Wechsler, Harold. (1977) *The Qualified Student.* New York: Wiley.

Wertheimer, Jack. (1987) "The Conservative Synagogue," In *The American Synagogue: A Sanctuary Transformed,* edited by Jack Wertheimer. Cambridge: Cambridge University Press.

———. (1993) *A People Divided: Judaism in Contemporary America.* New York: Basic.

Chapter 6

❦

British Jews or Britons of the Jewish Persuasion? The Religious Constraints of Civic Freedom

Geoffrey Alderman

This chapter examines some aspects of the Jewish condition in Great Britain, focusing particularly on the pressures—external as well as internal—that have shaped what is popularly termed the *Anglo-Jewish identity*, but what is in reality a mosaic of Anglo-Jewish identities. Although we all speak of "Anglo-Jewry," there is not—and never has been—one monolithic, monocultural Anglo-Jewish "community," but rather a series of communities that overlap to some extent. My concern is largely with that broad band of cohorts that comprise the identifying Jewish population of Britain. These people identify as Jews (usually but not necessarily through synagogue membership) and practice a variety of forms of Judaism, most of which could not be termed *Orthodox* in the sense of strict adherence to the *Halakic* norms. Using the fourfold typology of Jews developed in relation to the sociological analysis of Israeli Jewry—*haredim*, *dati'im*, *masoreti'im*, and *hilonim* (which I roughly translate as sectarian Orthodox, Orthodox, traditional, and secular)—my major concern, therefore, will be with the latter two categories, that have generally comprised and that certainly comprise today the overwhelming majority of the Jews in Britain.

Jewish identity in modern Britain is the product of history. Jewish emancipation in Britain proceeded in a way that was markedly different from that experienced by Jews on the European mainland. In Europe, legislative or legalistic emancipation, imposed from above, generally preceded economic, social, and cultural integration. In Britain, formal legislative enactments granting civic and legal equality to the Jews were almost afterthoughts—the acknowledgment by the state of situations that already existed in practice. Professing Jews could not legally vote in parliamentary elections until 1835, but there is plenty of evidence that they were doing so well before that date (Alderman 1983: 11; Endelman 1979: 113). Professing Jews were not legally enabled to hold municipal office until 1845, but there are many examples of Jews playing prominent parts in local government at much earlier dates (Alderman 1992: 53). Professing Jews were not supposed to engage in retail trade in the city of London before 1830, but we know that they habitually did so, the letter of the law notwithstanding (Endelman 1979: 113). T. B. Macaulay's famous plea in favor of permitting professing Jews to sit in the House of Commons was based on the argument that it was foolish to deny them this right when they already enjoyed so much economic power (Bettany n.d.: 170–76).

The struggle for political emancipation took roughly thirty years (1830–60) to be successful. In part this was because it was embedded within a much greater issue, namely, the extent to which Britain was to remain, constitutionally, a Christian realm. The eighteenth- and early nineteenth-century British state did not persecute Jews as such, neither did it compel them to live in ghettos. But it did treat in an inferior manner all persons who professed the Jewish religion. Such persons were perfectly free to practice this religion; to establish houses of worship; to set up religion schools; to train ministers of religion; to observe their dietary laws, their Sabbaths, and other holy days; to marry according to their religious laws, to purchase land for burial purposes; and to bury their dead in the manner their religion prescribed. All these things the Jews were free to do. But in doing them they consigned themselves to an inferior status in point of civic freedoms, along with all others who dissented from the established church of England. Legally the Jews were, as indeed they felt and declared themselves to be, neither more nor less than a section of "Nonconformist" society (Finestein 1986: 8).

During the eighteenth and early nineteenth centuries, the belief that heresy (the holding of religious views at variance with those of the established church) was tantamount to treason was finally laid to rest. In 1828 and 1829, most dissenting groups were admitted to full political equality. These groups, however, were all

Christian. Henceforth the United Kingdom of Great Britain and Ireland was a Christian realm, even if it was no longer a Protestant one. To admit the Jews (along with Unitarians and atheists) to the panoply of civic equalities and political freedoms required another half-century or so of national debate.

Jews were found on both sides of the argument, with adherents of Reform Judaism among the leading and most outspoken emancipationists. This identification was not accidental. The Reformers believed that British Jewry needed to accommodate itself to prevailing non-Jewish modes of worship, and to abandon its claim to a national destiny separate from the destiny of the Britons among whom it dwelt. By repositioning themselves as Britons of the Jewish persuasion, rather than as Jews who happened to live in Britain, the claim to full civic equality would (it was argued) be irresistible. British Reformers did indeed believe, passionately, that Reform Judaism would itself bring nearer the day of full emancipation (Gilam 1982: 42).

This argument was enough to arouse the suspicion and the ire of more conservative elements within British Jewry, led by Sir Moses Montefiore and Chief Rabbi Nathan Adler. While some members of the Anglo-Jewish clergy did go public in their support of civil and political equality, in general the religious leadership was either indifferent to the question or openly hostile. No one knew what the full effects of emancipation might be upon the religious identification of British Jewry. Fundamentalists argued that although British Jews could dwell among other nations, they were not permitted to sink their own identities within those of the nations among whom they dwelt: the Jew was not English and, if he tried to become one, his Jewish identity—and destiny—would be lost (Salbstein 1982: 42). It must be remembered that the eighteenth century had witnessed a stream of converts from Judaism to Christianity in England, that the first Members of Parliament of Jewish origin (e.g., the economist David Ricardo) were in fact converts, and that some of the leading non-Jewish champions of Jewish emancipation, such as Macaulay, were enthusiastic members of Christian "missions" to the Jews (in Macaulay's case, the Philo-Judaean Society, established in 1826). Against this background, the argument that the political emancipation of Anglo-Jewry would lead to assimilation and complete loss of religious identity seemed, on the face of it, highly plausible.

In fact, we know now that the more extreme fears of those— Jews and non-Jews—who had opposed emancipation were equally frustrated. The work of the missionaries appears to have had a

diminishing impact (Endelman 1990: chap. 5). Synagogue attendance (as evidenced in the 1851 religious census) remained low,
there was continued neglect of the dietary and other laws, and there
was continued indifference to Jewish education. Nonetheless, measured at least by the yardstick of observance of the rites of passage,
British Jews, while lax in their day-to-day practice of the Orthodoxy
to which they nominally subscribed, remained throughout the nineteenth century remarkably loyal to traditional values: they married
in synagogues, their sons went through a ceremonial Bar Mitzvah
at the age of thirteen, and the laws of mourning were observed at
least in part (Sharot 1971: 121-30). Strict adherence to Orthodox
practice (e.g., Sabbath observance) undoubtedly declined, and intermarriage remained at a significant level. But the *ethnic* identity of
British Jewry appears to have been affected little (if at all) by the
fact of emancipation.

This circumstance should not blind us to the fact that the wider
process of emancipation inevitably had profound effects upon British
Jewry, and in particular upon its relationship with the British polity
as well as with Gentile society. To begin with, although the emancipation had been, in the technical, legal sense, unconditional, the
state had (almost surreptitiously) exacted a price in return for full
civil equality. Nathan Adler feared that emancipation would entail
the erosion of religious freedoms in the name of equality before the
law. And so it was. If Jews wanted equality, they could have it; but,
in that case, the laws that applied to the Gentiles would also apply
to the Jews.

In relation to the religious autonomy of British Jewry, and
more particularly in the matter of personal and marital status, the
results were rather serious.[1] The 1835 Marriage Act, by rendering
null and void marriages "within the prohibited Degrees of Consan-
guinity" as defined by Canon Law (principally between and uncle
and niece) made it illegal henceforth for British rabbinic authorities to authorize, in England, marriages that were perfectly proper
according to *Halakha*. The freedom of Batei Din to authorize *gittin*
was heavily circumscribed by the terms of the Matrimonial Causes
Act of 1857, which created a civil Divorce Court which, inter alia,
could dissolve a Jewish marriage. The passage into law of the Metropolitan Interment Bill of 1850 (a response to the cholera epi-
demic of 1848) was deemed by the Board of Deputies of British
Jews to constitute a threat to the sanctity of rabbinic burial laws,
and there was audible relief when the act was repealed in 1852
(Gilam 1983: 147-56).

The price paid for equality before the law thus continued to be exacted long after the excitement generated by the granting of political emancipation had died down; the boundaries between the civil state and the realm of British Jewry were redrawn in the process. But we should note that the very redrawing of them was, and has continued to be, a matter of great dispute among British Jews. Sir David Salomons, the first Ashkenazi president of the Board of Deputies, and a religiously Orthodox champion of emancipation (in 1851 he became the first professing Jew to take a seat in the House of Commons) regarded statutory interference with Jewish burial rites as an unjustified infringement of religious liberty, but condemned any exemption of rabbinically sanctioned divorces from the general enactment of 1857 as a perpetuation, by law, of Jewish civil inequality.

Salomons was also critical of the continued existence of separate Jewish schools, which he saw as a barrier to the acculturation of Jews to British society and hence—in some sense—as an impediment to emancipation. This argument is as fresh today as when it was voiced in opposition to Nathan Adler's education policy one hundred forty years ago. Concerned about raising the level of religious observance, Adler made the expansion of religious education a cornerstone of his rabbinate, and placed his faith in the development of a network of Jewish "elementary" schools, catering to pupils from about five to twelve years of age. By 1870, as a result of his efforts, perhaps as many as half the child population of British Jewry attended such schools (Schmidt 1962: 302).

But this achievement was itself controversial. The patchwork of Jewish schools suffered from its association with mediocrity. It never proved attractive to more affluent British Jews, who employed private tutors or else dispatched their children to more select private Jewish academies. But from the mid-1870s there was an observable tendency for Jewish parents of middle-class status to send their sons to non-Jewish fee-paying schools such as University College and the City of London schools, and in the Manchester Grammar School (Singer 1986–87: 166). Jewish "houses" were established at the most prestigious "public" schools, such as Clifton College (Bristol), and schools in Harrow and Cheltenham.

The extent to which pupils at these schools received a Jewish education remains problematic. Even at the Jewish houses of the public schools, where kashruth was certainly observed, Jewish pupils probably received only a modicum of religious instruction, approximating to an appreciation of the outward forms of religious observance. The more observant parents or guardians made separate arrangements for the religious instruction of their children, but few refrained from sending their offspring to schools that offered the opportunity of entry into the highest levels of English society, and into the ancient universities of Oxford and Cambridge. Cecil Roth, who came from a very observant family, was privately tutored in both religious and secular subjects until the age of eleven before being sent to the City of London School, and then to Oxford and never attended a "Jewish" school (Loewe 1966: 2).

The argument that a system of Jewish schools would act as a negative force in the process of social integration, and would thus rob British Jews of the benefits of emancipation, was persistently deployed. Following the passage of the 1870 Education Act, which established a system of state elementary schools (attendance at which was, from 1891, free of charge to the parent), this argument carried even greater conviction. Thereafter, a relatively small number of Jewish day schools (which became eligible for some financial aid from the government from 1897) existed side-by-side with an expanding number of state schools, which alone could cater to the hundreds of children of those Jewish emigrants who reached British shores in the 1880s and 1890s. "It became established communal policy . . . to regard Jewish day-schools as appropriate only for areas of the foreign poor" (Finestein 1986: 15).

The Jewish day schools thus entered upon a new lease of life, as engines of assimilation rather than as preservers of cultural and religious difference; their rationale indeed, was no longer to inculcate a sense of religious or ethnic difference, but rather to accelerate the process of anglicization. By 1870 the Jews' Free School, in Spitalfields (the heart of the Jewish "East End" of London) had no less than 1,600 boys on its roll, and 1,000 girls, taught by a staff of 70; presiding over them all was the redoubtable Moses Angel, headmaster for 51 years, who made no secret of his belief that the school's overriding purpose must be to anglicize the children entrusted to its care. "Their parents," Angel told the newly established London School Board in 1871, "were the refuse population of the worst parts of Europe"; "until they [the children] had been Anglicized or humanized it was difficult to tell what was their moral condition . . . [they] knew neither English nor any intelligible language" (quoted in Gartner 1960: 223). Angel's reference to "refuse population" evoked communal disapprobation; but his condemnation of Yiddish as an unintelligible tongue had many supporters, and it was repeated, almost a quarter-century later, by his successor,

Louis B. Abrahams, who advised parents at a school award ceremony in 1905 to discard Yiddish, "that miserable jargon which was
not a language at all" (*Jewish Chronicle*, 7 July 1905: 21).

On the eve of the Russian pogroms, the Jewish population of
Great Britain was around 60,000; between 1881 and 1914 it was
augmented by the arrival of not less than 120,000 immigrants from
Eastern Europe—stark reminders of the alien origin of British-born
Jews whose families might have been settled in Britain for 150
years and more. "In 10 or 15 years," one communal leader warned
in 1893, "the children of the refugees of to-day will be men and
women, constituting in point of numbers the great bulk of the Jews
of England. They will drag down, submerge and disgrace our community if we leave them in their present state of neglect" (*Jewish
Chronicle*, 3 February 1893: 16).

The new immigrants practiced *multiculturalism* a century or
more before the term was coined in relation to the impact of other
ethnic minorities upon British society. But emancipation—it was argued—had been granted on the supposition that Jews differed from
non-Jews merely on account of their religious observance, and neither formed nor had any ambition to form a national subset:

> Ever since the conquest of Palestine by the Romans [Nathan
> Adler's son, Hermann, wrote in 1878] we have ceased to be a body
> politic: we are citizens of the country in which we dwell. We are
> simply Englishmen, or Frenchmen, or Germans, as the case may
> be. (Adler 1878: 134)

The task of the Jewish day schools was now viewed primarily in
terms of a new imperative. Pupils "enter the [Jews' Free] school
Russians and Poles," a Board of Trade report noted with evident
satisfaction in 1894, "and emerge from it almost indistinguishable
from English children" (quoted in Lipman 1954: 147). But of course
these schools could only cater to a small proportion of the Jewish
child population of Britain as the great emigration proceeded from
Eastern Europe. By 1911, the proportion of Jewish children, in London, attending primary schools operated by the London County
Council was over 75 percent. Although, under the legislation of
1897, financial help could have been obtained from the state to help
expand the number of Jewish day schools, the communal preference
was to provide a modicum of instruction in Judaism to Jewish children in the state schooling system. "The national system of compulsory and free education," the reverend S. Levy told the Conference

of Anglo-Jewish Ministers in 1911, was enabling thousands of Jewish children "to acquire English habits of thought and character"; this process, he added, "has inevitably a retroactive effect upon the parents in the home" (quoted in Lipman 1954: 144).

During the First World War the question as to whether there had indeed been an emancipation "contract" became a topic of intense debate within British Jewry, as a result of the progress of the Zionist movement. The Zionist claim, that Jews constituted a separate nation and were therefore entitled to a national homeland, was bound to encounter fierce resistance from Anglo-Jewish assimilationists. Following Hermann Adler's argument, they asserted that even if Jews had once constituted a separate nationality, such a status had long since been abandoned, that its abandonment had been a condition of the granting of civic equality, and, furthermore, that it was dangerous, now, to resurrect it. Alongside the Jewish day schools there had been established, in the 1880s and 1890s, a network of clubs and societies, catering to young people and adults. In these, not only was the learning of English encouraged, but the new arrivals were introduced to the panoply of British cultural and leisure pursuits, such as swimming, football, and cricket. That the Zionists should establish rival networks was inevitable. The rivalry between Zionist and non- or anti-Zionist clubs, more especially in London's East End, during the interwar period, was particularly intense.

The day school movement languished. In 1945, only two of the seven state-aided Jewish day schools that had existed in London in 1945 were still functioning; day schools in Birmingham, Liverpool, and Manchester were still functioning, but were suffering from falling enrollments (Steinberg 1989: 83). The farsighted 1944 Education Act held out the prospect of substantial state aid for denominational schools, but British Jewry failed to take full advantage of this opportunity. The Zionist Federation of Great Britain, searching for a new role for itself now that the State of Israel had been reestablished, determined to embark upon an ambitious school-building program. The growing sectarian-Orthodox community, led by the charismatic (and ruthless) rabbi Dr. Solomon Schonfeld, set about establishing a quite separate and unashamedly non-Zionist school system under the umbrella of the innocently named Jewish Secondary Schools movement.

Neither the Zionist nor the non-Zionist schools affected more than a fraction of the Jews in postwar Britain. What is remarkable, however, is the extent to which Jewish schooling has experienced a renaissance over the last quarter-century. Whereas in 1967 only a quarter of Jewish children in Britain were educated in day schools, by 1982 the proportion had increased to almost half (Waterman & Kosmin 1986: 39). Today, the demand for full-time Jewish schooling, at both primary and secondary levels, cannot be satisfied, while Jewish studies at the university level are probably greater now than at any previous period (Kadish 1990).

The causes of this renaissance are complex. The reawakening of a sense of Jewish identity in the wake of the Holocaust and the Six-Day War are well-known phenomena of Diaspora Jewries. In Britain, however, the internal pressures to acculturate were never stronger than in the immediate aftermath of the Second World War. But the immigration of Asians, Africans, and Afro-Caribbeans has created a multicultural society; more than that, it has helped foster a climate in which multiculturalism, and ethnic separatism, have become respectable. The result has been the creation of a society in which the *public* expression of religious or cultural differences has become normative: rabbis appear on television; Jewish cookery is featured in the media; there are a number of Jewish radio programs. Judaism is no longer something that is practiced merely in private, behind the front door of one's house.

In 1873 the *Jewish Chronicle* voiced its disgust at "the undignified and highly objectionable accompaniment of a public procession of Jewish (?) ceremonial through London streets on the Sabbath [i.e., Sunday] of millions of our fellow-countrymen" (*Jewish Chronicle* 19 September 1873: 413).[2] In 1992 the United Synagogue—the largest synagogal body in Britain, once a byword for "liberal conservatism" in religious matters—championed the cause of those who wished to establish an *eruv* (a symbolic boundary within which carrying is permitted on the Sabbath) in the London Borough of Barnet, in which lives one of the largest Jewish concentrations in Great Britain. The *eruv* (Sabbath demarcation) controversy still rages, and it is fair to say that the matter bitterly divides Jews in northwest London; but the divide is by no means simply between religious and nonreligious Jews. Rather, the fault-line separates those Jews who believe in the private practice of Judaism from those who believe in the freedom to display it publicly. Assimilationists and the sectarian Orthodox find themselves ranged as allies against the Orthodox and their allies now to be found among self-confessed "secular" Jews.

Notes

1. This paragraph summarizes arguments I deployed in "The Legacy of Jewish Emancipation in England," a paper read at a conference on the theme, "The Emancipation Contract: Anglo-Jewish Emancipation in a European Context," held at the Wiener Library, London, 6 September 1992.

2. The question mark occurs in the original text, and is itself a comment upon the Englishness of the United Synagogue at this time.

References

Adler, Hermann. (1878) "Jews and Judaism: A Rejoinder." *Nineteenth Century* (July).

Alderman, Geoffrey. (1983) *The Jewish Community in British Politics*. Oxford: Oxford University Press.

———. (1992) *Modern British Jewry*. Oxford: Oxford University Press.

Bettany, G. T. (n.d.). *Essays, Historical and Literary . . . by Lord Macaulay*. 2d ed. London: Ward, Lock.

Finestein, Israel. (1986) *Post-Emancipation Jewry: The Anglo-Jewish Experience*. Oxford: Oxford Centre for Postgraduate Hebrew & Jewish Studies.

Endelman, Todd M. (1979) *The Jews of Georgian England 1714–1830*. Philadelphia: Jewish Publication Society of America.

———. (1990) *Radical Assimilation in English Jewish History 1656–1945*. Bloomington: Indiana University Press.

Gilam, Abraham (1982) *The Emancipation of the Jews in England 1830–1860*. New York: Garland Publishing.

———. (1983) "The Burial Grounds Controversy between Anglo-Jewry and the Victorian Board of Health, 1850," *Jewish Journal of Sociology*, xiv.

Gartner, Lloyd P. (1960) *The Jewish Immigrant in England, 1870–1914*. London: Wayne State University Press.

Kadish, Sharman. (1990) *The Teaching of Jewish Civilisation at British Universities and Other Institutions of Higher Learning*. Oxford: Oxford Centre for Postgraduate Hebrew Studies.

Lipman, Vivian D. (1954) *Social History of the Jews in England, 1850–1950*. London: Watts & Co.

Loewe, Raphael, ed. (1966) *Studies in Rationalism Judaism and Universalism in Memory of Leon Roth*. London: Routledge & Kegan Paul.

Salbstein, Michael C. N. (1982) *The Emancipation of the Jews in Britain*. Rutherford, N.J.: Farleigh Dickinson University Press

Schmidt, Helmut. D. (1962) "Chief Rabbi Nathan Marcus Adler (1803–1890): Jewish Educator from Germany." *Leo Baeck Year Book* 7.

Sharot, Steven (1971) "Secularization, Judaism and Anglo-Jewry." In *A Sociological Yearbook of Religion in Britain*, iv.

Singer, Steven. (1986–87) "Jewish Education in the Mid-Nineteenth Century: A Study of the Early Victorian London Community." *Jewish Quarterly Review*.

Steinberg, Bernard. (1989) "Anglo-Jewry and the 1944 Education Act." *Jewish Journal of Sociology*, 31.

Waterman, Stanley, and Barry Kosmin. (1986) *British Jewry in the Eighties*. London: Board of Deputies of British Jews.

Chapter 7

∞

Reluctant Cosmopolitans:
The Impact of Continentalism,
Multiculturalism, and Globalization
on Jewish Identity in Canada

Stuart Schoenfeld

Research has indicated that Canada's 356,000 Jews are more distinctively Jewish than American Jews.[1] Canadian Jews have higher rates of in-marriage than American Jews, are more likely to send their children to Jewish schools (especially Hebrew day schools), are more likely to live near other Jews, give more per capita to the United Jewish Appeal, have been more likely to make aliyah, remain more conversant with Yiddish, and are more likely to report themselves as Orthodox or "just Jewish" and less likely to report themselves as Reform (Schoenfeld 1978). Recent research (Brodbar-Nemzer, et. al. 1993) indicates the continuation of these differences and reports in addition, higher levels of ritual observance in Canada than in the United States, and a greater likelihood of reading a Jewish newspaper, belonging to the Jewish Community Center, belonging to Jewish organizations, having Jews as closest friends, being able to converse in Hebrew, feeling close ties to Israel, and having visited Israel.

Some explain these differences by noting differing immigration histories. American Jews have, in general, been in the United States longer than Canadian Jews have been in Canada. In 1881, when there were about 250,000 Jews in the United States, there were only about 2,000 in Canada. During the 1920s, immigration to Canada was possible for several years after the United States passed legislation imposing restrictive quotas. Furthermore, the percentage of Holocaust survivors is higher in Canada than in the United States. One could conclude, therefore, that Canadian Jews are roughly a generation behind American Jews along the road to assimilation.

Some offer structural and cultural explanations. Canada has always had a less assimilationist idea of citizenship than the United States. The political tradition respects group rights; the cultural tradition sees group identification as meaningful. Public support in Canada has been available to religious as well as to ethno-linguistic groups. Consequently, Canadian Jews are in an environment that tolerates, and to some extent supports, their distinctiveness.

Over time, changes indicating a much less traditional and cohesive identity among Canadian Jews have taken place. Liberal Judaism has become more common. In 1953, there were only three Reform congregations in all of Canada. In 1993, there are more than a dozen. Family structure has changed—Canadian Jews marry later, divorce more, and have fewer children. The population of small town Jews has declined, while in urban areas Jews are not so concentrated as they used to be. Significant immigration of Israelis, Russians, and North Africans has made the population more ethnically diverse. As in the United States, there is much public discussion of Jewish continuity, with particular concern about intermarriage. Government of Ontario vital statistics from 1985 to 1989 show intermarriage rates,[2] by individuals, of about 27 percent for males and 22 percent for females. These figures are low by American standards, but are much higher than they were thirty years ago. It is possible to conclude, then, that the statistical indicators of a continuing involvement of Jews with Jewish organizations and the continuation of distinctive Jewish practices mask a transition that is taking place in Canadian Jewish identity.

The following analysis of change begins with the assumption that Canadian Jewish identity is shaped, sustained, and transformed by the cultural content of the social relationships that Canadian Jews have. As Canadian Jews have significant relationships with non-Jewish Canadians as well as with Jewish ones, shifts in the meaning of group identity in Canada are likely to be related to shifts in Jewish identity. This analysis then, differs from most other studies by focusing on the Canadian aspect of Canadian Jewish identity. If the cultural meaning attached to group membership in Canada is changing, these changes can be related to the transformation of Canadian Jewish identity.

The Meaning of Group Identity in Canada—
Past Perspectives

Canada has been described as "two nations," as "a mosaic society," and as "a community of communities." Notwithstanding important differences between the image of Canada that each of these phrases condenses, they connote some common features. They evoke a Canada where the cultural as well as social boundaries between groups matter, a Canada whose people understand themselves in the context of history and traditions.

These images have their beginnings in the conflict between the French and English empires that produced Canada. The defeat of the French Empire left a sizable French population under English control, unwilling to grant a further victory to their conquerors by giving up their cultural identity. The Canadian confederation created in 1867 acknowledged in its founding arrangements the lack of cultural homogeneity across the country and anticipated the continuation of differences.

Non-British, non-French immigrants arrived, coming in unprecedentedly large numbers from the 1890s until the outbreak of the First World War, to be sent to break the sod on the sparsely populated prairies or labor in the new urban sweatshops. The movement for their cultural assimilation was certainly more ambiguous than in the United States. The new immigrants were not fully accepted, since discrimination of the most overt kind was socially acceptable and widely practiced. Neither were they fully excluded, as they were granted citizenship, and some exceptionally talented individuals made the most of their opportunities.

For those who dreamed of a Canadian nation rather than a loose collection of provinces bound to an imperial center, or who dreamed of an independent French nation able to bring its citizens into the world unburdened by responsibility for the rest of Canada, the new immigrants could be perceived in various ways. For some, the new immigrants were simply a danger to the dream, as they were imagined to have little interest in the dream of nation, or to be too culturally different to fit in, or to be racially inferior. For others, the new immigrants were imagined as raw material, to be educated, converted, and otherwise mobilized around the dream of nationhood.

Yet in a practical way, and even in a tentative ideological way, the new immigrants were also left alone to be themselves. If their cultural differences were not accepted with enthusiasm, they were usually tolerated. For example, agricultural areas on the prairies were often settled in ethnically homogeneous blocs. The practical need for farmers and laborers was so strong that immigration could not be limited to the numbers that could be easily assimilated. There were even echoes in Canada of Horace Kallen's image of a multicultural society as an orchestra, composed of sections playing different instruments, making harmony together.

In these historical periods of imperial conflict and of nation-building, Canada was a place where the awareness of the demands of history was strong, where group was culturally as well as socially divided from group, where fundamental social relations and cultural experiences were in small-scale settings. This society did not dealt equitably with Jews (see Davies 1992). However, its assumptions about the fundamental importance of historical awareness, group boundaries, and the integrity of communities were consistent with strategies of survival practiced over thousands of years by Diaspora Jews.

The Meaning of Group Identity in
Canada–Emerging Issues

The context in which Canadian Jewish identity is now being formed has been changed by three trends. First, the Canadian economy and popular culture have become integrated into a U.S.–dominated North American market. Second, Canada has become a multicultural society. Third, Canadians have become increasingly aware of themselves as a people whose future will be made in a global rather than in a federal or continental context. Taken together, these trends have established a sociocultural environment that has implications for the ways in which individual Canadians construct their relationships to groups, and the ways in which Canadian Jews construct their relationships to each other (see Kaplan 1993 for the relationship between social structural and cultural change and group identities in Canada).

Cultural and Economic Integration into North America

Canada's initial strategy of economic development looked to the development of the east-west infrastructure necessary for the promotion of interprovincial trade in industrial and agricultural products. Protection against the importation of mass-produced goods from the United States was an essential part of this strategy. Despite this economic strategy, American corporations made significant acquisitions, leading to what nationalists described in the 1970s as a Canadian natural resource and branch plant economy. Despite the introduction of new rules to make foreign acquisition of Canadian businesses more difficult, continental economic integration triumphed in 1988, when Canada and the United States signed a Free Trade agreement.

Economic relationships have a direct impact on that part of identity that is shaped and expressed at work. Economic integration also has a direct impact on that part of the identity that is shaped through popular culture, as expressed through books, magazines, films, radio programs, and TV shows. Popular culture is a business in which enterprises able to produce and distribute in volume and that create demand through advertisement are able to drive out the competition. The Americanization of the Canadian economy is also associated with the Americanization of Canadian cultural industries. Canadian legislation in the 1970s mandated that specified amounts of "Canadian content" were to be incorporated into the songs played on the radio and in the shows on Canadian-licensed TV. Government subsidies have been used to promote film development. Despite the popular culture produced and marketed by these policies, popular culture in Canada remains much more American than Canadian. Magazine racks, bookstores, radio music programs, and video shelves are overwhelmingly stocked with American products. On cable television, American channels—which have no Canadian content—outnumber Canadian ones; and the Canadian ones themselves have a high proportion of American programming.

American popular culture comes with an identity kit—messages about ways of thinking, feeling, and acting. It promotes an identity that internalizes individualistic competition, insecurity, and the acquisition of stylish commodities as a defense against feelings of exclusion and low self-esteem. Theoretically, this type of character structure could be described as modern rather than American; concretely, it is most widely promoted through American popular culture (Ewan 1988; Postman 1979, 1988a, 1988b; Schoenfeld 1993a). In addition to being exposed to these general features of American popular culture, Canadian Jews, like American Jews, are exposed to images of Jewish identity filtered through "L.A. Law," "Thirtysomething," Woody Allen movies, "Love and War," "Seinfeld," and so forth.

The growing closeness of America and Canada is also seen in the institutional links between Jewish life on both sides of the border.

English language Judaica—books, magazines, newspapers, videos, computer programs, and Jewish schoolbooks—are almost all from the United States. Canadian Jewish federations participate in the continental wide structures and activities of the Council of Jewish Federations. Canadians may be found in prominent positions in the institutional structure of North American Jewry. To cite only two examples, the high-profile Conservative theologian Neil Gillman is from Montreal; the editor of the Reform movement's commentary on the Bible, Gunther Plaut, has had a distinguished career in Canada. Conservative, Reform, and Reconstructionist Jews are directly linked to their movements' central institutions and activities in the United States. The organizational structure of Orthodoxy is more diffuse, but there are also multiple cross-border ties (Schoenfeld 1978).

The tendency of Canadian Judaism to be more conservative than in the United States is reflected in the strong support in Canada for the Union for Traditional Judaism. However, the traditionalists in the Canadian Conservative movement did not break away and form their own organization when they felt that the Conservative movement had gone too far left; they aligned themselves with the U.S. faction that broke off. Similarly, while Reform Judaism is more traditional in Canada than in the United States, organizational ties are active and personal networks are strong.

The Multiculturalizing of Canada

Canada takes in about 250,000 immigrants a year, about 1 percent of its population. According to census figures, about 16 percent of Canadian residents are immigrants—significantly more than in the United States. Toronto is by far the most favored immigrant destination, but many immigrants settle in Montreal and Vancouver. For the past twenty years, Canada has been receiving most of its immigrants from the Third World, particularly from Asia. In addition to those who enter at low rungs on the occupational ladder, immigrants to Canada also fill important technical jobs for which no Canadian citizens are available, and thousands of "entrepreneurs" who agree to establish places of employment are actively recruited.

For a variety of reasons, it is possible for immigrants and their descendants to maintain significant social and cultural ties outside of Canada.

The ability to communicate with people at a distance is now much greater than fifty years ago. Competition in long-distance telephones, faxes, and computer networks provide cheap and quick means of contact. Relatively inexpensive air travel makes maintaining overseas business, friendship, or family ties much easier than a generation ago. Visits to Europe and other locations to study, to travel, to work, and to participate in voluntary service programs bring the Canadian born into contact with the rest of the world.

Cable television stations in Toronto now have over fifty channels, including separate channels for programming from Italy, France, and China, and a selection of imported programs on other channels. The Canadian television network includes many hours of religious programming about non-Western religion. To a lesser extent, cultural diversity is available on radio. In addition, video movies, magazines, and current newspapers from around the world are readily available.

The communication and technological progress that facilitates identification with spatially dispersed social networks has changed the experience of being in a minority culture. Minority ethno-cultural communities are now less "strangers in a strange land" and more diasporas, balancing their incorporation into one society with continuing connections to another. Cultural assimilation is still an option, chosen by many. However, the resources that are available to construct an identity with elements from a minority culture are richer and more varied than before.

The multicultural face of Canadian culture has developed at the same time as American popular culture has flourished and at the same time as more Canadian culture is being produced. The cultural landscape has become more complex, fragmented, and incoherent. Individual Canadians who are in the process of defining and redefining their identities have access to a remarkable diversity of messages about appropriate ways of thinking, feeling, and acting. The social networks in which Canadians participate give differential value to these messages. As Canadians move from one social setting to another, the value given to different messages about identity is likely to vary considerably, reproducing in individual experience the segmentation and fragmentation of the culture.

This changed technological and cultural environment has implications for Jewish identity. To begin with, Israel is more real. Israelis are recognizable as a group in the Jewish population. Among Canadian Israelis, the stigma of being *yordim* (ex-patriates) is fading, replaced with the view that Israel is a small country and that it is natural that Israelis be found all over the world. It is now easier to sustain and transmit Israeli identity in Canada. The Jewish day schools in Toronto, for example, employ about eight hundred teachers in Jewish studies. These positions create employment opportunities for Israelis in a Jewish (and partially Hebrew speaking) environment. A Hebrew language newspaper now circulates widely in Toronto; an Israeli film festival was recently held. Hebrew-heritage language classes are available in the public schools and the Israeli consulate helped establish an after school program for Israeli children in the public schools. Furthermore, Israel is no longer so far away. Travel has become more common. Computer networks link people in Israel to people in Canada at a far lower cost than international telephone calls. With the expansion of cable television channels, it will soon be feasible to broadcast Israeli shows in Canada. In a variety of ways, new relationships with Israel are likely to develop along the lines discussed by Arnold Eisen (1992).

Canadian cultural diversity also has implications for the religious dimension of Jewish identity. We can teach identification with a religious community to skeptics by teaching that religious communities are beneficial to society and to the individual and by teaching religion as metaphor. These strategies can work so long as the cultural environment sets up one functional metaphor (e.g., Christianity) as the standard, leaving religious minorities with the strong liberal argument that they should not be compelled to shift allegiance from one metaphor to another. In the form in which global culture is filtered into Canada, there is no longer a standard religious metaphor. Islam, Asian religions, and Amerindian religious teachings are now present in our newspapers, television screens, and public schools, where they are each presented as worthy of respect. How can we teach Jewish commitment to students and families who learn elsewhere that one religious metaphor is as good as another, and that it is intellectually backward and intolerant to privilege one metaphor over another? Note the title of Joseph Campbell's widely read study of comparative religion—*The Masks of God* (1964–69). Campbell's influential view of religion as essentially metaphor is consistent both with his dislike of the rigorous monotheism of Judaism and with the congeniality of his scholarship to a New Age, neopagan view of religion.

Canadian multiculturalism means more than a greater diversity of ethnic origins in the population, a high percentage of immigrants, the possibility of sustaining social ties outside of Canada, and cultural diversification. Multiculturalism is also official government policy. The Royal Commission on Bilingualism and Biculturalism, which served in the mid-1960s, was premised on the continuing division between the English and French groups and examined new ways of managing their relationship. In the process, the Royal Commission was forced to acknowledge those who considered themselves outside of either group and who made claims for recognition and public support. The establishment in 1969 of official Canadian bilingualism policy was one outcome of the Royal Commission. The initiation of federal multicultural policy in 1972 was another, indicating that the voices of "the other ethnic groups" had been heard. The 1982 Constitution Act included extensive provisions relating to English and French, but it also identified "the multicultural aspect" as a fundamental characteristic of Canada and made special mention of aboriginal status and of the rights of aboriginal Canadians. (Native people are approximately twice the percentage of the population in Canada as they are in the U.S.) In 1988, Parliament passed a formal Multicultural Act.

There are three ideological supports for multiculturalism. First, multiculturalism is seen as a resource for Canada as a whole. In an interconnected world, it is to Canada's advantage to have citizens who understand and can communicate with cultures and societies around the world. Second, multiculturalism is seen as a vehicle through which to achieve racial justice. Canada has a past history of being a "vertical mosaic." Moreover, it is argued that Canada continues to be a racist society (Simms 1993). Programs and policies designed to raise the status of racial minorities are seen, like programs and policies in the area of aboriginal rights, to be based on principles of social justice. Third, multiculturalism is seen as a logical extension of Canada's original compact between two founding peoples. If those of English and French descent are entitled to special group rights, new immigrant groups and native people are also entitled to claim group rights. This last ideological support for multiculturalism is explicitly challenged by those who speak on behalf of Canada's French minority (or Quebec's French majority). Consequently, it is rarely incorporated into public discourse.

Canadian multicultural policies include public financial support for a wide range of multicultural and antiracist organizations; affirmative action for "visible minorities" (as well as for women and the disabled); retraining of police forces and changes in their recruitment procedures; extensive revision of curriculum materials; the public support for "heritage language" classes (which meet on weekends, after school hours, and in some cases during the normal school day); and public financial support for the establishment of ethnic studies programs in colleges.

To be sure, there are counterideologies to multiculturalism. Some argue that immigrants who come to a new country should expect to live in its language and by its customs, and that contemporary Canadian attitudes and nondiscrimination legislation have closed the book on racism, making special preferences for designated groups unnecessary. Furthermore, it is argued that Canadians need to learn to accept each other as individuals and not to self-segregate (Bissoondath 1993).

Those who favor multicultural policy differ about priorities. The initial agenda of assisting the preservation of minority cultures was soon expanded to include the special problem of discrimination against visible minorities. Some view the needs to develop international language skills, to become sensitive to the many global cultures, and to manage growing internal Canadian diversity as needs that compete for the public resources that have historically been devoted to the management of French—English relations.

Policies promoting cultural survival, sensitivity to global diversity, and antiracism have implications for Canadian Jewish identity (see also Schoenfeld 1989). Policies to assist cultural survival bring resources into Jewish organizations. Antiracist policies specifically include anti-Semitism as a form of racism. On the other hand, antiracist ideologists sometimes see Jews as part of the white establishment, and antiracism is often accompanied by the promotion of intercultural blending that critiques the agenda of minority subcultural continuity.

Globalization and the Growing Awareness
of Global Insecurity

Canadians have increasingly become aware of themselves as participants in global society. The English language has become the dominant international language of business, technology, politics, and popular culture. Consequently, Canadians have easy access to development in these areas in most places in the world. French remains an important language in other places; both the governments of Canada and Quebec participate in "la francopohonie"—the international association of French-speaking countries organized by France. Those Canadians who know both English and French have access to developments in a large part of the world. Global business relationships are also developing, both in the area of Canadian expansion overseas and of overseas investment in Canada.

Global awareness, however, has a troubled aspect. Real issues, which effect the lives and future of Canadians, are global ones. They require, if not global policies, at least local policies that are coordinated and justified on the basis of a global ideology. Issues of pollution, resource depletion and environmental damage, refugees, human rights and population growth, economic stagnation, and declining standards of living are experienced locally, but are understood to be essentially global.

These aspects of global awareness have implications for Canadian identity. To be Canadian means to be a citizen of one of the more favored countries in the world. Canadians interpret that fact in different ways. It may mean a special obligation to share Canadian talents and resources with others. This interpretation leads to Canadian enthusiasm for the United Nations and for other international agencies, and to the many overseas volunteer programs in which Canadians participate. Or it may mean that Canadians have an obligation to protect their prosperity from the impoverished masses of the Third World. This leads to the revival of (so far) small racist and anti-Semitic groups, and a general turning inward toward particularistic loyalties and personal agendas. Or global awareness may be associated with the pessimistic observation that even in a favored country like Canada, a long-term economic decline is setting in, leading to higher rates of unemployment and downward mobility for many. These are all different responses to globalization; none deny the importance of the world context.

Jews may likewise interpret the meaning of Canada's openness to the world in different ways. The humanistic idealism that derives from Canada's awareness of itself as a favored country has elective affinities to liberal Judaism's understanding of the social mission of the chosen people. Jews are represented in numbers far out of their proportion in movements that mobilize Canadians to address urgent worldwide socioeconomic problems. Other Jews, struggling to get on the economic ladder or to maintain their toehold there, are preoccupied with personal challenges. Multicultural relativism and a climate of insecurity stimulate other Jews to identify more within their own group. To some, the revival of anti-Semitism is a reminder of a specifically Jewish vulnerability. Some seek the kind of integral and coherent identity provided by social groups that offer ideological clarity and practical social support. Despite the defections that take place in an open society, the Orthodox community in Canada continues to be optimistic and energetic, and many liberal Jewish congregations are also centers of activity. Given this variety of possible responses, one might project polarized choices. However, since all of the possibilities offer something valuable to the individual, one might better expect fluid instability instead of polarizaton, with changes according to differing life circumstances.

Among Canadian Jews, globalization also facilitates the traditional awareness of being part of a globally dispersed community. Canadian Jews are numerous enough, affluent enough, and Jewish enough to produce individuals who are active in the Jewish issues in the United States, Israel, Europe, the states of the former USSR, and elsewhere. These activities are known within Canada and have become part of the understanding that Canadian Jews have of the meaning of their group identity.

Reluctant Cosmopolitans:
Jewish Identity in Canada and Elsewhere

Taken together, the trends of continental integration, multiculturalism, and globalization have an additive effect. Canadians remain physically in Canada, but their social networks and reference groups are on a larger scale. Within Canada, the population is not only more diverse, but is held together less by common cultural models.

The writer Neil Bissoondath notes, "It has become a commonplace that we who share this land—we who think of Canada as home—suffer an identity crisis stemming from a fragile self-perception" (Bissoondath 1993: 375) He further concludes that in Canada we find "a divisiveness so entrenched that we face a future of multiple solitudes with no central notion to bind us" (Bissoondath 1993: 385). The cultural critic Robert Fulford, surveying the history of different attempts to formulate a Canadian identity, observes that Canada is now a "post-modern dominion" (Fulford 1993). He explains, "we recognize the 'indeterminacy'. . . of our history and utterly reject . . . one agreed-upon 'master narrative' that would enslave all of us to a single vision." He notes the "'questioning of any notion of coherent, stable, autonomous identity (be it individual or national)" and asks "what could be more Canadian than that?" (Fulford 1993: 118).

These observations could not be made in England, France, the United States, or in other countries with strong traditions of being nation-states. At least not yet. The influence of American business and popular culture, the presence of multiple minorities who are not assimilating, and the awareness of being in a global context—are phenomena that are found in many places in the world. It may be that Canada—for historical and geographic reasons—is one of the places where these trends are most pronounced, have gone furthest in transforming sociocultural structures, and are most visible to the observer.

Marshall McLuhan, three decades ago, foresaw the emergence of an electronically linked global village (McLuhan 1962, 1964). His compatriots, somewhat reluctantly, are now living in it. People in other parts of the world are living in it too, but perhaps with less awareness. McLuhan predicted that the identity emerging in the global village would be cosmopolitan—world-wide and tolerant—but not integrated. Plurality would be experienced as incoherence; diversity as fragmentation. In discussing the implications of continental-ism, multiculturalism, and globalization for Canadian Jews, a variety of specific transformations in Canadian Jewish life have been noted—ranging, for example, from the impact of American popular culture images of Jews to multiculturalism's mixed messages about how Canadian society manages diversity to the awareness of the participation of Canadian Jews in worldwide Jewish social networks.

Beyond the specific implications that have already been dis-cussed, the more general debate and confusion about Canadian identity resonates in the discussion of Jewish identity. The model of Canadian social structure based on historically grounded distinct communities is constantly becoming a less and less accurate de-scription. The tolerance for diversity that is associated with multi-culturalism and global awareness is justified by an ethical rhetoric of individual choice. Communities are valued, but only if they are chosen. Historically derived cultures are resources for identity, but not for sources of obligations. The perspective of American popular culture is resolutely individualistic, promoting the goals of personal security, self-gratification, and self-actualization.[3]

The cumulative effect of continentalism, multiculturalism, and globalization is, then, the presentation to the individual of a cul-tural landscape that is experienced as inconsistent and fragmen-tary, which has many options for identity, which presents all (or most) options as of relatively equal value, which discourages a strong commitment to a particular historical culture, and which promotes a way of being in the world in which individuals may ei-ther change their understanding of themselves radically over time or go through life without feeling that their identities are organized around a meaningful center of gravity.

Implications For Jewish Education

Canada is becoming more of a sociocultural environment where identity is fragmented; where there is greater pessimism about indi-vidual and collective futures; and where there is a desire for values to live by, but in which values are relativized. This adds to the challenges of choosing the appropriate strategy of Jewish education for the next generation of Canada's Jews.

For a minority of Canada's Jews, Jewish education may not be problematic. For some, Jewish identity is based on the four-thousand-year Jewish struggle to live as a holy people completely dedicated to observing divinely revealed commandments. The strategy for Jewish education that follows from this is simple—the maximum separation of Jewish children from the relativizing, fragmenting influences of the surrounding sociocultural environment (see, e.g., Shaffir 1974, 1987; Bauer 1984). Another minority for whom Jewish education is not problematic are those who deny any but vestigial meaning to Jewish identity; they will choose minimal involvement in Jewish education, if any, for their children. Most Canadian Jews, however, expect their children to participate as Jews in Canadian life and look to Jewish education, especially formal education, to help prepare the next generation to be Jewish while they are at the same time Canadian.

In a Canada in which the image of a mosaic society was prominent, parents could understand Jewish education as a way of grounding the child in the community of origin—of keeping faith with memories of pious ancestors, with relatives murdered in Europe for the sole "crime" of being Jews, and with the strong group feelings of the grandparents who may be helping to pay the tuition. Jewish education, while not denying the importance of acquiring the skills to succeed in Canadian society, could also be seen as a way of of giving the child the knowledge and feelings to be connected to Diaspora Jewish communities around the world and in Israel.

The role of these kinds of feelings in the subculture of Jewish education is likely to diminish, however. In young families that are of increasingly mixed background and where the Jewish partner is likely to be third or fourth generation, there are fewer elements around which to build nostalgic and national sentiments. And as important as Holocaust awareness is, it is not an identity defining event to the extent that it was a generation ago. When the universalistic implications of the Holocaust are internalized, as they should be, identification can be directed toward a global reference group, rather than toward a particularly Jewish or Israeli one. This likelihood is stronger when the Holocaust is linked to the specter of disasters unfolding now or looming in the foreseeable future. As a consequence of these changes and of the increasing presence of a fragmented, relativizing culture, Jewish schools—day and supplementary alike—encounter more and more the challenge of the nature of the Jewish identity of the children enrolled in them (see also Glickman 1979, 1981; Hirschberg 1990; Schoenfeld 1983, 1992, 1993b). The issue of Jewish identity may be evaded if Jewish schools are reshaped around what is sometimes called "the Jewish option"—providing services in the Jewish community that are not only Jewish but are of higher quality than the public alternative. In the present climate of economic insecurity, schooling may become an even more competitive setting than it is now. For example, minimum grades for admissions to Ontario universities went up markedly in 1993. Newspapers reported that students were switching schools to go where they could have high marks, retaking courses in order to upgrade, and dropping out of extracurricular activities. Jewish schools are seen by many parents as settings where their children will be better prepared than in public schools to do well in their later education. In addition to the perceived academic superiority of the schools, parents may also anticipate that the friendships formed with other superior students will support high achievement in school and relationships with other students that will be important later in life. These perceptions have been associated with the shift over the past generation from a majority of Canadian Jewish students enrolled in public schools and receiving supplementary Jewish schooling to a majority enrolled in Hebrew day schools. Parents may continue to be attracted to Jewish schools on the basis of a superior Jewish option and may bring this expectation with them in their relationships with teachers, principals, and school boards.

There may be some difficulty in maintaining the perception of a superior "Jewish option" in education. An analysis of Jewish education in Montreal (Weinfeld & Zelchowitz 1993: 144–147) concluded that the Jewish day schools, which enroll about two-thirds of the eligible elementary age population and almost a third of the secondary school age population, cannot be considered elitist. They draw from a wide mix of income backgrounds, contain many students from minimally Jewish homes, contain many average and below average students as well as intellectually superior ones, and usually have physical plants that are less adequate than those of other private schools and many public schools. In Toronto, where elementary Jewish day school enrollment is slightly larger than supplementary school enrollment, it is similarly difficult to acquire the financial resources to maintain the existing quality of day schools, even though almost half of the local federation expenditures are directed toward subsidies to day school students. In recent years, the amount of the subsidy has been capped, with schools reporting that they must consequently cut services, raise fees (thus reducing enrollment), or both. Moreover, the Toronto federation has been moving away from its almost exclusive financial support of day school education as a strategy of Jewish continuity to support of a broader range of approaches (Jewish Federation of Greater Toronto 1994).

The competition to get into college also raises problems for the Jewish option at the high school level. Many students in the Toronto Jewish community high schools transfer out before graduation so that they may focus their efforts on those subjects that will determine college admission. On the other hand, Jewish enrollment in elite private schools was uncommon a generation ago; this is no longer the case. For many superior or wealthy students, the private school option is more attractive than the Jewish option.

It is possible to imagine Jewish education that responds to the problems of community, insecurity, and relativistic values in the larger environment. Students who live in a fragmented; incoherent; relativistic; and insecure cultural, familial, and occupational environment bring into our schools needs for an organizational culture that is concerned as much with identity as it is with information (see Heilman 1993 on feeling comfortable and part of a community in Jewish schools). Bernard Reisman (1994) has listed the following characteristics of schools that effectively promote identity as well as the transmission of information: They are schools that act like communities rather than institutions; which balance caring and mastery; which strengthen families (both as families and as Jewish families); which are at least as well managed as comparable non-Jewish schools, where different stakeholders and units in the system work together; where there is a clear ideological commitment shared through the school; and where value is placed on the spiritual dimension of Jewish identity.

This option for reshaping Jewish education may be the most demanding; it is certainly not the path of least resistance or least expense. It implies that schools, in a time of financial difficulty and cultural relativism, should be adding additional activities to work with families, to cultivate a school community, and to articulate spiritual values that are present in the school community. This option poses challenges to Orthodox schools that have been reluctant to engage minimally Jewish parents or have failed in their attempts so far (Grysman 1989); to Conservative and Reform schools that have tacitly accepted the perception of their movements as standing for something "less" rather than something "different"; and to day and supplementary schools alike that will have to ensure that they are more than just schools. This is, however, the only option that responds to the full range of needs which our analysis of emerging structural changes in the socio-cultural environment projects.

Notes

1. About 45% of Canada's Jews live in "greater" Toronto, another 10% elsewhere in Ontario. About 30% live in Montreal, Quebec, and the remainder are found mainly in the other large urban centers in Canada. The Jewish population of the Pacific rim city of Vancouver is growing; that of Winnipeg, on the midwestern prairies, is declining.

2. The marriages tables by religion show the religion of the bride and groom at the time of marriage. Those who converted prior to the marriage (in either direction) appear as religious in-marriages. These data indicate that the survey data reported in Brodbar-Nemzer et. al. (1993) underrepresent those marginally connected to Jewish social networks.

3. See Thomas Luckmann (1967) for a discussion of the relationship between individualism and the personal construction of identity.

References

Bauer, Julien. (1984) "De la deviance religieuse: le sous-systeme Hassidique a Montreal" (On religious deviance: The Hassidic subsystem in Montreal) *Cahiers de recherches en sciences de la religion* 5: 235–60.

Bissoondath, Neil. (1993) "A Question of Belonging: Multiculturalism and Citizenship." In *Belonging: The Meaning and Future of Canadian Citizenship*, edited by William Kaplan, 368–87. Montreal: McGill-Queen's University Press.

Brodbar-Nemzer, Jay, Steven M. Cohen, Allan Reitzes, Charles Shahar and Gary Tobin. (1993) "An Overview of the Canadian Jewish Community." In *The Jews in Canada*, edited by Robert J. Brym, William Shaffir, and Morton Weinfeld, 39–71. Toronto: Oxford University Press.

Campbell, Joseph. (1964–69) *The Masks of God,* 4 vols. New York: Penguin.

Davies, Alan. (1992) *Antisemitism in Canada: History and Interpretation*. Waterloo, Ontario, Canada: Wilfrid Laurier University Press.

Eisen, Arnold. (1992) *A New Role for Israel in American Jewish Identity.* New York: American Jewish Committee.

Ewan, Stuart. (1988) *All Consuming Images: The Politics of Style in Contemporary Culture.* New York: Basic.

Fulford, Robert. (1993) "A Postmodern Dominion: The Changing Nature of Canadian Citizenship." In *Belonging: The Meaning and Future of Canadian Citizenship,* edited by William Kaplan, 104–19. Montreal: McGill-Queen's University Press.

Glickman, Yaacov. (1979) "Ethnic Boundaries and the Jewish Parochial School in Toronto: The Inevitability of False Expectations." In *Emerging Ethnic Boundaries,* edited by Danielle Juteau Lee, 92–116. Ottawa: University of Ottawa Press.

———. (1981) "Jewish Education: Success or Failure?" In *The Canadian Jewish Mosaic,* edited by Morton Weinfeld, Schaffir, and Cotter, 113–28. Toronto: Wiley.

Grysman, Charles. (1989) "The Orthodox Day School and its Non-Observant Population." *Jewish Education,* 57: 32–38.

Heilman, Samuel. (1993) "Inside the Jewish School." In *What We Know about Jewish Education,* edited by Stuart Kelman, 304–30. New York: Behrman House.

Hirschberg, Jack. (1990) "Religious Education and Jewish Ethnic Identity." In *Essays in the Social Scientific Study of Judaism and Jewish Society,* edited by Sincha Fishbane and Jack Lightstone, 251–76. Vol. 1. Montreal: Concordia University, Department of Religion.

Jewish Federation of Greater Toronto. (1994) *Report of the Task Force on Jewish Continuity.* Toronto: Jewish Federation of Greater Toronto.

Kaplan, William, ed. (1993) *Belonging: The Meaning and Future of Canadian Citizenship.* Montreal: McGill-Queen's University Press.

Luckmann, Thomas. (1967) *The Invisible Religion.* New York: Macmillan.

McLuhan. Marshall. (1962) *The Gutenberg Galaxy.* Toronto: University of Toronto Press.

———. (1964) *Understanding Media.* New York: McGraw-Hill.

Postman, Neil. (1979) *Teaching as a Conserving Activity.* New York: Dell.

———. (1988a) "The Disappearance of Childhood." In *Conscientious Objections: Stirring up Trouble about Language, Technology and Education,* 147–62. New York: Knopf.

———. (1988b) "Future Shlock." In *Conscientious Objections: Stirring up Trouble about Language, Technology and Education,* 147–62. New York: Knopf.

Reisman, Bernard. (1994) "Policies and Programs to Reaffirm the Centrality of the Jewish Family for the Jewish Community." In *The Jewish Family and Jewish Continuity*, edited by Steven Bayme and Gladys Rosen, Hoboken, N.J.: KTAV.

Shaffir, William. (1974) *Life in a Religious Community: The Lubavitch Chassidim of Montreal*. Toronto: Holt.

—— (1987) "Separation from the Mainstream in Canada: The Hassidic Community of Tash." *Jewish Journal of Sociology*; (1987), 29, 1, June, 19–35). Reprinted from (1993) *The Jews in Canada*, edited by Robert Brym, WIlliam Shaffir, and Morton Weinfeld. Toronto: Oxford University Press, 126–41.

Schoenfeld, Stuart. (1978) "The Jewish Religion in North America: Canadian and American Comparisons," *Canadian Journal of Sociology* 3 no. 2: 209–31.

——. (1983) "The Transmission of Jewish Identity in a Non-Jewish Neighbourhood." *Contemporary Jewry* 6 no. 2: 35–44.

——. (1989) "Jewish Identity in a Multicultural Canada: The Implications for Assimilation and Intermarriage." In *Canadian Jewry Today: Who's Who in Canadian Jewry*, edited by E. Y. Lipsitz, 92–98. Toronto: JESL.

——. (1992) "Best Practices Project—Bet Sefer Solel." In *Best Practices in Jewish Education: Supplementary Schools*. New York: Council for Initiatives in Jewish Education.

——. (1993a) "Jews, Jewish Texts and the Emergent Media Culture," *Agenda: Jewish Education* 1, no. 2: 14–19.

——. (1993b) "Some Aspects of the Social Significance of Bar/Bat Mitzvah Celebrations." In *The Bar/Bat Mitzvah Handbook*, edited by Helen Lenneman. Denver: Alternatives in Religious Education. Reprinted (1990) *Essays in the Social Scientific Study of Judaism and Jewish Society*, edited by from Simcha Fishbane and Jack Lightstone. Montreal: Department of Religion, Concordia University.

Simms, Glenda P. (1993) "Racism as a Barrier to Canadian Citizenship." In *Belonging: The Meaning and Future of Canadian Citizenship*, edited by William Kaplan. Montreal: McGill-Queen's University Press.

Weinfeld, Morton, and Phyllis Zelchowitz. (1993) "Reflections on the Jewish Polity and Jewish Education." In *The Jews in Canada*, edited by Robert J. Brym, William Shaffir, and Morton Weinfeld, 142–52. Toronto: Oxford University Press.

Chapter 8

✺

From Commandment to Persuasion: Probing the "Hard" Secularism of American Jewry

Henry L. Feingold

To become modern, societies undergo a wrenching process of change in the way in which they are organized and view the world. The attitudinal aspect of that change process is sometimes called "secularization." It takes different forms in different societies but everywhere it requires the dethroning of traditional mind-sets. Because America is different, so is its secularism. I have called it "hard" secularism because of its libertarianism and the high degree of individuation it aspires to and to its lesser willingness to let old forms and institutions stand. It is that hardness that creates the powerful solvent that poses a survival challenge to all religious and ethnic cultures in America. The former is desacrilized, the latter, denuded. That is what has been happening to American Jewry since its origins in the seventeenth century.

To speak of *secularism* in a Jewish historical context poses nigh insurmountable problems of definition since that term has prior usages in Jewish history. It implies irreligion or adherence to a particular socialist ideology. So we must state at the outset that the secularism we speak of here is only remotely connected to such ideologies as Bundism or Socialist Zionism. Secularists in our sense may not observe the rules of their church, but they need not be strangers to spirituality or to a concern for existential questions. In

the secular person, a religious sensibility is internalized to become
an integral part of the individual self. He or she may continue to enjoy the aesthetic celebratory aspects of formal institutionalized religion and may even sing in the synagogue choir, but being free, one
is not ready to be commanded. The myriad laws of the *halakha*
would impinge upon the autonomy that is central to a secular person. For the same reason, secular people do not lightly surrender to
the praxis element of modern ideologies, whether they preach the
need to participate in the "revolution" or to halt the killing of
whales. They cannot long obey these exhortations because the secular mentality is in fact already an ideology that preaches the development, or better, the liberation of self from all that would fetter it.

A separate study could be done on what secular Jews choose to
give up and what they retain. Life cycle ceremonies, for example, are
not easily surrendered. Even the most secular prefer to be married
under a *chupah* and buried in a Jewish cemetery. And many secular
Jews light Sabbath candles before they attend a movie or turn on the
TV. The pattern would be determined by the design of modern life in
the particular community. If an automobile is a necessity rather than
a luxury then most Jews, there are many Orthodox exceptions, will
drive to services. A favorite Jewish joke used to be that the difference
between Orthodox, Conservative, and Reform Jews lies in the distance they park their cars from the synagogue.

Sadly, it is not a static process. As the secular spirit grows more
intense, the distance from the religious and ethnic culture widens
and both are emptied of their content and deprived of their special
language. Once particularity has been ground down, it becomes easier to comingle with other subcultures that have undergone a similar detribalization process. Intermarriage that grows naturally out
of such circumstances is actually not the last step in the dissolution
of a once distinctive and separate culture. It is merely part of a
process of cultural dilution that is marked by a loss of communal
memory. The tribe no longer knows who it is or why it should be.

Historians can best contribute to an understanding of the secularization process that acts as the motor force behind the changes in
modern Jewish life, by describing a specific instance of its workings. In
this discussion we begin with the growing "crisis of faith" during the
interwar period that was marked by a sharp decline of religious observance. We do so to gain a glimpse of the "hard" pervasive character of
American secularism at work. The stage is then set for a broader discussion of how that process has shaped American Jewish life.

* * *

During the twenties, the American Jewish *church* grew with startling rapidity. I use that alien term because it best describes the institutional shell—the seminaries, courts, rabbinic assemblies, and unions of congregations—in which the religion is institutionalized. But supported by a divided and scattered people and having lost its hierarchical structure, the American Jewish church had less power to command than Christian churches. In America, a society that developed in a postenlightenment setting, a Jew could leave the fold with comparative ease. Indeed they were often encouraged to do so by Christian missionaries. There was little that could coerce adherence or observance. Eventually the idea of the church and synagogue holding on to its adherents by anything other than persuasion would prove to be impossible. The lack of direct power over its worshipers and the existence of a welcoming secular world enhanced the Jewish appetite for life outside the synagogue, a secular life. Jews ultimately became America's most avid secularists.

Withal, the twenties witnessed an increase in Jewish congregations, especially in its Reform and Conservative branches. Both experienced a veritable "edifice complex," the construction of houses of worship to shelter these newly organized congregations. The Orthodox branch lagged somewhat behind in imposing organizational structure. Its minyans were communities of faith that hardly required a fancy edifice and a "spiritual leader" but they were often also poor and transitory. Each branch had established a rabbinic seminary to produce an indigenous rabbinate. The Jewish church was establishing itself but did not seem to be able to avoid the plague of denominationalism that splintered the Protestant churches. That fragmentation became more apparent with the failure of the Jewish Theological Seminary and the Isaac Elchanan Yeshiva to unite in 1927. That failure forced the leaders of the Jewish Theological Seminary to think of themselves as a third or middle branch of American Judaism. It then rapidly expanded into areas of second settlement where geographically mobile Jews were establishing new communities.

In 1921, Mordecai Kaplan had established the Jewish Renascence Center that soon evolved into the Society for the Advancement of Judaism. Based on an organizational principle copied from Felix Adler's Ethical Culture Society, it became the core of the Reconstructionist movement that Kaplan wanted merely to be an influence rather than another branch of Judaism. Its ethos seemed to be fashioned to keep secularizing Jews in the fold. Jewish centers, also advocated by the Reconstructionist movement, proliferated. It was hoped that the "shul with a pool and a school" that combined secular and religious activity under a single cultural umbrella, might become the wave of the future. That is at least what the new, usually American-born, "professional" rabbis would have liked to believe. But the Jewish Center movement, which sought to combine all secular Jewish culture and religious activities, proved to be a failing strategy. In the centers secular activities tended to overshadow purely religious ones such as morning services (Scult 1993).

Little in the economic situation of the children of immigrants, who were assuming leadership positions in the congregations and organizations, suggested such a "crisis of faith." Most Jews knew about the anti-Semitic rantings of Henry Ford and the limitations policy of Harvard University. They understood that the restrictive immigration law of 1924 might have, despite denials, been aimed at excluding their brethren. But that was nothing to get excited about. There were no Black Hundreds, no pogroms, and why would Jews want to attend institutions where they were unwanted. One could establish one's own university or country club, and even build one's own new neighborhood. That is in fact the path American Jews often followed during the twenties and after World War II (Moore 1981). Almost yearly the *American Hebrew*, a popular Anglo-Jewish weekly, featured a review of the new posh Jewish country clubs all over the nation. *It's a free country* was a favorite observation of "alrightniks," the satiric term applied to those who acculturated too rapidly with often comical results. Most Jews of the "Jazz Age" had confidence in the American system and remained blithely unaware that it was the very freeness they so cherished that posed special problems for Judaism, a prescriptive faith based on religious law. A free autonomous citizen did not need to adhere to the long-established ethical principles of his church. Free meant that one could develop one's personal code of ethics and behavior and even a personalized idea of God.

At the grass roots, anti-Semitism was palpable and often painful to Jews seeking employment, especially with large firms. But by and large its proponents seemed unable to deny access to the instruments of socioeconomic mobility. Jews flooded into medical and law schools. A DDS, "disappointed doctor or surgeon," was usually available as a second choice for those who were rejected by medical school. The barriers to professionalism gradually crumbled. Perhaps it is more accurate to say that Jewish candidates for the professions worked their way around them. The proportion of Jews in the independent professions, law, medicine, and accountancy grew to em-

barrassingly high levels. At the height of the Harvard quota deba-
cle, President Lowell liked to point to the fact that even after the
new enrollment policy was implemented, the number of Jewish students at Harvard would remain disproportionately high (Synnott
1979). That was also true in the new dependent professions like
teaching and social work that Jewish women found especially attractive. What Lowell could not fathom was that the drive to
achieve middle-class station that shaped the lives of these secularized Jewish students was so powerful that it would, like steam seeking to escape, find some way to come to the surface.

When a Harvard student accused Jewish students of underliv-
ing and overworking, he was probably unaware of the enormous
pressure to achieve that these students had imposed upon themselves. Such students were actually doubly driven. Achievement
through learning was inherent not only in the Judaic culture from
which they were often distancing themselves, but also in the quest
for self-realization peculiar to the secular spirit of America. This
doubly motivated drive for professionalization among second-generation Jews was in fact only the tip of the iceberg. It could also be observed in the aspirations of the Jewish work force. During the
interwar years an occupational upgrading converted finishers into
cutters and filing clerks into secretaries. A second perhaps larger
stream used small business to achieve middle-class station.

The result was that no other immigrant group was so successful in sharing the prosperity of the twenties. It was as if Jews knew
instinctively how to prime themselves to function in the emerging
complex market economy. When the economy collapsed in 1929,
Jews were already better equipped than other immigrant groups to
sustain themselves through the lean years and then to recover their
former position.

The inordinate drive to rise out of the ghetto and to achieve a
secure place in America's middle class was the most powerful moti-
vational force that shaped the lives of second-generation American
Jews. That spirit of self-improvement, of viewing oneself as incomplete but perfectable, associated here with American secularism, re-
leased enormous new energies and ultimately altered the way in
which Jews saw themselves and the world. What these driven Jews
could not foresee is that the priority given to self-development carried with it the potential for asociality that would have a profound
impact on Jewish communalism.

Beyond the prosperity of America that second-generation Jews
shared fully, beyond the proliferation of temples and synagogues, a

communal and religious crisis was brewing. The noted historian Lucy Dawidowicz observed that a religious depression preceded the economic one. Religious observance was less important in the secular worldview. Paradoxically, while that secular spirit was pervasive, its impact remained hidden from most observers, just as the weaknesses in the economy were not fully realized until the great market crash and the depression that followed. Mordecai Kaplan first sensed something amiss while counseling troubled rabbinic students at the seminary. They often complained that they could get little meaning or guidance from their faith to confront the challenges of their daily lives. Their malaise, which was rooted in the dissonance between the demands of the faith and the requirements of daily life, was not limited to rabbinic students. To remain observant often meant having to give up not only the material comfort of middle-class life but also its promise for self-betterment.

By the thirties the massive synagogue-building crusade tapered off and with the deepening depression there was concern about how the mortgages would be paid. But the decline in observance and synagogue attendance could not be attributed to the high annual cost of synagogue membership alone. The decline in piety and observance, much in evidence in the Old Country, was hardly a new phenomenon. What was new in the America of the twenties and thirties was that second-and third-generation Jews no longer possessed backgrounds that rooted them firmly in the religious culture. By the thirties nigh everyone had become an "alrightnik." Most knew less of Judaic texts and religious laws and customs than their parents. Few continued to turn to the east three times daily to pray or to put on phylacteries every morning as if by Pavlovian conditioning. Often they no longer knew how to pray. There was thus even less to pass onto their children who would be compelled to carry on the tradition armed with only a memory of a memory. Most important, something in the new mind-set prevented them from seeing themselves as members of a special tribe. By the midtwenties rabbis frequently complained that their synagogues were empty. An editorial in the *American Hebrew* (29 May 1925) recommended the building of accordion-shaped synagogues because they had the possibility of expansion during the High Holy days, when everyone attended services, and contraction for the weekly Sabbath and daily services, when comparatively few did.

Much that was recognizably Jewish remained in the daily lives of the Jews of the interwar period. They ate Jewish foods and told Jewish jokes. But the Yiddish press would be compelled to convert to English, the prefered language of the "alrightniks." The Yiddish theater, the "jewel in the crown" of immigrant culture, experienced a sharp decline in attendance in the late twenties. The decline in religious observance and synagogue attendance occured in tandem with the weakening of Jewishness, the ethnic culture. In contrast to the situation in Eastern Europe, in America secularizing Jews would find no ethnic cultural net to catch them. That falling away could take various forms. Some became involved in Jewish organizational life or in the Zionist movement that could delay the assimilation process for a generation or two.

Sometimes it seemed as if the familiar Jewish zeal for faith and mitzvoth (good deeds) was transmuted to political idealism embodied in the doctrines of socialism, often in one generation. Led by college students, whose mobility had been blocked by the collapse of the economy, young Jews flocked in disproportionate numbers to the social justice and peace movements that proliferated during the interwar period. The familiar role of Jews as the most conspicuous activists on the left side of the political spectrum began in earnest during the depression years of the thirties. But the quest for social justice was not sought through Jewish institutions or organizations like the American Jewish Congress, or the Reform movement whose theology had made a special place for it. Young Jews became active through secular nonsectarian parties and groupings. Jewish students were conspicuously present in the American Student Union, the American Youth Congress, and the Young Communist League (Cohen 1993). The peace strikes and protest rallies in which Jewish students participated with such fervor may have had a familiar religious enthusiasm about them but they were secular and espoused radical universalism. Ultimately "falling" Jews fell out of Jewish space and into the cosmos. Jewish cosmopolitans were concerned about the world, not about a particular tribe within it.

In 1942 a rudimentary "state of the faith" survey of New York Jewry found that over 40 percent checked none of the items customarily associated with practicing Judaism such as lighting Sabbath candles, observing kashruth or giving to charity. When the puzzled interviewers asked what then made them Jewish the response was inevitably that they felt "Jewish in their heart." They were promptly dubbed "cardiac Jews" (Steinbaum 1942). It was apparent that it was not a heart that beat very strongly. Zionism, a secular ideology that served in other democratic Western democracies to break the fall of the newly secularized, also reached a low point in America during the early thirties. Having already found its

Zion, American Jewry understood little of Zionist ideology and fairly
neglected the agencies and organizations that were associated with
the world Zionist movement. When they finally flocked to the Zionist banner in the late thirties, they did so because of the Jewish
refugee problem created by Berlin's heartless extrusion policy.

Generally, its response to the Holocaust, especially by native-
born Jews, was unorganized and largely ineffective. The closer Jews
were tied to families in Europe, that is, the less acculturated they
were, the more visceral the response. It was the American Jewish
Congress, whose membership was composed of the secularized children of "downtown" Jews, who organized and attended the rallies to
protest what Berlin was doing to its brethren. For native-born secularized Jews who came under the influence of universalist left-wing
ideologies the response was different. The fought the "scourge of fas-
cism," not in a proposed Jewish army that was much spoken about
after 1940, but in the Lincoln Brigade. They fought and died in
Spain for universal right and justice for all (Avni 1982). The specific
threat that Nazism posed for the Jews of Europe was merely part of
that. If they were Jews at all they were logical Jews, not biologic.
Later American Jews enlisted in the American armed services in
disproportionate numbers.

A special agency was created to remind the nation of the Jewish
contribution to the war effort. It was, they believed, the failure to do
that during the First World War that led to charges of malingering
and war profiteering. The use of public relations to ward off the
slings and arrows of a hostile host culture, even the notion that they
could be counteracted, had been developed by Louis Marshall in his
fight to stop Henry Ford's campaign of anti-Semitism in the twenties (Feingold 1993). It was a matter of manipulating images that
were infinitely malleable. Even defense strategies had become modernized. But there were no strategies to counteract the negative impact of secularism on the religious culture. That required
commitment and faith that secularized Jews gave to the development of self.

* * * *

Was American Jewry's crisis of faith inevitable? Secularization,
the kind we speak of here, after all, entails less willingness to allow
life to be shaped by command of faith or ideology. American Jewry's
survival conundrum would be better managed if the link between
temporality, so much part of secularism, and the remarkable success of Jews in business and the professions were better understood.

Secularization's this worldliness, the privatization and distancing from tribal identity it brings in its wake, affects everything on the Jewish agenda, from the way in which Jewish leadership responded to the Holocaust, to the Jewish performance in the business arena. Nothing is left untouched. How modern American Jews see themselves and the world has undergone a profound change especially since World War I. That change stems from the continuing impact of America's "hard" secularism on its vision. To grasp it fully, its principles and value orientation requires our special attention.

Unlike the single unifying sensibility of observant premodern Jews, their modern counterparts have multileveled identities and matching plural loyalties that are often in conflict with observance. The secular world of work knows not of sacred time. An emergency call to a doctor or lawyer, the tax season for an accountant, or the possibility of overtime for a cutter in the garment industry may conflict with Sabbath observance. Secular identity formation also differs from the premodern in that it is not organically of one piece. The secular persona is necessarily split and divided to enable him and increasingly her, to function in the complex modern world. The tensions involved in this multiplicity of roles for secularizing Jews is only partially resolved by the postemancipation response that calls for duality—being a Jew at home and a man or woman in the world. Of all the roles he plays, it is the professional or working role that is the integrative one. Ask modern man who he is and he is likely to tell you what he does.

A tribe unto himself, he is autonomous. The guidance of family and tribe are diminished. The quest for self-actualization becomes the prime organizing principles of secular life, playing the role that tribe or church did for premoderns. People choose their mates on the basis of romantic love rather than on the need to enhance the family or tribal position and coffers. They can choose to be unencumbered by communal, church, and even family ties and increasingly do so. They must be persuaded to affiliate or give to charity and they do so on their own terms. Since democracy is the secular spirit's favorite offspring, the well-being of the laity becomes more urgent than placating the deity. One cannot be commanded; one must be persuaded. Tribal bonds have been replaced by voluntary association. The family ceases to be the arena of primary association and soon loses its role as an agency of social control.

Though some of these elements may be familiar, there are few who touch all bases of the "complete" secular Jew. A composite portrait of such Jews would show them as neither totally secular nor

traditional. Most station themselves somewhere on the axis between the two poles. They find what is comfortable by picking and
choosing from religious and secular modalities, as if in a cafeteria.
Some rules are obeyed, others are disregarded, still others are
transmuted. Exile becomes priestly mission; exodus, a search for
freedom; prophetic exhortation, a quest for social justice. The religious garment is retailored to fit. The important thing is that the individual secular Jew, not the community, is the tailor. The centrality
of the individual person is quintessentially what America's "hard"
secularism is about.

Secularism, then, is the attitudinal core behind modernity. It
shapes the identity and alters the sense of self and place in the
world. Moderns, we have seen, are more concerned with the present
and less with the Hereafter, more with material well-being and less
with things of the spirit. In 1691, anxious to save souls, the College
of William and Mary petitioned the Lords of Treasury for a charter.
Back from London came an exasperated reply: "Souls, damn your
souls; make tobacco" (Sperry 1963: 36). That appeal for material
wealth might be the cry of a secular priest hood, were it possible for
secular people to cherish a priesthood.

But the actual profile modernization would assume and the
character of the transition differed widely from culture to culture.
Israel, Spain, and England, for example, do not make a fetish of the
separation of church and state as is done in America. While the
motor force of America's "hard" secularism is individual self-realization, the former Soviet Union sought class well-being and preoccupied itself with creating an egalitarian society. Russia, without
socialism, remains strongly collectivist and egalitarian, while America is still passionately libertarian and individualistic.

The high degree of individuation and freeness it advocates,
which produces America's hard secularism, is related to its historical proximity to Calvinist Protestantism. There we find the separation of public from private behavior, and indeed our first notion of
behavior as differentiated from feeling. America's tolerance of pluralism also can be traced ultimately to its Protestant roots. In a
sense, what we have witnessed in the American Jewish experience
is the gradual Protestanization of its Judaism. That is what American Jews acculturated to. It went beyond the concern of Charleston
Reformers with decorum and family pews (Hagy 1993; Meyer 1988).
What was important was how things looked and how people behaved was not necessarily linked to how they felt. That is directly
linked to another bifurcation of modernity, that of ethics from eti-

quette; the bifurcation of what is believed to be right from what looks right. Premodern Jews cared little for such concerns and many of the ultra-Orthodox still don't. It also separated Jewishness, the tribal, ethnic, folk culture, from Judaism, the religious aspect. That too was a distinction unknown in ancient Israel.

The transitional immigrant culture continued to weakly nourish the Jewish spirit and culture of the second and third generation. In the twenties and thirties one could still feel Jewish by going to the Yiddish theater, or by reading a Yiddish newspaper, or by eating "Jewish" food. But clearly that culture would not live beyond the life of the language whose users were passing from the scene. Oddly, though mutually antagonistic, the religious and the secular-ethnic cultures were in the same boat and were somehow dependent on each other. They were both challenged, as noted by the sociologist Talcott Parsons, by the spirit of "universal otherhood" that secularism sought to substitute for "tribal brotherhood." But all attempts to bridge the chasm between them, including, as we have seen, Mordecai Kaplan's, Jewish Center movement, failed. They prefered to face the uphill battle to sustain themselves alone.

So unobtrusive yet pervasive, so seemingly natural, was the gradual acceptance of the spirit of secularism, that few realized that it had penetrated the inner recesses of even the most religious communities. The speed and intensity with which the children of immigrants adopted secular values and aspirations and abandoned the synagogue startled and worried church leaders who saw it as a cause of Jewish crime and political radicalism. Some have speculated that the special Jewish penchant for the secular spirit may be attributable to the early place it found in Jewish history. It actually emanates from the split life maintained by generations of Marranos that gave them a strong this worldly disposition, a fragmented religious identity, and other characteristics of the modern mind-set. It was already manifest in the thinking of philosophers like Baruch Spinoza (1632–77), centuries before the Enlightenment and emancipation (Yovel 1989; Seltzer 1980).

Yet in contrast to Eastern Europe, the secularism of American Jews was not embodied in a particular ideology. Rather it was something in the air, a way of seeing, a new mind-set or mentality that shaped reality. At its core was the idea of self-fulfillment, the notion that every citizen had the right and the obligation to develop his talents, to be what he could be. Such a scheme required that the citizen be fully assured of his freedom; today interpreted as the right to unencumbered access to opportunity for education or business enterprise. That is the promise of liberalism, some form of which is America's prefered political ideology in both parties.

Liberalism, which also has become the most distinctive remaining fingerprint of American Jewish identity, is a peculiar ideology when compared to those of Eastern Europe because its primary burden is not to shape behavior but rather to make free, to liberate. Extending opportunity or access, whether to former slaves or to the handicapped, is a strong force in American politics. The individuation that such a libertarian secularism brings in its wake has special implications for the Jewish enterprise. It makes the intrusive legalistic and corporate character of Judaism difficult to sustain. It is also a key to the survivalist dilemma of American Jewry. Jews might legally be those born to Jewish mothers, but they cannot be forced to assume the responsibility of their birthright. They can reject membership in the corporation. They are free and must be persuaded to voluntarily associate themselves. It is in that sense all secular Jews in American are "Jews by choice," not merely regarding the degree of affiliation, but whether they want to be affiliated at all.

A mind-set that places self-realization at its center was bound to pose a challenge to any intrusive religious dogma or political ideology that insisted upon praxis, a linkage between theory and action. Understandibly, free secular citizens could not easily permit their newly won freedom to be refettered by the claim of dogma or ideology. Churches and political movements that insisted on claiming such control did not fare as well with American Jewry as those that managed to make room for the free secular spirit by what Henry Kissinger called "creative ambiguity." The comparative success of the Conservative movement in the thirties and fifties is probably attributable in part to the very uncertainty of its ideology that some bemoan today. Conversely the ultimate failure of Orthodoxy to attract and hold American Jewry can be traced directly to its need to intrude deeply into the personal lives of its adherents.

Most interesting is how Zionism, which in its socialist incarnation contained an imperative to resettle in Palestine, was refashioned by Louis Brandeis to fit the American reality. Just as the non-Orthodox branches developed a Judaism without the "yoke of Torah," so Brandeis developed a Zionism without the "yoke of aliyah." Brandeis understood that the secular American Jew could no longer be commanded as were his ancestors at Sinai. He had to be persuaded. Often what is most persuasive is what is believed to bring happiness or contentment in contemporary vogue. It could be the ownership of a cadillac or a Ph.D. The point is that individual Jews, wisely or foolishly, determine the content of their lives. Their power goes beyond choosing the rabbi and determining his or her salary. They choose as well what to consider sacred or profane. The church is democratized; the "people" stand where once was the deity. It is they who command and they who may choose to obey.

The democratic command structure of modern secular American society is profoundly at variance with the one in which the synagogue was born and grew to maturity. Predictably, in the American Jewish world it was the Orthodox branch that was least able to accommodate the change. It takes some getting used to and some rabbinic leaders never did. In the 1920s the Vaad HaRabonim, fearing that the Isaac Elchanan yeshiva was being tainted by secularism, tried several times to intervene. Earlier, in 1902, a similar group brought Rabbi Jacob Josef to the United States to be the chief rabbi. Both attempts, like those before and after them, to revert to a premodern command structure failed.

For some this secular outlook, especially the notion of freeness, brought confusion. But for the majority it brought personal confidence and the release of new energies. The sense of being at the center of the cosmos brought with it a sense of being in control accompanied by a willingness to assume risks that is requisite for the entrepreneurial spirit. But having mastered the temporal world of the professions or business, secular people man can no longer easily view themselves as mere specks of dust before a commanding God. They can neither pray nor obey. The humility and sense of proportion, which ultimately forms the essence of faith, is lost to them. It is in that sense that they have become irreligious. But that does not mean that they are unspiritual or immoral. It simply means that the religious spirit, once housed in the church or synagogue, has been privatized or internalized. In our time one can name few moral giants that have stemmed from the synagogue. Andre Sakharov and Natan Sharansky, who fit that description, derive from intensely secular backgrounds.

All of America's religions have been affected by its "hard" secular spirit; but for Jewry, the subculture that has embraced secularism with an adoration their ancestors reserved for their commanding God, its assets and liabilities seem amplified. On the other hand, Jews are also the first to confront the growing disorder in personal and communal life that it brings in its wake.

For American Jewry, the decline in the strength of the family has special significance since it is the traditional incubator of identity as well as of social controls. The internalization of these controls is especially important since without such a process there can be no communal life. Like all communities, Jewish communal life is based on the assumption that the process of maturation is based on widespread self-governance. Good citizens stop for red lights and pay their taxes without having to be policed to do so. Jews were particularly good at such internalization. But lately we have seen traces that all is not well. As a community, synagogue and family life weaken and disrupt the internalization process is disrupted.

Predictably some Jews, like the recent cohort of Jewish inside traders, have gone too far in the quest for self-actualization. They and thousands of other Jews who have broken the law were too avid in the "pursuit of happiness," which for them meant the accumulation of wealth. They did not possess the internal controls, the moral compass, to prevent themselves from tipping into crime. But they are the exception rather than the rule. Generally Jews in America have successfully combined remarkable success, achieved in acceptable secular terms, while assuming the high degree of civic responsibility that free communities require. They are self-governing. But it is predictable that as the secularization process continues and institutions like family, community, and synagogue decline in influence, American Jewry will be faced with an increase in asocial behavior. Paradoxically, the community itself might be too fragmented to concern itself with it. After all, in secular terms, what a Bolsky or any of a group of indicted inside traders did, he did as a free modern secular individual, not as a Jew.

It is then virtually predictable that America's most upwardly mobile group, its Jews, is also its most avidly secular one. Jewry's secularity is linked to its formidable success in achieving middle-class station through business and professionalization. Understandably, that success is written almost exclusively in secular terms. One can actually graph the reverse correlation between the rise of its annual per-capita income and the decline of religious observance. Secularization, as used in this chapter, explains the relationship between the two.

A clear understanding of the impact of "hard" secularism sheds new light on virtually every problem area of contemporary Jewish life in America. The decline of observance is merely one example, probably the most direct one, which can be presented to illustrate the impact of secularization. The burgeoning intermarriage rate is but its latest manifestation. But there are less direct linkages as well. The sequence of problems that shook the synagogue in the last few decades, from the ordination of women to the organization of gay congregations, even the move to proselytize among the un-churched, is related to it. Each of these extensions of freedom to pre-viously excluded or partially excluded groups, pushed foreward by secular liberalism to extend the bounds of freeness, requires yet a new accommodation that entails a difficult alteration of founding principles.

In another arena, the failure of the world Zionist movement to generate mass aliyah (immigration to Israel) from America and the related massive yerida (emigration from Israel) from Israel cannot be understood apart from the comparative opportunities for self-realization. That desire, we have noted, is central to the secular imagination and until now it has been more realizable in America. It goes without saying that if the conditions for self-realization through business or education were expanded and personal security were assured in Israel, yerida would decrease and immigration would increase. These are the necessary preconditions of the secular life-style.

Like the weakening of the synagogue and the Jewish all-purpose organization, the weakening of Jewish family is related to the new secular mental set that leaves nothing untouched. The secular per-son often feels a need to free himself of all fetters including those of community and family. He becomes a lonely tribe of one. The con-temporary contraction of Jewish organizational life can also be laid at its doorsteps. Secularized and therefore autonomous American Jews prefer to organize their own social lives and to purchase their medical insurance and cemetery benefits, which drew them to the large fraternal orders, on the open market. They have become suffi-ciently universalized to socialize with similarly reprocessed Gen-tiles. There is no longer much that actually differentiates the two groups. In a word, a pervasive spirit of secularism, whose meaning goes far beyond merely being irreligious, affects every aspect of modern personal and communal life. It dictates the values, the style and the basic content of modern life.

* * *

Can contemporary Jews be taught a culture they once imbibed naturally with their mother's milk? Historians can give no satisfac-tory answer to that question. But of one thing we can be fairly cer-tain: If the Judaism that emerges from a newborn Jewish education system bears only a tenuous relationship to what went before, if the connection is allowed to be completely severed by the sheer force of secularism, then there is little hope. A great deal will depend on how much of its basic beliefs and practices can be transmuted or otherwise altered while still authentically retaining a strong link to the original culture as it was laid down in Judaic texts. The fundamental question, then, is not whether a Jewish education system can teach the culture or enhance identity. It is, rather, whether Jewish education can mute the most extreme demands of secularism so that a recognizable Jewish/Judaic culture remains, on the one hand; and whether Jews on the observant side of the spectrum can be convinced to accept these secularized Jews as Jews, on the other.

A muting of the secular agenda is unlikely to happen. The education system that can reverse the values of modernity has not been invented yet and probably never can be. American schools seem to pick up and transmit secular values and style earlier than most communal institutions. But the open secular society prides itself on its tolerance. It encourages pluralism and change. Some space for the development of a separate ethnic culture is proffered, even encouraged. The problem is that we no longer know what to plant in a Jewish garden. Ultimately too it will be the second problem, the gaining acceptance of secular Jews by the observant, which poses the more serious obstacle to revitalizing American Jewry.

First we ought to note that the notion that identity can be taught or enhanced by education is itself a secular notion. It assumes the existence of a human spirit and intellect infinitely malleable or improvable. The very idea of a separate psychological identity, related to the self, is modern. One rarely hears mention of problems of "Jewish identity" in premodern texts. In that era, identity was a given stemming directly from life within the Jewish community and family. They were Jews because they lived as Jews together with other Jews. Each member of the Jewish community was an identifiable part of the whole. Clearly such a community and family no longer exists in America. Thus what we do when we link Jewish education to survival is to assign a ramshackle school system the impossible task of doing what the community and family can no longer do.

What we need to understand is that even the most effectively organized and adequately funded Jewish education system, armed with the best curricula, methods, and teachers, cannot create Jewish identity. That much we can learn from the failure of the far-flung Catholic school system, now in the process of being dismantled. It did not produce better Catholics. Group identity stems from belonging to the group. That is the reason why the Orthodox branch in America consistantly creates people with stronger Jewish identities then other branches. It has retained a sense of community especially in the need to live in close proximity to each other and to the shul. When the group's sense of self has been so weakened that it can no longer act as an incubator for identity, there is little purpose in contriving and then teaching such an identity. It is inauthentic as is the penchant for copying elements of the separatism of the ultra-Orthodox and their resistance to modernity. That entails a price that most "modern" Jews are unwilling to pay. Given the choice, and the secular insist that there must be such choices, most American Jews would not surrender their freeness.

If no system of education strong enough to withstand the basic values of America's "hard" secularism is conceivable, then what kind of Jewishness can be enhanced by Jewish education? It will have to be one that fits into the postsecular world—a world composed of highly individuated people who strive for self-fulfillment and resist fetters that would curtail their individual freedom, but that also has room for subcultures that do not infringe on the freedom of others. In such a world many things are permissible but few are mandated.

The Jewish day school is especially appropriate, not because it is successful in teaching a culture that is no longer lived. We have seen that its success in this area is problematic. But nothing prevents such schools, while they are teaching Jewish culture and values, to also teach skills that enhance the possibility of self-realization in the secular world. It is precisely in the area of self-realization that there is a confluence between Judaic and secular values. It is conceivable that secular Jews, enrolling their children in the subsidized day school, will be attracted more by the SAT scores of the graduating class than by the Jewish content of the curriculum. But, given the continued failure of the public school system, secular Jewish parents may have no choice but to place their children in an environment that is willy-nilly Jewish. The problem for Jewish educators will be to conceive and implement a Jewish education that does not dislocate the students in the secular environment in which they have to live. If they cannot do that, these students will abandon the Jewish school the way their grandparents abandoned the heder (part-time Jewish school) and the yeshiva.

Despite the pervasiveness and inexorability of this "hard" secular environment, can room be found within it for a Judaic religio/ethnic culture, many of whose basic tenets and practices do not fit easily into modernity? It does not require great prescience to predict that the twenty-first century will witness a movement away from the more extreme forms taken by American secularism, even while its underlying assumptions remain in place. The rising violence of American urban life, with which American Jewry has cast its lot, suggests that national life organized around the extreme selfness at the core of America's "hard" secularism cannot be sustained. The percentage of citizens who do not internalize controls or who allow the quest for fulfillment to get out of control is simply too great. For whatever reason, too many people cannot heed the basic commandments of the secular mind-set: "invent thyself" *and* "control thyself." The primary goal of the secular person, self-realization—which is usually thought of in the sense of achieving economic security or professional fulfillment—may be less possible in the economy of the future. The next generation of American Jews may need to modify some of their basic aspirations.

Despite their avid secularism, most Jews will continue to belong to religious congregations and blithely disregard the fact that they are no longer believers and know little of Jewish culture. Such a disjuncture is possible because America's secularism, unlike its Eastern European counterpart, does not demand atheism or view the church as the "opiate of the people." It becomes merely another formerly sacral, but now largely social activity secular Jews partake in more out of habit than reason. A free society leaves ample room for inconsistent and even irrrational behavior. That may be its most important advantage.

The secular spirit of American Jewry has served it well. Its economic station; its affluence; the central place of its adherents in the operational, scientific, and cultural elites of the nation attest to that. They enjoy a measure of tolerance and belonging unprecedented in Jewish history. Yet clearly America's "hard" secularism has exacted a price in community adhesion and coherence.

Jewish educators need to be aware of the primary assumptions that shape America's unique form of secularism. Its two basic ingredients—libertarianism and individuation—might be reshaped in the years to come, but they are too central to be lightly abandoned. It is what Americans of all faiths want. Recent events indicate that these aspirations have become universal. As long as they remain in place, the "old-time religion" based on faith and obedience will remain outside the life options for most American Jews. What Jewish educators face is the challenge of dealing with tribes of one, with an individuated and often culturally deracinated person. That is what most American Jews have become. It is that reality, and that strong continuing insistance on remaining free, that any attempt to restore Jews to the enriching culture that once was theirs must confront.

References

Avni, Haim. (1982) *Spain, the Jews, and Franco.* Philadelphia: Jewish Publication Society.

Cohen, Robert. (1993) *When the Old Left Was Young: Student Radicals and America's First Mass Student Movement, 1929–1941.* New York: Oxford University Press.

Feingold, Henry L. (1993) *A Time For Searching: Entering the Mainstream, 1920-1945.* Baltimore: Johns Hopkins.

Hagy, James W. (1993) *This Happy Land: The Jews of Colonial and Antebellum Charleston.* Tuscaloosa: University of Alabama Press.

Meyer, Michael. (1988) *Response to Modernity: A History of the Reform Movement in Judaism.* New York: Oxford University Press.

Moore, Deborah Dash. (1981) *At Home in America: Second Generation New York Jews.* New York: Columbia University Press.

Scult, Mel. (1993) *Judaism Faces the Twentieth Century: A Biography of Mordecai Kaplan.* Detroit: Wayne State University Press.

Seltzer, Robert M. (1980) *Jewish People, Jewish Thought: The Jewish Experience in History.* New York: Macmillan.

Sperry, William L. (1963) *Religion in America.* Boston: Little Brown.

Steinbaum, I. (1942) "A Study of the Jewishness of Twenty New York Families." *YIVO Annual of Jewish Social Science* (September).

Synnott, Marcia G. (1979) *The Half Opened Door: Discrimination and Admissions at Harvard, Yale and Princeton, 1900–1970.* Westport, Conn.: Greenwood.

Yovel, Yirmiyahu. (1989) *Spinoza and Other Heretics: The Adventures of Immanence and the Marrano of Reason.* Princeton: Princeton University Press.

Chapter 9

∞

Family Economy/Family Relations:
The Development of American Jewish
Ethnicity in the Early Twentieth Century

Riv-Ellen Prell

We drank too much but we and our friends, especially those
of us who were Jewish—and that was most of us—are not to
be confused with characters in a Hemingway novel. No Jew I
knew drank with the abandon and virtuosity of the people in
Hemingway. Indeed, Jewish men were at that time said to be
free not only of alcoholism but also of schizophrenia; Jewish
women were thought to be immune to cancer of the cervix.
We were old enough to go to speakeasies and even to marry
but there was an important sense in which we were still children, good Jewish children, within quick and decisive call of
our parents. At whatever geographic remove from our homes,
we carried our mothers and fathers with us. . . . We and our
friends were passionately in search of lives unlike those of
our parents. Our parents were nonetheless always with us,
as we made our journeys of self-creation.

—Diana Trilling, *The Beginning of the Journey:*
The Marriage of Diana and Lionel Trilling

What Walden Pond is to Thoreau or the West End of London
to Henry James, a family situation is to the Jewish writer;

the homestand of his or her confrontation with life as well as
the repository of distinctively Jewish and cultural norms.

—Ted Solotaroff, Introduction, to *Writing Our Way Home:*
Contemporary Stories by American Jewish Writers

Jewish ethnicity was woven in the New World on the warp of
turn-of-the-century economy and of the woof of family relations. The
century, which forever separated home and production, assigned to
the domestic domain the task of articulating and representing values. Public settings, whether schools or factories, assimilated differences and in this sense hastened acculturation. The home, however,
was one setting where cultural uniqueness might be transmitted.
Hence the Jewish family was an important locus for translating; in-
venting, and/or maintaining practices, relationships, and ideas that
came to be understood as American Jewish identity. Despite a growing number of voluntary associations and synagogues that were
available to immigrants, men in particular, the home had the potential to offer family members an altered, but persistent and palpable Jewishness through experiences such as food, language,
holidays, and daily life.[1]

Jews came to the United States as families to a greater extent
than other immigrants (Kessner 1977). The various crises and up-
heavals experienced by Jews for the most part did not destroy their
families, but challenged some of their basic assumptions and relationships.[2] The Jewish family was therefore not surprisingly a
source of great interest to social welfare workers, journalists, and
Jewish professionals. Throughout the twentieth century, both during the difficult adjustment period of immigration and the post-
World War II era of increasing affluence, experts have viewed the
Jewish family as the source of Jews' successful acculturation and
the cause of their pathologies. Nevertheless, little American Jewish
history has been written in terms of Jews' private life—culturally
rich matters of family, courtship, leisure, and gender.[3] A study of
Jewish American identity that assumes the importance of the family to social mobility, but that omits a wider understanding of its
place in the development of American Jewish culture, excludes one
of the significant, if elusive, foundations of that world. The construction of middle-class identity for Jews, and with that the critical
place of gender, have not been paid sufficient attention in spinning
the story of American Jewish life.

I pursue this problem in a speculative and suggestive fashion, emphasizing certain features of Jewish experience over others. I look at mobility not as a demographic problem (a well-mined area), but as a cultural one. By examining how mobility intersects with family I intend to present and only partially answer the question: how was American Jewish identity developed in relationship to two powerful poles of Jewish life, the workplace and the home?

Jewish Identity and Social Mobility

The most persistent and pervasive form of American Jewish identity linked Jewishness to (aspirations for) middle-class socioeconomic status. Indeed, Americanization itself was experienced by Jews in relationship to upward mobility. Of course being middle class and being Jewish were not synonymous. Yet, being Jewish in America came to be associated by Jews with remarkably specific types of work and success, consumption patterns, and life-styles. Particularly following World War II, Jews understood these neutral markers of middle-class life to be characteristically (but not exclusively) Jewish, even as they attended synagogue fewer than five times a year or not at all.

The task of understanding American Jewish identity in the twentieth century—seeking out the core elements that shape and drive Jewish meanings systems—is inevitably a nonlinear but thoroughly historical one. The model is not so much archaeology, digging down through the layers in search of the bedrock, but seeking out the simultaneity of identities that tethers Jewishness to multiple realities. Those who embrace their Jewishness do so through their social class, their gender, their families, and their social practices and beliefs. Those accounts of Jewishness that are institutional, ideological, or occupational will narrow our understanding of what it means to be a Jew in the late twentieth century. Jewishness has persisted in the United States as an identity constructed in relationship to private and public life through an astounding variety of choices made both by families and individuals. An account of American Jewish identity depends on understanding what the choices are, how and why they are reproduced generationally, and what social and cultural conditions created and continue to create these choices.[4]

The strategies that led to this mobility made the reproduction of traditional Judaism extremely difficult. Hence the family, for immigrants as well as for other generations, increasingly redefined Jewishness in relationship to work, family loyalty, and community, but not necessarily in relationship to Judaism. American Jewish identity emerged more vividly in the intimate relations of family and of the public relations of community and institution building, than in the sacred realm of prayer or in the individual experience of personal and communal observance.[5] The middle-class articulation of Jewishness turned out to be gender specific, linking men and women to different expressions of both class and ethnic identities. Inverting Eastern European patterns dramatically, American Jews linked their gender roles to the primary requirements of an economic, rather than a ritual system. To achieve a middle-class life in America, men went to work and produced a family wage, and women overwhelmingly chose to stay at home and raise families until the 1970s when women returned to the work force in greater numbers.[6]

Ironically, what is particularly striking about American Jewish identity is its persistence. Lacking external pressures for maintaining separation, and without the ability to maintain a wide range of Jewish cultural resources through education and a shared calendar, Jews continued to construct identity in highly specific social relational terms. Nearly the majority of Jews resisted simply being folded into either the working class, or the middle class, and continued to define themselves as Jews. They maintained and symbolized their uniqueness, in large part, through gender and family relationships.[7] At the same time, these very relationships have consistently been a matter of concern to professionals and commentators on Jewish life because they have been placed at the root of Jews' "maladjustment" to American life.

In the immigrant generation then, American Jewish identity rested on two fundamental transformations. First, generational conflicts over religion were resolved in favor of work and against observance. Secondly, gender relations were transformed by separating production and consumption and by coding them by gender (male and female, respectively). Jewishness was both domestic and institutional, and gender determined how and in what arena one articulated Jewishness. Therefore, American Jewish identity was not simply tied to Americanization, but to the very process of upward mobility that restructured both social and economic relationships and that reconstituted the meaning and domains of Jewishness within the industrializing nation.

Mobility and Intimacy

Those scholars and professionals who have scrutinized the American Jewish family, fall into two opposed camps. The very same Jewish families that inhabited real time and space were differently understood as the source of either successful acculturation, or the failure of Jews to thrive in the New World. These interpretations of the Jewish family can be neatly divided between two "narratives" of American Jewish life; one about intimacy and the other about mobility. Those studies of Jews that focus on mobility credit the Jewish family with values and outlooks that were responsible for successful acculturation created by a fundamentally middle-class orientation inherent in European Jewish life and transported to the New World. They define Jewish ethnicity as Jews' capacity to enter the mainstream while maintaining a distinct cultural/religious identity.

Those studies of Jews that focus on Jewish family relations themselves find evidence of pathology—generational conflict, suffocating religious values, and excessive attachments. Some analysts saw these phenomena as transitional and others as persistent, but all argued that the Jewish family proved to be an obstacle to at first Americanization, and then to normal development.

These positions may be understood as "narratives" because each offers a totalizing scheme for understanding the experience of immigration. The notion of narrative heightens the constructed and discursive formulations of Jewish experience. Even when expressed through census figures and demographics, the interpretation of Jewish success or failure imposes on Jews' lives a sense of the quintessentially Jewish (read culture or values) which sets in motion a way of life. I define narratives very broadly, focusing on post-1960s American social history, on 1920s social work theory, and on the Jewish press of the 1910s and 1920s, among others.

The Mobility Narrative

The mobility narrative is both scholarly and defensive. Early social welfare and sociological works about Jews underlined Jewish mobility for the obvious purpose of combating anti-Semitic views of Jewish immigrants as physically and mentally inferior. Lists of Jewish professional and financial successes were presented to reveal the self-evident falsehood of accusations of Jewish inferiority.

But protection of Jews from anti-Semitism was hardly the only motive for the study of mobility. Indeed, scholarly work on Jewish mobility, particularly after World War II, was tied to a significant turn in historical studies toward the lives of ordinary people. In *The Other Bostonians: Poverty and Progress in the American Metropolis 1880–1970*, Stephen Thernstrom explored the American opportunity structure and the place of immigrants within it (1973).[8]

Historical work on Jewish mobility is particularly interesting because it appeals in part to cultural and familial values in order to help explain economic success. Thernstrom, for example, looked at the importance of the family in supporting education as a source of mobility (Thernstrom 1973: 145–75). William Toll's study of Portland Jewry underlined the significance of changes in women's lives—their patterns of participation in voluntary associations, for example—in creating a middle-class life. (Toll 1982). Judith E. Smith examined the "family culture of work" to explain how immigrants in Providence, Rhode Island sustained themselves until children began to seek out their own opportunities (Smith 1985) Joel Perlmann's (1988) analysis of ethnic differences in schooling in Providence suggested that ethnicity did in part account for variations between children's years in school, and its impact on their subsequent occupations. He concluded that Russian Jews' high educational attainment was related to particular cultural values regarding education.

This research explicitly and implicitly reveals very specific strategies used by Jews as they pursued upward mobility. Historical works published after 1970 certainly demonstrated that women and children participated in Jews' economic climb by contributing their wages and domestic and paid labor. The story embedded in this narrative suggests that both middle-class aspirations and attainments were the product of a family unit. Works written before 1970, whether by sociologists or historians, tended to focus on mobility as a male phenomenon with little attention to the participation of the entire family in supporting male achievement. For example, educational attainment was high both for Jewish boys and girls in Perlmann's study of Rhode Island, but Jewish males were educated for a longer period and their courses allowed them to go on to college and professional schools. Girls who stayed in high school were directed by their families to a commercial course that led them to become wage earners directly out of high school. Daughters and fathers worked in order to secure mobility for sons and brothers. Whatever resentments were experienced, and oral histories attest to the pain many women felt who were deprived of an education

(Weinberg 1988), the family operated together to create economic opportunities for sons.

The mobility narrative is in large measure the dominant story of American Jewish life. Jews climbed a social ladder and arrived in the middle class rapidly. That striking success provides the structure for understanding where Jews live, worship, how they relate to the Jewish community, and how they express their loyalty to other Jews in the United States and elsewhere. Jews, for example, rarely attend synagogue but more frequently pay membership dues, contribute to Jewish causes, or join Jewish organizations.[9] Their participation in Judaism was transformed in relationship to the demands of the marketplace. Post-World War II studies of Jewish life underscored loyalty to Jewish community and uniqueness even in the absence of an active religious life. Institution building, including the development of synagogues and educational programs to help children understand their religion, were all products of Jews who channeled a portion of their resources toward Jewish ends. The mobility narrative emphasizes the fact that Jewish uniqueness persists even with economic success. It is the story of Jewish men's experience because their work histories form the basis for that economic success. Women and children disappear from this narrative, reconstituted as appendages to the male worker who hoists them up the economic ladder.

The Intimacy Narrative

The second narrative focuses on intimacy, the nonpublic connections of family members. By contrast with studies of mobility, very little is written that investigates the cultural significance of the private lives of Jews, although countless experts appeal to the Jewish family as a unique phenomenon. Mobility studies guess at family patterns, but few satisfying studies of families exist.[10] When Jews were immigrants and perceived as at risk for a variety of problems from theft to prostitution, the Jewish family was a matter of concern primarily to social workers.

The work on the immigrant family written by those whose job it was to assist them renders these people's story poignant. A survey of social work texts and articles about Jews of the period written in the early decades of this century, overwhelmingly by Jews, reveals that these immigrant families were perceived as chaotic and troubled as a result of immigration and Americanization. Most articles

emphasized the troubling chasm created by the generational strug-
gles between parents and children. An East Side social worker and
director of New York's Educational Alliance, David Blaustein, wrote
in 1904,

> The children of the neighborhood are very progressive, and this of-
> ten results in tragic conflicts between parent and child. After six
> months in this country the parents and the children often no
> longer understand one another. . . . The children look forward too
> much and the parents look backward too much; the parents be-
> come more conservative, and the children more progressive in
> their ideas. (Blaustein 1904: 118)

In 1917 Boris D. Bogen, a Jewish social worker, described the
same problem.

> A social worker, coming into close contact with the life of the Jew-
> ish immigrant, cannot help deploring the widening of the gap be-
> tween the old and the young, the parent and the child. The home
> influence, which is in a great measure responsible for the integrity
> of the immigrant family is weakening from year to year. The par-
> ents are unable to keep up with the rapid Americanization of the
> younger generation; their children are rapidly acquiring new
> tastes and tendencies, and are losing their attachment and respect
> for their mother and father. (Bogen 1917: 248–49)

These comments are typical of social service literature written
for both professionals and Jewish philanthropists. There is nothing
abstract about the separation between parents and children. What
concerns these professionals is the well-being of children who lack
the guidance that will keep them from danger—to themselves and
their community. Delinquency and crime were both associated with
the alienation of American children from their immigrant parents.
Bogen recounts the potential dangers.

> Insolence, disobedience, defiance of parental authority, bad lan-
> guage, late hours, are all forerunners of delinquency, culminating
> in the one fatal step from which we would fain save every girl. We
> interested some of our good women in the "borderline" cases. By
> giving such girls a chance under better environment, taking them
> away from homes of grinding poverty, where the parents have lost
> control over them, and providing new interests for them, it has
> been possible to reduce the number in our city and state training
> schools by more than seventy-five per cent. (Bogen 1917: 291)

In 1907, a probation officer, Miss. N. A. Portell wrote for the English language Philadelphia weekly, *Jewish Exponent*, about the attraction of the street to boys and girls.

> How could they resist the temptation to leave their own dark ill kept, dreary rooms called home—their tired irritated mothers—to go out into the world and indulge in their desire for recreation and play. After awhile their desire assumes a vicious turn and then the boy or girl is lost to us forever. (Portell 1907: 1)

Miss Portell, like other professionals, often advocated the removal of children from their families. Barring that expensive step, however, the creation of neighborhood settlement houses would suffice.

Functionaries within the Jewish community also shared concern about the inability of the family to offer a healthy environment for their children. Moses Levin, principal of a Chicago Talmud Torah, postulated that the Hebrew school might be able to offer an alternative to the chaotic family. In 1913 he wrote in the *Daily Jewish Courier*,

> The American father leaves early in the morning and when he comes home from work the son is either sleeping or out on the street. Neither Sabbath nor holidays exist. He is always on the hustle, bustle, harnessed down to his work just as the ox to its cart. And the poor mothers, who are enslaved, who have enough work to do in the house by preparing food and taking care of the babies, are highly pleased when the children go out on the street to fulfill their hearts' desire. The Jewish teacher should be the father of this living orphan. The Hebrew school should supersede the home training. (Levin 1913: n.p.)

The Jewish child as an orphaned delinquent lacking parental guidance was a common image used by professionals during this period who were simultaneously supportive and judgmental. Indeed, immigrants themselves reflected on their childhoods in these terms.

Mary Antin, the "exemplary immigrant" of her time, wrote about her own experience as a member of the younger Americanized generation. The quintessential spokesperson for the importance of the immigrant's "second birth" as an American, Antin is surprisingly ambivalent about the painful costs of Americanization, and shares at least part of Levin's analysis of the immigrant family.

The price that all of us paid for this disorganization of our family life has been lived in every immigrant Jewish household where the first generation clings to the traditions of the Old World, while the second generation leads the life of the new. In Polotzk we had been trained and watched, our days had been regulated, our conduct prescribed. In America, suddenly, we were let loose on the street. Why? Because my father having renounced his faith, and my mother being uncertain of hers, they had no particular creed to hold us to. My parents knew only that they desired us to be like American children and seeing how their neighbors gave their children boundless liberty, they turned us also loose, never doubting but that the American way was the best way. In their bewilderment and uncertainty their needs must trust us children to learn from such models as the tenements afforded. More than this, they must step down from their throne of parental authority, and take the law from their children's mouths. For they had no other means of finding what was good American form. (Antin 1912: 247, 270–71)

Mobility and the Immigrant Family

Unlike other public officials, Jewish social workers rarely assumed that there was something inherently problematic about Jews or Jewish families. These social workers were at pains to deny any "racial" foundation for Jewish poverty, a popular theory of the time. For example, Bogen suggested that recently arrived immigrants were more high-minded than those who had Americanized. America offered the dangers of "ragtime, drama by vaudeville, and similar stunts" (Bogen 1917: 275). If Jews could simply be removed from the ghetto to "the so-called higher strata of society," they would no longer be prey to the "crushing influences that are unavoidable in a neglected neighborhood" (Bogen 1917: 271). Their families could be restored to domestic tranquillity and again influence "the development of strong character" (Bogen 1917: 251–52). He argued that once out of unsavory neighborhoods Jews did not return. Their achievements led to constant progress.

He asserted that Jews were not inherently poor.

In Russia for instance, the Jews, notwithstanding political restrictions and persecutions, do not represent the lowest strata of society, and while on the whole, poverty among the Jews is appalling, still in the matter of education, art, and morals, the Jew stands very much higher than the peasants and city workers. (Bogen 1917: 251–2).

Removing Jews from poverty in the United States would allow their return to the influence of the family and to the assumption of their rightful place in the moral hierarchy.

> As early as 1903 Lee K. Frankel argued that the small percentage of Jewish dependency (poverty) was entirely to be blamed on causes extraneous to the individual, and which are mainly the product of their environment. What these causes are will develop subsequently. . . . Given the opportunity and the proper surroundings, the immigrant Jew will become an addition to the body politic and not a menace. (Frankel 1903: 52–53)

Other social workers provided empirical proof that there were no American-born Jewish poor, and demonstrated as well that family members were the primary sponsors of immigrants who were not a burden to the society.

> Immigrants themselves reported the intense pressure they felt to find work immediately upon arrival. Work was the answer to all problems, and from the point of view of the Americanized Jews and social welfare workers, those who failed to work failed to Americanize. Heinze claimed that work and mobility were on the minds of Jewish breadwinners who, though more than half were blue-collar workers, clearly aspired to white-collar work. (Frankel 1903: 102)

The solution to chaos advocated by both communal workers and immigrants rested on economic success. Mobility and intimacy turned out to share the same seams. The family found joint cause in one shared desire, even as it fractured around the lack of a common language of gender, power, authority, and Judaism.

Jews brought with them from their European lives a desire for enhanced status. Samuel Kahn's MA thesis was in part based on oral interviews, which he called "biograms," with fifty immigrants who arrived in America between 1901 and 1925. One man's biogram dealt with finding appropriate work in the United States. He explained the importance of the status of an occupation to Eastern Europe Jews.

> In those years, such people were very ashamed to teach their children a trade. Except perhaps for the poor people, who gave away a child for a longer period to a manual worker to learn a trade. And if a person believed in the saying "A man should always teach his son a trade," he looked for a clean trade, a holy trade, as a slaughterer of kosher meat, a scribe of holy scrolls. (Kahn 1954: 75–77)

Because tailoring was a low status trade, most immigrants aspired to higher-status occupations for their children in the United
States, although no longer religious ones.

Andrew Heinze argued that the senior generation of immigrants wanted their children to have work "higher than dirty work
in a factory." Based on a 1908 *Jewish Daily Forward* article on the
occupational goals of Jewish newcomers, Heinze argues that immigrants identified themselves with the middle class, and that identification supported their commitment to upward mobility for their
children. The Jewish press had many examples of the happy success
stories of families "rising" through the sacrifices of the parents and
the successes of their children.

Leopold B. Lazarus writing for *The Jewish Forward* recounted
the story of the Stolnicks (1924). They were "extremely ambitious"
for their children, having "slaved" to send their children to school.

> For their children they aspire for the to them—unattainable pres-
> tige, comforts, social positions. (Lazarus 1924: n.p.)

Lazarus continues that the Stolnicks have been "elevated."

> The Stolnicks have reached their land of milk and honey. They
> have risen in the world through the ascent of their children. They
> are one of the thousands upon thousands of immigrant families
> who have been given wings by their American-bred children.
> (Lazarus 1924: n.p.)

Mobility studies more than bear out that these aspirations were
realized. The immigrant laborers were neither the sons nor the fathers of workers. While Jewish family relations, combined with
poverty and ghettos, were often seen as the cause of Jews' problems,
in retrospect the family did not inhibit success.

The Child-Centered Family

As Jews left the dense quarters of the ghetto in New York in the
1910s, and as immigration ground to a halt in the 1920s, their role
as vulnerable Americans changed. Their educational and occupational attainment began to be noticed, and Jews increasingly
emerged as an "exemplary" minority, those who stayed in school and
maintained families.

There is at least some evidence of a new profile emerging as Jews became more middle class, that of the "neurotic" family. *The National Conference of Social Work's Proceedings in 1924* carried a series of articles on immigrant families during this period. Dorothy Kahn, director of Baltimore's Hebrew Benevolent Society, wrote that on the basis of work done at a "famous psychiatric clinic" that treated primarily Jewish children, that there was evidence that the most common "diagnosis" was that they were "spoiled" (D. Kahn 1924: 286).

Kahn linked the parental pattern of Jews spoiling their children to "a tendency to regard them as links in a chain of hereditary development, the product of a long line" (D. Kahn 1924: 286). As generational links these children, she argued, were the object of "idolatrous attitudes" on their parents' part, and in turn, parents felt shame when faced with their children's "defects" (D. Kahn 1924: 286). These attitudes produced parents who spoiled children and who were "ineffectual" in handling their problems. Kahn's case study of Oscar, a child of a prosperous shopkeeper-father, who stole, was resolved by teaching his parents to punish his theft and to reward appropriate behavior. Kahn assured her readers that child spoiling was not innate to Jews, since European children were not spoiled. The parents simply needed to learn how to become effective by learning how to punish (D. Kahn 1924: 287).

Elizabeth Ewen in her history of Jewish and Italian immigrant women argued that social workers of the period insisted that immigrants set aside their "preindustrial notion" that the interests of the individual family members had to be subordinated to the economic needs of the whole family. In the new order, children's needs would come first (Ewen 1985: 85) Children were to be liberated from the family.

Jews appeared to do just that; to make children's education and aspirations for the middle class a significant priority. But Kahn complained that Jews did not do this on an individualist model, but rather saw their children as "products of a long line," "links in a chain." This collectivist, cultural vision of children was unacceptable to the early twenthieth-century Progressive prescriptions for the nation and its citizens.

Ironically, close to forty years later, a psychologist attributed mobility among children of Jewish immigrants to the "feelings of disequilibrium and tension in the individual family member." (Hurvitz 1961: 229). Like the "unmarried career women" who experienced upward mobility, the Jewish man is motivated by conflicted interpersonal relationships in the family of orientation (Hurvitz 1961: 229–30). Hurvitz claims that Jewish children are raised in "individuated-entrepreneurial" homes emphasizing self-reliance and an active relationship to the environment (Hurvitz 1961: 232).

The immigrant family, then, paradoxically created an environment that was thought to encourage independent achievement at the same time as its members created a sense of obligation and connection to the generations. Tensions and loyalty both aided children (sons) in achieving mobility because they both provided motivation for success.

Nathan Hurvitz and Kahn offered psychologized portraits of cultural and economic phenomena. Their responses are interesting (rather than convincing) precisely because they each attempt to understand how the tensions in immigrant families can be understood in light of educational and economic attainments. They link families, Jewishness, and mobility to the transformations in immigrants' lives and to how they are passed onto the children.

Their diagnosis of the Jewish family underlines the problem of understanding American Jewish identity in this critical period. As the variety of Jewish identities, from religious to secular, lost salience in the United States, the definition of Jewishness was clearly undergoing dramatic changes. Kahn, for example, described group efforts, like the Zionist and youth movements, which offered the content of a new reformulation of Jewish identity (D. Kahn 1924: 286).

But Jewish identity, whatever public, religious, and secular forms it would take, was still produced and reproduced within the family. As Irving Howe reflected on his own experience of the 1930s, he recalled that "what was left of Jewishness came to rest in the family," the domain in which immigrants and their children could, if briefly, share some continuity (Howe 1982: 4).

What Jewish content remained in the family is what, for example, the sociologist Richard D. Alba claimed in the 1990s were the persistent features of ethnicity for all groups—food, family ties, and memory. And yet much more seems to be at stake than the "symbolic ethnicity," represented by these remaining features, mere crumbs of a once coherent cultural/nationalist identity. For beyond the soup and kinship was a sense that achievement was linked quite systematically and not accidentally to being a Jew. The bridging figure of the Jewish mother came to be satirized and attacked by World War II for her interest in achievement. Even as early as 1930 the Yiddish Press published letters from disgruntled American-born young men and women who decried their parents' preoccu-pation with financial success and achievement.[11] The two powerful novels of postwar Jewish American life, *Marjorie Morningstar* (Wouk 1955) and *Goodbye Columbus* (Roth 1989) presented the con-flict between Jewish men and women as at bottom caused by men's desire to be free of the demand for mobility and by women's clinging to those aspirations. Jewishness was as much an ethnic cuisine as it was the fiction, humor, and drama of Jewish families embattled over achievement and success.

The achievement message was not invented in isolation by im-migrant Jewish families. They were bombarded with their inferior-ity by professionals, by German Jews, and by Americans. The very debate over closing immigration that began at the height of Euro-pean Jews' entry to the nation articulated every vicious stereotype possible—from mental inferiority, to distorted character, to Jewish disloyalty. Theodore A. Bingham, New York's police commissioner, writing for the *North American Review* in 1908 proclaimed:

> Wherefore it is not astonishing that with a million Hebrews, mostly Russian, in the city (one-quarter of the population), perhaps half of the criminals should be of that race when we consider the ignorance of the language, more particularly among men not physically fit for hard labor, is conducive to crime. (Bingham 1908 969)

The more moderate *Outlook*, advocated intelligence tests for immigrants in 1908 claiming,

> They dig American ditches, they mine American coal, they cut American garments, but they no more become Americans thereby than a cow becomes an American because she eats American grass. (Outlook 1908: 970)

Behind every disavowal of the inherent problems of Jews in the writings of Jewish social workers was an overwhelming anxiety that these immigrants had to prove that they were worthy of be-coming Americans. Jewish success, particularly as it was linked to overcoming the perils of delinquency and prostitution, was proof of their suitability for American life.

In response, social workers, rabbis, journalists, and a host of other spokespersons proclaimed that Jewish family life supported Jewish organizational and community life. And Jews appeared to use their economic success to support both domains. If Jews created

new avenues for articulating their identity through building synagogues, or through fund-raising efforts for building Jewish institutions, they were able to do so because the private domain of
intimate relations supported the Jewishness of achieving success.[12]
Psychological, cultural, and capital investments in children promised not only a future for individuals, but for Jews who were asked
to prove their worthiness in a homogenizing culture.

Nevertheless, success proved to be insufficient to determine
worthiness. With affluence the acculturated Jewish family again
came under scrutiny. Child-oriented families required a rather specific division of labor for the entire middle class, and Jews followed
suit by keeping women out of the work force and men mostly out of
the house. This typical division of labor became the source of an
open attack on Jewish women's appropriation of "power." A range of
commentators—rabbis and scholars included—noted the growing
power of Jewish women in America. They formulated this power as
a travesty related ironically both to the weakness of immigrant men
and to their economic success. In either case these commentators
noted that men were absent, ill suited for American family life, and
otherwise unavailable. From Stephen S. Weiss's 1922 parents' man-
ual to Albert Gordon's (1959) study of the Jews of the suburbs in the
1950s, the family was re-created as a potentially dangerous, and
certainly problematic arena because of the father's absence and the
mother's power. The family, even after economic mobility, was re-
created as the locus of Jewish problems, even though it was also
sentimentalized and hailed for its uniqueness. Once again the family became the arena to explain why Jewish children had adjustment problems, or why they were or were not motivated for success.
Parents' adaptations to American life, both the foreign and native-
born, were in some sense pathologized because of a perception of a
change in family power that left men outsiders to the domestic
sphere, the dominant norm of the twentieth-century American middle class.

As the meaning, object, and even practices of Jewishness were
dramatically privatized alongside community building in the public
domain, Americanization overdetermined the linkage between Jewish identity as achievement and Jewish continuity realized through
family. With middle-class gender roles dramatically differentiating
public and private spheres, the family's dominance in that identity
became associated with women, and was continually pathologized,
just as the desire to succeed in the public arena was also made problematic for women by the 1950s. Americanization created a scenario

by which the source of success and the source of uniqueness was the family, the domain constantly under scrutiny for its failure to produce healthy Americans and for its ability to produce successful ones.

Conclusion

American Jewish life has had innumerable narrators. Perhaps the most popular historical accounting is that of the institutions built by the Jewish community that were the sources of ethnic identification and ethnic solidarity. The builders of these institutions were the successful Jewish men who made effective use of the opportunity structure.

This picture of American Jews is incomplete because its emphasis on mobility and institution building leaves out the hidden counterpart narrative of the immigrant family. Divided in innumerable ways, they were bound by the necessity and possibility for mobility. Nevertheless, that economic opportunity wrought dramatic transformations on the lives of Jews that determined the shape an American Jewish identity would assume. Central to that identity was Jews' experience of a powerful conjunction of success with a Jewishness produced in the family and articulated in institution building.

This newly emerging Jewishness had dramatically different implications for men and women. This Judaism was domesticated, requiring women to direct their energies to marriage and the family, and to extend those roles in voluntary associations. Women were consumers who required male-produced capital to achieve a middle-class status for themselves and to ensure their children's futures. Men were the producers, and their arena of status was a public organizational world in which capital could translate into prestige. Jewish identity was inseparable from the mobility that differentiated genders and generations and that promoted Americanization, even if not total assimilation that most Jews rejected.

If the family is the "homestand" of Jews' interaction with American life it is because at the core of American Jewish identity is uniqueness and difference from a dominant culture. American Jews came to understand their uniqueness in part through their economic mobility, the only definitive proof that they were not racially and morally deficient. Jews learned from their rabbis, therapists, social workers, and social scientists that their families were responsible for that mobility. Their families clearly supported the importance of mobility as an individual and collective achievement. Therefore the very trappings of middle-class life took on the peculiar aura of Jewishness for Jews and became a significant arena for creating Jewish life.

This set of circumstances grounded in necessity and intolerance became the staging ground for a post-World War II reconsideration of Jewish identity whose overdetermined links to the American dominant culture and the Jewish family, became the source of that critique.

Notes

1. I am of course aware of the fact that one might equally argue that the home was the source of acculturation. A variety of attacks on Jewish women throughout the early decades of the century emphasized that the home was no longer Jewish. In these portraits, the hardworking, European-born father is out of place in his own home dominated by Americanized children and a wife. Despite the pervasiveness of this image, the home was a very important site of cultural reproduction.

2. Two recent historical works offer contrasting approaches to these transformations. Arthur Hertzberg (1989) suggests that the Jewish family in America was entirely transformed by male desertion, "corrupting" Judaism in the process. Susan Glenn (1990) argues that a new Jewish womanhood was articulated through changing relationships due to women's employment.

3. Paula E. Hyman and Steven M. Cohen's collection does include articles that do some of this work.

4. See Ewa Morawska (1990) for a discussion of recent theories of ethnic identity and immigrants in the United States.

5. See Charles Liebman and Steven Cohen's (1990) discussion of familism as a core meaning in American and Israeli Jewish identity.

6. See Hyman (1995), Susan Glenn (1990), and Charlotte Baum Hyman, and Sonya Michel (1975) for discussions of how gender affected the development of an American Jewish culture.

7. For an interesting parallel in Imperial Germany see Marion A. Kaplan (1991).

8. For a critique of Stephen Thernstrom's approach and a review of other critics see Micaela di Leonardo (1984).

9. Steven M. Cohen (1988). See Calvin Goldscheider and Alan S. Zuckerman (1984).

10. In the 1980s historical work was produced that did trace work patterns, including men and women's labor and voluntary associations such as William Toll (1982). However, studies of Jewish family life have not been written in the United States, although much speculative work by sociologists seeps into their work, and the sociopsychological literature focuses on family life.

11. A more complete discussion of these letters may be found in Riv-Ellen Prell (1999).

12. See Deborah Dash Moore (1981) for a discussion of the period of synagogue and institution building among second-generation New York Jews.

References

———. (1908) "The Making of Americans." *The Outlook* 74, 22 August, 969–71.

Alba, Richard D. (1990) *Ethnic Identity: The Transformation of White America.* New Haven: Yale University Press.

Antin, Mary. (1912) *The Promised Land.* Boston: Houghton.

Baum, Charolotte, Paula Hyman, and Sonya Michel. (1975) *The Jewish Woman in America.* New York: Plume Books.

Blaustein, David. (1904; reprint, 1952) "Preventive Work on the East Side." In *Trends and Issues in Jewish Social Welfare in the United States, 1899–1952. The History of American Jewish Social Welfare, Seen Through the Proceedings and Reports of the National Conference of Jewish Communal Service,* edited by Robert Morris and Michael Freund. Philadelphia: Jewish Publication Society of America, 115–16.

Bernheimer, Charles S. (1948) *Half a Century in Community Service.* New York: Association Press.

Bingham, Theodore A. (1908) "Foreign Criminals in New York." *North American Review* 634 (September): 383–94.

Bogen, Boris D. (1917) *Jewish Philanthropy: An Exposition of Principles and Methods of Jewish Social Service in the United States.* New York: Macmillan.

Cohen, Steven M. (1988) *American Assimilation or Jewish Revival?* Bloomington: Indiana University Press.

————, and Paula E. Hyman. (1986) *The Jewish Family: Myths and Realities*. New York: Holmes and Meier.

di Leonardo, Micaela. (1984) *The Varieties of Ethnic Experience: Kinship, Class and Gender among California Italian-Americans*. New York: Cornell University Press.

Ewen, Elizabeth. (1985) *Immigrant Women in the Land of Dollars: Life and Culture on the Lower East Side, 1890-1925*. New York: Monthly Review Press.

Frankel, Lee K. (1903) "Jewish Charities." *The Annals of the American Academy of Political and Social Science* 21 (January–June): 389–406.

Fromenson, A. H. (1904; reprint, 1952) "East Side Preventive Work." In *Trends and Issues in Jewish Social Welfare in the United States, 1899-1952. The History of American Jewish Social Welfare, Seen Through the Proceedings and Reports of the National Conference of the Jewish Communal Service*, edited by Robert Morris and Michael Freund. Philadelphia: Jewish Publication Society of America, 118–29.

Glenn, Susan. (1990) *Daughters of the Shtetel: Life and Labor in the Immigrant Generation*. Ithaca: Cornell University Press.

Goldscheider, Calvin, and Alan S. Zuckerman. (1984) *The Transformation of the Jews*. Chicago: University of Chicago Press.

Gordon, Albert. (1959) *Jews in Suburbia*. Boston: Beacon.

Griswold, Robert. (1993) *Fatherhood in America: A History*. New York: Basic.

Hertzberg, Arthur. (1989) *The Jews in America; Four Centuries of an Uneasy Encounter: A History*. New York: Simon & Schuster.

Heinze, Andrew. (1990) *Adapting to Abundance: Jewish Immigrant Mass Consumption and the Search for American Identity*. New York: Columbia University Press.

Howe, Irving. (1982) *A Margin of Hope: An Intellectual Autobiography*. New York: Harcourt.

Hurvitz, Nathan. (1961) "Sources of Motivation and Achievement of American Jews." *Jewish Social Studies* 23, no. 4 (October): 217–34.

Hyman, Paula E. (1995) *Gender and Assimilation in Modern Jewish History: The Roles and Representations of Women*. Seattle: University of Washington Press.

Kahn, Dorothy. (1924) "Special Problems in the Adjustment of the Jewish Family." *Proceedings of the National Conference of Social Work*. Chicago: University of Chicago Press.

Kahn, Leonard. (1954) "The Role of the Family in the Adjustment of the Jewish Immigrant in the United States." Master's thesis, Columbia University.

Kaplan, Marion A. (1991) *The Making of the Jewish Middle Class: Women, Family and Identity in Imperial Germany.* Oxford: Oxford University Press.

Kessner, Thomas. (1977) *The Golden Door: Italian and Jewish Immigrant Mobility in New York City, 1880–1915.* New York: Oxford University Press.

Lazarus, Leopold R. (1924) "Parents Rise in Station Together with Their Children." *Jewish Daily Forward* 27, 24 August (English page).

Levin, Moses. (1913) "Living Orphans," *Daily Jewish Courier.* Translated by Works Progress Association, n.p. *Daily Jewish Courier,* 20 May.

Liebman, Charles, and Steven Cohen. (1990) *Two Worlds of Judaism: The Israeli and American Experiences.* New Haven: Yale University Press.

Moore, Deborah Dash. (1981) *At Home in America: Second Generation New York Jews.* New York: Columbia University Press.

Morawska, Ewa. (1990) "The Sociology and Historiography of Immigration." In *Immigration Reconsidered: History, Sociology, and Politics,* edited by Virginia Yans-McLaughlin. New York: Oxford University Press, 187–240.

Perlmann, Joel. (1988) *Ethnic Differences: Schooling and Social Structures among the Irish, Italians, Jews, and Blacks in an American City: 1880-1935.* New York: Cambridge University Press.

Portell, N.A. (1907) "Jewish Children in the Juvenile Court." *The Jewish Exponent* 45, no. 17: 1.

Prell, Riv-Ellen. (1998) *Fighting to Become Americans: Jewish Women and Men in Conflict in the Twentieth Century.* Boston: Beacon.

Roth, Philip. (1959; reprint, 1989) *Goodbye Columbus.* Boston: Houghton.

Smith, Judith E. (1985) *Family Connections: A History of Italian and Jewish Immigrant Lives in Providence Rhode Island 1900–1940.* Albany: State University of New York Press.

Solotaroff, Ted, and Nessa Rapoport, eds. (1992) *Writing Our Way Home: Contemporary Stories by American Jewish Writers.* New York: Schocken.

Thernstrom, Stephen. (1973) *The Other Bostonians: Poverty and Progress in the American Metropolis 1880–1970.* Cambridge: Harvard University Press.

Toll, William. (1982) *The Making of an Ethnic Middle Class: Portland Jewry Over Four Generations*. Albany: State University of New York Press.

Trilling, Diana. (1993) *The Beginning of the Journey: The Marriage of Diana and Lionel Trilling*. New York: Harcourt Brace.

Weinberg, Sidney Stahl. (1988) *World of Our Mothers: The Lives of Jewish Immigrant Women*. Chapel Hill: University of North Carolina Press.

Weiss, Stephen S. (1922) *Child Versus Parent*. New York: Macmillan.

Wouk, Herman. (1955) *Marjorie Morningstar*. New York: Doubleday.

Part III

Regional Variations in the United States

Chapter 10

∞

Inventing Jewish Identity in California: Shlomo Bardin, Zionism, and the Brandeis Camp Institute

Deborah Dash Moore

This chapter employs a case study to explore educational innovation explicitly designed to change the Jewish identities of its participants. Through its focus on a charismatic figure in Los Angeles and the camp he created in the Simi Valley, the chapter approaches central issues of individual initiative and communal organization to test the claims of theory. Close attention to local history not only allows us to reclaim the past in its rich detail to see how ideas and dreams were translated into actual institutions, but it also provides a solid ground for subsequent generalizations. Shlomo Bardin and the Brandeis Camp Institute, the subjects of this chapter, were part of a larger American movement in adult Jewish education that flourished after World War II. Such mass membership Jewish organizations as Hadassah and B'nai B'rith embarked on ambitious efforts to educate their members; to train a new generation of leaders; and to foster basic Jewish literacy, ritual competence, and ideological commitment (Moore 1981: 231–40; 1997). Yet Bardin's decision to locate the Brandeis Camp Institute just outside of Los Angeles took him on a different path from that of adult Jewish education. Responding to the character of Los Angeles Jewry and in partnership with local leaders, Bardin developed a form of spiritual recreation specifically tailored to address the needs of uprooted Jews of

Los Angeles. These Jews retained only faint memories of Jewish life in the Northeast and Midwest, their home towns. Most had received a minimal Jewish education and few knew how to practice any forms of Jewish ritual observance. Yet, because of World War II and the Holocaust, they were not ready to abandon Jewish life and a connection with the Jewish people. Entrepreneurs like Bardin, who set out to reach these Jews, recognized that they would be future leaders of American Jewry, and, therefore, of Diaspora Jews. Thus he tried to develop educational institutions to inspire Jews to be Jews, to link them with Jewish peoplehood, to whet their appetite for more learning, and to encourage them to bring up their children as Jews.

I characterize these innovative methods as spiritual recreation because this approach to Jewish education integrated it into the leisure pattern of living typical of Los Angeles. Indeed, the city's associations with leisure, epitomized in the tall palm trees lining the streets, attracted thousands of Jewish newcomers each month after the end of the war. Yet Jewish recreation differed from other, popular forms: it was spiritual. It inspired, uplifted, transformed. From an easterner's perspective, it often appeared shallow and superficial, with a touch of Hollywood dramatics. From our contemporary perspective, it might appear typically Californian: eclectic, experiential, experimental, and popular. I argue that it was remarkably effective. Whether it is exportable or serviceable as a model of Jewish education depends, in part, on how one assesses the condition of American Jewry today. If most American Jews now resemble those postwar pioneers who moved to Los Angeles, then spiritual recreation may indeed point to the future. Bardin certainly thought of himself as a pathfinder. Perhaps he was right. His one unfinished dream was to build a model Jewish preparatory school, as good as Choate or Exeter, which would attract and train the cream of the crop, the future leaders of the American and Jewish world. In 1970 such dreams could not be realized; now the idea seems far from impossible and thus may be implemented by figures who don't recognize that they are following Bardin's footsteps.

Before turning to Bardin and the Brandeis Camp Institute, some theoretical reflections are useful. First, I think it is important to emphasize the disrupted character of Jewish culture throughout the world (Elazar 1998). Even when we think we see continuity, as in the United States where the majority Jewish population is at least two and often three or four generations removed from the dislocations of immigration, an ongoing process of disruption is occurring. The high mobility of American society guarantees that each generation is encouraged to make its own way physically removed from their parents. Only a minority of Jews live in the same city as their parents and grandparents, and even mobility from one neighborhood to another causes some dislocation. Jews who moved to California after World War II left behind a Jewish cultural world that many of them actually rejected. They did not seek to replicate the world of their parents in Los Angeles, one of the reasons why they were open to the innovation and personal charisma of Bardin. So if a disrupted culture characterizes Jewish life, identity formation will resemble Levi-Straus's bricoleur more than any organic, holistic process of intergenerational transmission. I need not add that Bardin was a bricoleur, scavenging bits and pieces of his own past—perhaps in a way analogous to Harvey E. Goldberg's persuasive account—to produce a formula that worked (Goldberg 1998).

Second, I think that Daniel Elazar's substantivists and experientialists are valuable categories of analysis as long as we recognize them as gendered terms (Elazar 1998). Thus the split between the two involves a gendered division. Substantivists are male, that is, the educational ideals they subscribe to come close to masculine Jewish traditions of education—traditions that are now increasingly open to women. The experientialists are female, trying, in Elazar's words "to give people a good feeling about feeling Jewish." That is exactly what many Jews took away from their homes, where women traditionally were educated. Recognizing this gendered reading of the educational debate might be productive because it might encourage us to look at how Jews behaved in their homes, points made by Riv-Ellen Prell (Prell 1998). Bardin chose to focus upon Shabbat because he believed in it deeply, because it provided that specific point of Jewish spirituality and peoplehood that was potentially transformative, and because one could *enjoy* it with all of one's senses. Not only did Bardin want people to feel good about feeling Jewish, he also wanted them to feel good.

This brings us to Prell's two narratives of mobility and intimacy, both gendered accounts. Mobility produced leisure time, a mark of middle-class status in postwar America, a desired goal of not having to constantly work. One of the attractions of a city like Los Angeles to American Jews was its leisurely atmosphere: the climate, patterns of work intermixed with recreation, casual clothing styles, and socialization opportunities out-of-doors, all pointed to the breakdown of rigid categories associated with work and urban life in the Northeast and Midwest. There "going out" involved getting "dressed up" to engage in leisure activities in places that were special, an utter contrast to the situation in Los Angeles (Nasaw 1993). Ultimately the two narratives propel Jews to L.A. where Judaism and Jewishness can both become leisure-time pursuits. If Judaism and Jewishness are leisure-time activities, they will change. They will become part of a Jew's identity, but a special part, providing certain rewards and satisfactions tailored to each individual.

Finally, Arnold Eisen spells out some of the rewards, including meaning, community, and religious experience, which can be acquired as a leisure-time activity. Bardin recognized the value of all three and tried to provide these to young adults who came on "aliyah" to Brandeis. He explicitly used drama—theatrics, is another name—and music to reach people quickly because he had to work his magic in four weeks with young people and in the space of a weekend with adults. Bardin produced Judaism—he staged it—so that those watching were simultaneously participants and observers.

To summarize the relevant theory for this case study of Bardin and the Brandeis Camp Institute: the Brandeis Camp directed its attention to Jews whose culture was disrupted, which meant most L.A. Jews who were migrants to the city, and created an experiential female-gendered program that spoke to young Jewish women, future homemakers, helping them to feel good about feeling Jewish. The Brandeis Camp Institute implicitly understood Judaism and Jewishness to be leisure-time activities; it blended drama and music, because of their ability to transform observers into participants, to produce Shabbat. Judaism and Jewishness were experienced through Shabbat, necessarily a distinctive form of Shabbat that provided meaning, community, and religious experience.

Now to the case study of Bardin and the Brandeis Camp Institute, often abbreviated as BCI. Its story is suggestive and provocative, for it reveals not only what happens to intentions and ideology in California but also what possibilities exist for ambitious leaders in such virgin territory as postwar L.A. The history has a subtext worth pondering: the significance of women and Jewish women's modes of learning for Jewish education. The BCI educated mostly women, thus contributing to women's changing status within the Jewish world.

The camp, started in the East and transplanted to the West, eluded denominational and ideological definition. Under Shlomo Bardin's charismatic leadership, the institute synthesized its innovations into an eclectic package of summer camping, adult education, holiday workshops, programs in Jewish creative arts, and even experimental religious rituals. Bardin deliberately set out to arouse emotions: to awaken interest in the Jewish people, to stimulate a desire to pursue Jewish knowledge, and to instill a sense of responsibility for the Jewish future. "Above all," he explained, the institute "attempts to create an atmosphere which enables the young Jew to gain new insight into himself, . . . " (Bardin 1946: 27). The institute tapped the talents of Jews working in the motion picture industry. Bardin enlisted them to create the "atmosphere," to write scripts and stage pageants, to compose music and design rituals, and to inspire the art of Jewish living in their own lives and in the lives of others. Bardin grasped the manifold possibilities of Jewish spiritual recreation.

The future BCI began as an experimental summer leadership training program initiated by the recently established American Zionist Youth Commission and run by its energetic director, Shlomo Bardin. The camp institute intended to demonstrate to campers the compatibility of their Jewish and American identities. It intentionally catered to young adults, aged eighteen to twenty-five, whose Jewish ties were most vulnerable. This vision owed something to Louis Brandeis's version of Zionism. The goal was "to give the young a feeling of belonging; . . . to make him feel at ease as a Jew in an American environment" (Bardin 1958a). Bardin later credited Brandeis with an enduring concern for American Jewish youths and insisted that Bardin's own involvement with the youth commission and camp institute resulted from Brandeis's efforts on his behalf (Bardin 1958c, 3:7). In the early years every camper received a copy of Brandeis's essay, "True Americanism." So when Brandeis died after the successful first summer institute in 1941 held in Amherst, New Hampshire, Bardin asked for the use of the justice's name (*California Jewish Voice*, 1947c). Renamed the Brandeis Camp Institute, the one-month summer program carefully blended aspects of Bardin's own education: his memories of growing up in Zhitomir, Ukraine; his adult years in Eretz Yisrael, marked by the values of the kibbutz; his doctoral studies at Columbia University's Teachers College where his Ph.D. dissertation studied the experiential educational methods of the Danish folk high schools (especially the importance of music); and his admiration for the informal give-and-take of American discourse (BCI Masterbooks 1947, 1952; Bardin 1946: 27).

Born and raised in Zhitomir, Bardin left Russia after World War I for Palestine. He briefly attended and taught at the Reali School in Haifa before leaving Palestine for Berlin. After several

years of study in Berlin, Bardin went to London to further his education. Eventually he landed in New York where he was accepted as
a graduate student at Columbia University's Teachers College.
Bardin studied under the impressive group of educators gathered at
Columbia in the early 1930s, especially George Counts, who encouraged him to examine the Danish Folk High School. While in New
York, Bardin married Ruth Jonas, the daughter of a wealthy Brooklyn lawyer. He returned to Haifa with a wife, an advanced degree, a
book on *Pioneer Youth in Palestine*, and the determination to start a
school modeled on Brooklyn Technical High School. A meeting with
Frieda Warburg, who had read his book, prompted her to provide
the funds. Bardin established Haifa Technical High School in 1936
and a special nautical school two years later. In 1939 he returned to
the United States for financial reasons and remained when the war
began. Bardin's manner and accomplishments impressed American
Zionist leaders who considered him a model of the new Jew created
in Palestine. He can also be seen as the prototypical *yored*, the
Palestinian (and later Israeli) who leaves the homeland to seek his
fortune in the diaspora. Bardin's credentials as a pedagogue made
him the perfect choice to direct the new American Zionist Youth
Commission (Bardin 1958b, 1958d).

By the middle of the second summer Bardin knew that he had
the formula guaranteeing success. In a letter to Judith Epstein,
vice-chair of the commission and president of Hadassah, Bardin
wrote that the group was typical of the rank and file members of Junior Hadassah as well as the leadership. "[W]ithout hesitation we
may say that whatever has been achieved with this group could be
achieved with any similar group," he told her. Bardin reiterated his
conviction that now "we have a very effective instrument for our
Zionist youth education" (Bardin 1942). His success was recognized
by Abraham Goodman, a wealthy New York businessperson, a Zionist, Reconstructionist, and supporter of Jewish creative arts. Goodman arranged to purchase a camp in the Poconos for Brandeis. In
1943 Bardin transferred his entire program to the new site, even re-
naming the lake, Kinneret, the Sea of Galilee in the Poconos (*The
Hancock Herald* 1943a).

Each session, meticulously planned no less as an emotional than
as an educational experience, was designated an *aliyah*, clearly an
unorthodox use of the Zionist term. Bardin subscribed to the Zionist
doctrine that "there is only one homeland for the Jew, and that is the
ancient homeland in Palestine." He also admitted that although "we
don't expect our young people to return to Palestine, . . . there should

be a tie with the homeland" (*Hancock Herald* 1943b). He fostered this connection through an extensive reading list on Zionism, study of Hebrew, and cultivation of elements of Palestinian Jewish culture, "because of the normalizing character of [its] Jewish community" (Bardin 1958b, 1958d, 3:10). As one contemporary put it, Bardin was a small "z" Zionist (Kelman 1988).

Bardin's approach turned Brandeis into a surrogate homeland and Jewish home rolled into one, letting campers taste previously unfamiliar experiences. His program made campers responsible for the camp's physical needs (except its food) and included a healthy dose of gardening. Bardin thought doing menial work acted "like a tonic" inside the campers' souls by giving them the feeling that Judaism was rooted in real life. It counteracted the tendency of young Jews "to associate Judaism with wealth" (Bardin 1958d, 3: 9–10). It also linked camp life to the kibbutz's notion of physical work as a creative and redeeming enterprise. The program ran on a rigorous schedule. Before breakfast there was a dual flag-raising ceremony honoring the American and Zionist symbols. Then came lectures, study, work, and singing in the morning, followed by rest, recreation, and workshops in the afternoon. The evenings, except for Shabbat, and Thursday nights that were reserved for the campers' campfire program, consisted of informal but structured gab sessions, Hebrew lessons, discussions with lecturers, and singing and dancing (BCI Masterbooks 1952a). Michael Meyer recalled that Bardin allowed for no deviation. Attempting to organize fellow campers to decide what evening programs they would produce—the type of leadership he was accustomed to exerting—Meyer encountered Bardin's resistance to what might have been praised as initiative in a different type of camp. Bardin disarmed Meyer's planned revolt (Meyer 1994).

The Sabbath was the focal point of the week. Bardin used his considerable dramatic skills to evoke a sense of reverence, spirituality, and beauty among the campers. During the week they learned Shabbat melodies so that the Friday night and Saturday morning rituals could be participatory. To close the Sabbath Bardin developed a *Habdalah* ceremony whose emotional stagecraft regularly brought campers to tears. Standing in a circle, with arms on each other's shoulders, Bardin's *Habdalah* became "a symbol of a great camaraderie" (Bardin 1958b, 1958d, 3:13). He even orchestrated the lighting to produce the desired emotional effect. Irma Lee Ettinger, girls head counselor from 1948 to 1955, recalled how exacting Bardin was in regard to raising and lowering lights and how upset he would get if she missed a cue (Ettinger 1989).

Bardin wanted a national constituency. He expanded his recruitment efforts to reach the local Zionist Youth commissions scattered in over 100 cities throughout the United States and Canada. In 1943 only 20 percent of the 150 campers came from the New York metropolitan area. Among the first campers recruited from Los Angeles was the daughter of Julius and Mollie Fligelman, active Zionists and members of the L.A. Commission (*The Hancock Herald*, 1943a). The Fligelmans were so impressed with the program's impact on their daughter that they sponsored scholarships for other young people. Julius also began to correspond with Bardin. Buoyed by success, Bardin envisioned a network of half a dozen camps around the United States. By 1946, he was ready to bring the BCI to the West Coast. Moshe Davis, a member of the Youth Commission, recalled that at the meeting "the vote was even—on the line, an absolutely neutral vote. As a matter of fact, a neutral vote meant a negative vote, and Bardin was not going to get his camp on the west coast. At that point," he continued, "I said to them rather formally, 'Ladies and Gentlemen, before you reach a final decision I want you to know that the Seminary has just decided to establish the West Coast branch. . . . We believe that Los Angeles is going to be the second largest city of Jews in the United States." Davis's persuasion worked. A second vote was called for, and this time the meeting was completely in favor of the West Coast camp (Davis: 7).

Bardin arrived in November for a series of parlor meetings with potential supporters organized by the indefatigable Mollie Fligelman. He told all who would listen about his plan to establish an all-year-round camp, the "largest Jewish camp of its kind in the United States and the first of its kind in the West" on the outskirts of Los Angeles. At Sinai Temple, at Hadassah and Zionist meetings, in the Fligelman's home, to Max Laemmle and other Jews in Hollywood, Bardin brought his message of youth redemption and education for leadership (*California Jewish Voice* 1946). By February, he had generated enough support for a gala "Stars for Youth" dinner in the Ambassador Hotel, hosted by the comedian Phil Silvers, with such well-known stars as Danny Thomas and Chico Marx, and with a rare appearance by Al Jolson. The goal was to raise two hundred fifty thousand dollars to purchase a camp site (*California Jewish Voice* 1947a, 1947b).

The enthusiasm of local leaders and the enormous untapped wealth of Los Angeles Jews soon turned Bardin's vision into reality. After many weekends of driving around hunting for a site, the local committee purchased Oak Park Ranch, a two-thousand-acre estate in the Simi Valley that included tennis courts, riding stables, and the hunting lodge of a former beer baron. Rapidly, the land was readied for the first session in the summer of 1947 (*California Jewish Voice* 1947c). The local Ventura county paper, its interest piqued by the arrival of a Jewish camp, interviewed Uri Ariav, a twenty-six-year-old Sabra and agriculture student hired as the gardener. The reporter discovered that Ariav hoped to "bring some American boys and girls to Palestine" because they were desperately needed. "Now, when we need men to perform some act of sabotage in the city," Ariav explained, "we have to get them from the farms and that leaves them short-handed there." Young American Jews could help facilitate plans for sabotage (*Star-Free Press* 1947). The newspaper story threatened the entire enterprise. Bardin worked furiously to repair the damage, firing Ariav, giving a talk before the local Rotary club, cultivating area churches, and even inviting an area folk dance group to use the camp facilities. Eventually, he quieted the outcry and the first "aliyah" received good press.

Bardin transported not only his program but most of his staff from the Poconos to the Simi Valley. Max Helfman, appointed music director of the Hebrew Arts Commission of the Zionist Youth Commission in 1944, brought his considerable talents to the West Coast. He shared Bardin's assessment that young Jews "are atrophied emotionally. They have lost their will for passionate living as Jews" (*California Jewish Voice* 1947d). Helfman brought this passion, combined with a love of music, Palestine, and philosophy, to the campers. One camper from Winnipeg called him "the soul" of the camp. Even onlookers, watching him rehearse a choral group, sensed the enormous enthusiasm he evoked (Sokolov 1949a). "If the Brandeis Institute would have done nothing more than present Helfman to the West Coast, it would have been 'dayenu'!" (enough!) exclaimed an excited local-fund raiser. But Bardin did more. He brought the dancer Katya Delakova and the well-known philosopher, Horace Kallen. In addition, he started to nurture his own staff from among the most promising campers, sending a select handful—among them, Irma Lee Ettinger—to Palestine for a year to soak up its culture (Ettinger 1989).

Yet even while he looked to Palestine for its rich Jewish culture, Bardin started to reinterpret Zionist categories. Chava Scheltzer, whom Bardin recruited as a representative of the Yishuv in 1945, struggled to introduce *halutziut*, or "preparation for pioneering" in Palestine, into the camp. Bardin opposed such efforts although he "claims that he is for *halutziut*. In truth, he is not for it," she

observed, but sees the pioneer as standing for a *halutziut* that exists
in all areas of life (Scheltzer 1946). Scheltzer understood Bardin. As
representative *shalichim*, Bardin specifically requested "young men
from rural settlements or colonies who, in their very appearance,
personify the new Palestine. . . ." For Bardin, "the ability to sing and
dance, and particularly to convey the spirit via singing and dancing,"
was "essential. With all this," he astutely noted, "they cannot be par-
tisans in a political party sense. They must be broad enough to include all Palestine, with all its groups and factions" (Bardin 1945). In
his mind, Bardin had reconstructed Zionism in American terms.

The potential of the California camp excited Bardin; he wanted
to develop it into a year-round institute. But members of the Zionist
Youth Commission balked at the prospect. So Bardin talked several
of the major supporters, including Abe Goodman and Judith Epstein, into establishing a separate Brandeis Youth Foundation to
run the camps and related programs (Brandeis Youth Foundation).
By the summer of 1948, as the State of Israel fought its war of independence, Bardin severed the remaining Zionist connections (Ettinger 1989). Even the rhetoric of the camp changed, as did the
reading lists. "The orientation of the camp is definitely towards Israel, but it is not a Zionist camp," wrote a camper, David Sokolov.
"The accent is on Hebrew culture, not because Yiddish is inferior,
but because [of] an unfortunate and almost unshakable association
. . . with the call of the ghetto, with persecution, and shame. . . ."
(Sokolov 1949b).

Bardin evidenced a remarkable ability to respond to the needs,
styles, and tastes of American Jews. His starting point was his audience, his potential campers and supporters. Zionism, in its classical European and even American form, served Bardin as a resource
to be winnowed and transformed. Thus Bardin took the language of
Zionism—of *halutziut*, of aliyah—and used it to promote individual
growth and self-knowledge with a Jewish flavor. Bruce Powell, a
former camper and counselor at Brandeis wrote that Bardin "interpreted Zion as the spiritual center of one's mind; Zionism was simply a return to that center." Powell thought that "Bardin created a
'Jewish Zionism,' a yearning to return to one's own personal center
of Judaism and Jewish vitality" (Powell 1979: 174).

Aware of the institute's transformative impact on young people,
Bardin solicited testimonials. These letters spoke in moving terms
of a profound change in Jewish identity produced by the institute,
akin to a conversion experience. One woman even used such religious language in an article she wrote on the institute when she re-

turned to college. "I was born again," she affirmed (Zigmond 1948).
An articulate young man, Sokolov wrote: "We lived like . . . Sabras
. . . to whom the meaning of anti-Semitism has to be explained. Although our atmosphere is completely Jewish, paradoxically, we do
not think as Jews here the way we do in the 'outside world.' We
think as human beings, not colored by particular pressures"
(Sokolov 1949a). Bardin used to say to campers, "let's strike a contract. You give me twenty-eight days and I'll give you an experience
that will last a lifetime" (Ettinger 1989). Indeed, one woman later
reported that "Brandeis was the turning point of my life . . . ." Her
message confirmed Bardin's bargain and the power of an institute
experience. "Brandeis charted the way for me," she explained. "Because of it I still attend school, I feel relatively secure as a Jew, and
my family has enjoyed a Brandeis 'feeling' about religion, Shabbat,
and festivals. They have learned a positive Judaism," she concluded. "I believe your scholarship to me paid off in producing four
positive Jewish children and our home has provided an example for
many of our friends" (quoted in Levine 1971: 25–26).

Brandeis attracted a majority of women, partly a result of the
draft (both for World War II and the Korean War), partly due to recruitment through Junior Hadassah and alumni, and partly stemming from the character of its program. According to a 1971 survey
women represented 68% of the institute's enrollment and men only
32% over the course of three decades. However, in the early years
during the Second World War there were as many as 190 women to
10 men (Levine 1971: 9). In many respects, Bardin's experientially
based and emotionally structured education consciously articulated
the unarticulated mode of traditional learning for Jewish women.
For a month the camp became home to campers who learned by doing and living. Bardin and his staff turned themselves into the ideal
Jewish parents, aunts, uncles, cousins, and grandparents who
transmitted a love for Jewishness in all of its rich variety as much
through example as through specific didactic instruction. Bardin
mandated that his staff memorize the name and face of every
camper before an institute began so that campers were addressed
on a first-name, intimate basis from the moment they arrived (Ettinger 1989).

"It would not be an exaggeration to say," wrote one observer,
that Bardin "induces his young people to surrender themselves to
him for one month and during this period he and his staff replace
feelings of estrangement with a love for Judaism. . . ." Brandeis nur-
tured as it taught, inspired as it educated. "Charisma and seduction

are hard to resist and most of those who experience this combination at Brandeis succumb," the eastern observer concluded (Berger 1968). Bardin wanted to reach the hearts of his American-born campers even more than their minds, one reason why he chose to work with youths at what he called "the plastic age," the "age when the young person makes his great decisions" (Bardin 1958b, 1958d 2:5).

Graenum Berger, an eastern executive in Jewish communal recreation, visited Brandeis in the 1960s and astutely observed how Bardin linked the centrality of the Sabbath with traditional women's learning. "One prepares for it all week, but officially it begins on Friday morning just like it used to in the traditional home," he noted. "Brandeis changes its bed sheets and laundry on Friday. Not on Tuesday or Thursday or any other day. Along with clean sheets, clean clothes, the buildings and grounds are all cleaned up in preparation for the Sabbath." Berger understood the importance of such a routine. "These are so-called mundane things which most of the youngsters never did," he wrote. "It wasn't done in their own homes, unless a traditional grandmother lived with them. It is something which they had to experience as part of the Jewish Sabbath." The result was a sense of the Sabbath's sacredness, its sanctification of time. "No vehicles scurry within the campgrounds on that day. There is a festive air and there is a Sabbath quiet. Food is different too." Berger concluded that this spiritual recreation "is religious in the traditional sense, despite all disclaimers" (Berger 1968). Bardin also extended the traditional education for women. With girls over half of the campers, he quickly discovered that they had nothing to do during Friday night and Saturday morning services. So he included them in the Sabbath services. Female campers read Torah (in English) and joined in the singing of Hebrew prayers (Bardin 1958b, 3:12; BCI Masterbooks 1952a).

By 1951 with his marriage disintegrating, Bardin was eager to move to Los Angeles from New York. Only the L.A. camp had the year-round potential he sought to exploit and a circle of men and women dedicated to him. At the fall meeting of the Board of Governors, Goodman recommended accepting Bardin's proposal to move himself and the national office to Los Angeles and to introduce a year-round program in 1952. As Goodman reiterated, Bardin intended not to create a local institution for southern California and the West, but a national one (Brandeis Youth Foundation 1951). Without Bardin's presence, the eastern supporters found it difficult to raise funds, though Goodman remained enthusiastic. He was particularly impressed with what he considered the unusual cooperation of different types of Jews united in one enterprise and under one roof. In 1953 he recommended selling the eastern camp and suggested, in a compliment to Bardin's accomplishment, that a site be found an hour from New York City to duplicate the Los Angeles program (Brandeis Youth Foundation 1953a).

Bardin, however, was concentrating on developing and extending the Los Angeles program. Hollywood provided a congenial milieu for his own showmanship. He diligently recruited supporters who could contribute their creative talents as well as finances and particularly courted Jews working in the movie industry. These wealthy men would drive out to the Simi Valley in their limousines and Bardin would make them send their chauffeurs home. Then, he would have them dig in the garden. "They loved it!" Wolfe Kelman recalled (Kelman 1988). Los Angeles offered opportunities for individual entrepreneurship that Bardin, a natural entrepreneur, could hardly resist. In 1952 he introduced a tree-planting ceremony for families that combined Tu B'Shevat with Lag B'omer, the holiday of trees with the scholars' holiday (Brandeis Camp Institute of the West 1952). Michael Blankfort, a left-wing screenwriter, came to the camp, fell under Bardin's spell, and started to contribute scripts for various pageants, including one on Maimonides. "The first five hours I spent with Shlomo Bardin were apocalyptic," Blankfort recalled (Blankfort 1956: 4-6). He responded by spreading the message, recruiting Dore Schary and the writer Norman Corwin, as well as the writers Fay and Michael Kanin. Schary and Corwin developed a ceremony for the tree-planting ritual; Blankfort also wrote programs for Purim and Hanukkah and other holidays and contributed his services to the camp over the summer (Brandeis Youth Foundation 1953b).

With weekend institutes for couples inaugurated in 1952, Bardin could reach effectively into the Hollywood community. To cultivate supporters he worked with the lawyer Joseph Rifkind, and especially his wife Betty, a wealthy Beverly Hills couple whose son Robert attended Brandeis in 1948 and served as a staff member in 1949. The Rifkinds would recruit a prospect to a weekend institute. Then on Sunday after the institute had ended, Bardin, who loved to cook, would invite the selected couple up to his private apartment (Ettinger 1989). There, in rooms decorated with Navaho rugs and other items of Western Americana, Bardin would converse over a nonkosher dinner (in contrast to the institute's meals) (Elazar 1994). If the couple were moved by the Shabbat experience and by Bardin's charisma, he would ask them for just one favor—to introduce one friend to Brandeis. Bardin could "inspire people. He was a Pied Piper," Fay Kanin recalled. The camp "really celebrated all the cultural richness of being Jewish, and that kind of appealed to us. Through it we were exposed to some of the ritual that I had had a little of in my home—the Friday night candle-lighting and all that," she remembered. "We enjoyed them again, and we brought them home and did them for a while with our children, . . . " (Kanin: 57–58).

An ardent supporter, Fligelman recruited the old-timer, Max Bay. "I went most reluctantly," the physician recalled. "I was not particularly dedicated." Then, in 1954 "a stag weekend at Brandeis, turned me around completely." The stag weekends melded Shabbat celebration and learning with male camaraderie; it introduced Jewish men to the warm fellowship of a Jewish world their fathers might have known in the synagogue. Max Bay dated his Jewish education from his first weekend at Brandeis. Bay subsequently brought his wife to a couples weekend at Brandeis and that transformed her and she became involved in the Jewish community. "Experiencing a Shabbat at Brandeis is what it is—it also gave you a sense of pride in your heritage," he explained. "[O]ne of the feelings I had from my weekend was a sense of remorse for the lack of education that we had given our son. As a result, when I came home, and told the family about it, I sounded like a holy roller, because I suddenly had gotten religion, born again, born again before Carter!" (Bay 1979: 4, 8). Not everyone was touched by Bardin's charisma and showmanship. Ted Thomas, a writer and director, and friend of the Kanins, visited the camp but left unimpressed. Thomas remembered Bardin as "an arrogant son-of-a-bitch Israeli." The son of the famous Yiddish theater couple, Boris and Bessie Thomashevsky, Thomas had his own vibrant memories and didn't care for Bardin's spiritual re-creation of the Sabbath (Thomas 1989).

By the midfifties, a decade after moving to Los Angeles, Bardin completed the transplantation. Brandeis contained all of the year-round components he originally had envisioned: weekend institutes for adults—couples, stag weekends, and sorority weekends; a summer camp for children; special holiday-related events and workshops for families; and the original leadership program for youths. Financial support came from individuals loyal to Bardin; the leadership consisted largely of West Coast figures (Brandeis Youth Foundation 1953c).

Despite the remarkable continuity of program and personnel, the Brandeis Camp Institute, in its migration westward, lost its

Zionist ideological thrust though it retained a Zionist reputation. In the midsixties the non-Zionist lawyer and communal leader, Walter Hilborn, went to a weekend institute "with my tongue in my cheek, because I thought that he [Bardin] was going to try to make me a Zionist." But Hilborn discovered that Bardin "didn't try to do that. What he did was to make me feel much more interested in why I was a Jew, and what it meant to be a Jew, and he got me reading history about it." Not only did Hilborn read, but he also was inspired to study regularly for several years with Rabbi Max Nussbaum on the Sabbath (Hilborn 1974: 216).

In Los Angeles, Brandeis became a vehicle for Bardin's individual entrepreneurship. Its eclectic, inspirational programs led by a charismatic figure made Jews with minimal Jewish knowledge feel good about being Jews, offered a heterogeneous clientele a wide range of ways to be Jewish, and affirmed through drama, dance, and especially music, the spiritual values of Judaism. One reporter recognized that the institute fostered "an appetite for things Jewish—music, literature, traditions. . . ." (*San Francisco Jewish Tribune* 1947). A supporter considered the transformation wrought by Brandeis to be "a miracle." Participants became "real Jews, many of them for the first time in their lives" (Meltzer 1948). As one oldtimer observed, "You come, you get the inspiration and the thrill of real total Jewish living, without interruption and without influences being brought to bear" (Broidy 1979: 2–3). Bardin's status as a secular lay leader—he was not a rabbi—enhanced the power of his spiritual message.

Eventually easterners interested in programmatic efforts to foster Jewish identity and to revitalize American Jewish life found their way to Brandeis. Berger's visit was not unusual. In the 1960s several other eastern Jewish leaders came to Brandeis to learn from the camp experience. One astute observer examined the Institute for the American Jewish Committee. He summarized succinctly the assumptions of its educational program: "1. To understand Judaism, you must experience it. 2. Judaism is not primarily a creed or theology; it is concerned, mainly, with the art of living with one's fellow men." He went on to point out that Brandeis tried to restore two lost Jewish traditions: a lay leadership and a Jewish home culture revolving around Shabbat and the festivals. To revitalize the home, and thus all of Jewish life in America, one had to start with the Sabbath (Hurvitz: 11–12). "I definitely feel that we should make a very serious effort to introduce the Sabbath into our own lives," Bardin affirmed, "and, maybe, through us, it will spread to the whole of

America, for it is not merely the Jews who need it" (Bardin 1958d, VI:1). This meant, of course, that women and their home domain now occupied a crucial, central place in American Judaism. At the heart of Bardin's program lay the conviction that women held the key to the Jewish future. Only women really possessed sufficient leisure time to be Jewish now that Judaism had become a form of spiritual recreation.

An American Jewish folk religion developed in Los Angeles. Popular, eclectic, and experiential, this new Judaism drew upon spiritual modes traditionally associated with women. Such modes emphasized the centrality of experience to knowing. Without experiencing Judaism—be it the joy of the Sabbath or the thrill of hearing an inspiring lecture or the pleasure of singing Jewish songs—it would be impossible to be Jewish. Since such experiences with their attendant emotions of solidarity and feeling good about being Jewish did not fill the homes of L. A. Jews, institutions like the Brandeis Camp Institute sought to convey them. In Los Angeles, Judaism gradually lost much of its elite, male, theological, and halakic form and substance. At the time, the difference between Judaism in the City of Angels and Judaism back home appeared to be a difference between East and West, center and periphery, even, perhaps, between parent and child. Only later would observers realize that as Jews pursued their spiritual recreation, they also were changing the character of Judaism (Liebman 1990; Hammond 1988).

In Los Angeles the delicate balance that usually animated American Judaism—between the claims of tradition to transform the Jew and the demands of the individual Jew to modify tradition—shifted decisively in favor of the latter. As Bruce Powell noted enthusiastically, Bardin enjoyed "the freedom to 'select' from the best in Jewish culture instead of having to take it all, . . ." (Powell 1979: 120). And what guided Bardin's choices was the audience— those uprooted Jews living in a Jewish desert on the edge of paradise. He devised programs that would reach them, move them, inspire them, transform them. If the process also transformed Zionism—this was one of the unexpected outcomes. Zionism was a resource to be exploited, not a constraint.

If there was a measure of chutzpah in these experimental endeavors, it fit comfortably into the L. A. milieu where anything appeared possible, even the reimagination of such an ancient religion as Judaism. Unencumbered by tradition, Los Angeles Jews proved receptive to an innovative eclecticism that crossed denominational and ideological boundaries. Bardin deliberately chose Shabbat as his central focus as a common denominator. It was *the* Jewish moment when the joy of Jewish living could be grasped, when passion might be evoked, when beauty and truth coalesced. Yet Bardin knew better than merely to reproduce Sabbath rituals; rather, he produced them using his own melodies, his own ceremonies—especially in *havdala.* He aimed to create a sense of longing, camaraderie, and beauty through special music and lighting effects. The candles and the gradual dimming of lights evoked a palpable sense of loss, sustained by all of the campers standing in a circle with their arms on each other's shoulders. Yet each participant was here a creator as well as an observer. The effects of *havdala* bounced back to one. Recently, the emergence of *havdala* rituals at federation meetings aims for similar effects. American Jewish organizational culture appears to be recognizing the experiential power that Bardin employed at the institute.

Several observations are in order. When Bardin struck his bargain with his campers, he wanted to control the dynamics of the camp as much as possible. He even demanded no coupling for the four weeks, although this requirement was honored more in the breach than in observance. Given the ages of campers, it indicates Bardin's desire for control rather than for any realistic expectations. Bardin also freely criticized his lecturers, telling them when they were effective and when he thought they were ineffective. He tried to make them entertaining or inspiring; merely to be knowledgeable and competent was inadequate. Although Bardin continually invited new people to the camp, he clearly had his favorites—effective, persuasive, moving, witty, engaging, dynamic speakers—and these would regularly return.

Bardin was a pedagogue, but he was also an entrepreneur. It was a compelling combination. He knew how to use the national organizational machinery of American Jews for his own personal ends and he could also reach individuals who became his loyal supporters and followers. Perhaps we need more such educational entrepreneurs devoted to reaching young Jews aged eighteen to twenty-five. Bardin wanted to create a lay leadership, an elite. He designed the Brandeis Camp Institute to nourish lay leadership, not as universal Jewish education. In the early years, all of the students who came on "aliyah" received a scholarship raised by hometown leaders or Hadassah, and this undoubtedly increased their sense of commitment. The Jewish community had invested in them and expected them to do some community service on their return. Finally, Bardin welcomed—indeed, sought out—Jews who were successful in other cultural fields. As already noted, he particularly appealed to Hollywood Jews, those who were unaffiliated, and he asked them to write pageants, to stage ceremonies, and to develop dramatic ways of telling Jewish stories. That a Michael Blankfort or Dore Schary or Norman Corwin knew nothing to speak of about Judaism didn't deter Bardin. They knew how to write or produce popular movies that grabbed an audience. Bardin was confident that he would inspire them to learn enough to create the products he needed. His embrace of successful "secular" Jews engaged in cultural production was a central component of his entrepreneurial and pedagogical strategy. Bardin deliberately worked to undo stereotypes of American Jews. If Jews were thought of as rich, then he had campers work in the garden to get their hands dirty. If Jews were thought of as cowardly, he had campers read about Jewish heroes to feel proud and free.

Bardin's experiment in spiritual recreation invites reflection on the Jewish condition of exile, and on its meaning for personal identity and reinterpretation. I think Bardin imagined American Jews as permanent tourists, an oxymoron. Like all tourists, Jews in Los Angeles temporarily bracketed a portion of their identity in order to be open to new experiences, to discover new worlds. Often, the piece of identity bracketed was their Jewishness—left behind in the hometown of their youth. Bardin invited these permanent tourists to reclaim that Jewish part of their identity by reinventing it as something intriguing, inspiring, and even compelling.

References

Bardin, Shlomo. (1942) Letter to Mrs. Moses Epstein, 31 July, House of the Book, Brandeis Bardin Institute.

———. (1945) Letter to Abe Herman, 1 September, S32/536, Central Zionist Archives.

———. (1946) "The Brandeis Camp Institute." *Jewish Education* 17, no. 3 (June): 26–27.

———. (1958a) Interview by Jack Diamond, 2 February, House of the Book, Brandeis-Bardin Camp Institute.

———. (1958b) Interview by Jack Diamond, 11 February, House of the Book, Brandeis-Bardin Institute.

———. (1958c) Interview by Jack Diamond, 10 May, House of the Book, Brandeis-Bardin Camp Institute.

———. (1958d) Interview by Jack Diamond, 20 May, House of the Book, Brandeis-Bardin Institute.

Bay, Max William. (1979) Oral History Interview, 25 July, Oral History of the United Jewish Appeal, Oral History Archives, Institute of Contemporary Jewry, Hebrew University.

BCI Masterbooks. (1947) Brandeis-Bardin Institute.

———. Masterbooks. (1952) Brandeis-Bardin Institute.

———. Masterbooks. (1952a). BCI West, Brandeis-Bardin Institute.

Berger, Ramon F. (1968) "An Aliyah to the Brandeis Camp Institute," ed. Graenum Berger, Santa Susana.

Berger, Graenum. (1968) "An Aliyah to the Brandeis Camp Institute," Santa Susana.

Blankfort, Michael. (1956) *The Strong Hand.* Boston: Little, Brown.

Brandeis Camp Institute of the West. (1952) Minutes of Meeting, 7 June, House of the Book, Brandeis-Bardin Institute.

Brandeis Youth Foundation. (n.d.) Summary of Activities, House of the Book.

———. (1951) Minutes of Meeting of the Board of Governors, 26 September, House of the Book, Brandeis-Bardin Institute.

———. (1953a) Minutes of Meeting of National Board, 23 February, House of the Book, Brandeis-Bardin Institute.

———. (1953b) Minutes of Meeting of Members in Los Angeles, 15 April, House of the Book, Brandeis-Bardin Institute.

———. (1953c) Minutes of Meeting of the Executive Committee, 7 June, Members of Board of Directors, 1954, House of the Book, Brandeis-Bardin Institute.

Broidy, Steve. (1979) Oral History Interview, 27 July, Oral History of the United Jewish Appeal, Oral History Archives, Institute of Contemporary Jewry, Hebrew University.

California Jewish Voice. (1946) 22 November.

———. (1947a) 28 February.

———. (1947b) 7 March.

———. (1947c) 8 August.

———. (1947d) 29 August.

Davis, Moshe. (n.d.) Oral History Interview.

Elazar, Daniel. (1994) Conversation at Conference on National and Cultural Variations in Jewish Identity and Their Implications for Jewish Education, Jerusalem, 6 January.

———. (1998) "Jewish Religious, Ethnic and National Identities: Convergences and Conflicts." In *National Variations in Modern Jewish Identity*, edited by Steven M. Cohen and Gabriel Horenczyk. Albany: State University of New York Press.

Ettinger, Irma Lee. (1989) Interview with author. 7 July.

Goldberg, Harvey E. (1998) "A Tradition of Invention: Family and Educational Institutions among Contemporary Traditionalizing Jews." In *National Variations in Modern Jewish Identity*, edited by Steven M. Cohen and Gabriel Horenczyk. Albany: State University of New York Press.

Hammond, Phillip E. (1988) "Religion and the Persistence of Identity." *Journal for the Scientific Study of Religion*, 27, no. 1: 1–11.

The Hancock Herald. (1943a). Article on 22 July, in Scrapbooks, House of the Book, Brandeis-Bardin Camp Institute.

———. (1943b) Article on 5 August, in Scrapbooks, House of the Book, Brandeis-Bardin Camp Institute.

Hilborn, Walter. (1974) "Reflections on Legal Practice and Jewish Community Leadership," Oral History Interview with Malca Chall, Regional Oral History Office, Bancroft Library, University of California, Berkeley.

Hurvitz, Jacob I. (n.d.) *Brandeis Camp Institute*. New York. House of the Book, Brandeis-Bardin Institute.

Kanin, Fay. (n.d.) Oral Memoir, William E. Wiener Oral History Library of the American Jewish Committee.

Kelman, Wolfe. (1988) Interview with author. 5 March.

Levine, Gene N. (1971) *An Adventure in Curing Alienation* (summer).

Liebman, Charles S. (1990) "Ritual, Ceremony and the Reconstruction of Judaism in the United States." *Studies in Contemporary Jewry* 6:272–85.

Meltzer, Edward. (1948) Quoted in *B'nai B'rith Messenger*, 6 August.

Meyer, Michael. (1994) Conversation at Conference on National and Cultural Variations in Jewish Identity and Their Implications for Jewish Education, Jerusalem, 6 January.

Moore, Deborah Dash. (1981) *B'nai B'rith and the Challenge of Ethnic Leadership*. Albany: State University of New York Press.

———. (1997) "Hadassah." In *Jewish Women in America: An Historical Encyclopedia*, edited by Paula E. Hyman and Deborah Dash Moore. New York: Routledge.

Nasaw, David. (1993) *Going Out: The Rise and Fall of Public Amusements*. New York: Basic.

Powell, Bruce. (1979) "The Brandeis-Bardin Institute: A Possible Jewish Model for Multicultural Education." Ph.D. diss., University of Southern California.

Prell, Riv-Ellen. (1998) "Family Economy/Family Relations: The Development of American Jewish Ethnicity in the Early Twentieth Century." In *National Variations in Modern Jewish Identity*, edited by Steven M. Cohen and Gabriel Horenczyk. Albany: State University of New York Press.

San Francisco *Jewish Tribune*. (1947). 14 September, in Scrapbooks, House of the Book, Brandeis-Bardin Institute.

Scheltzer, Chava. (1946) Letter to Lev (Abe) Herman, 24 September, S32/1205, 1 June 1946–30, September 1946, 10235/62, Youth Matters, U.S.A.; Central Zionist Archives. (Hebrew)

Sokolov, David. (1949a) "Brandeis Camp Gives Youth Direction." *The Jewish Post*, 20 October.

———. (1949b) "Brandeis Camp Notes." *The Jewish Post*, 27 October.

Star-Free Press. (1947) 19 July, in Scrapbooks for 1947-48, House of the Book Library, Brandeis-Bardin Institute.

Thomas, Ted. (1989) Interview with author, 13 July.

Zigmond, Maurice. (1948) Letter to Rabbi Theodore H. Gordon quoting Rosalyne Eisenberg, 1 April, included with cover letter to Members of the National Youth Commission from Shlomo Bardin, 26 April 1948, F25, 162, Central Zionist Archives.

Chapter 11

∽

Jewishness in New York:
Exception or the Rule?

Bethamie Horowitz

In November 1993, Ehud Olmert, the mayor of Jerusalem, sent a greeting to Rudolph Guiliani, the newly elected mayor of New York City: "Congratulations, from the mayor of the greatest Jewish city in the world to the mayor of the second greatest Jewish city." Although he may have antagonized the residents of Tel Aviv, his comment showed that he recognized an underlying similarity between the Jewish environments of these two places.

The idea of place has a certain resonance in Jewish history. We find it in the image of the Israelites carrying the ark around with them as they moved from place to place in the desert, which initiated the recurrent Jewish theme of wandering versus stability. One of the circumlocutions for the name of God is Ha-Makom—the Place, the Omnipresent. The Temple was also called *ha-makom*; rather than calling God by his unspeakable name, the rabbis apparently felt it more appropriate to identify him by his address. Yehuda HaLevy's poignant lament, "My heart/essence is in the East but I am (located) at the far edge of the West," throws into relief the contrast between physical place of residence and spiritual homeland. Even the expression from Jewish folklore, "A change of place brings a change in fortune," makes the point that place does it fact matter.

Despite its importance in the collective conscience of the Jewish people, the idea of place has played only a minor role in the American social analysis of the Jews. Mobility—both physical and social—is a topic that gets more attention, perhaps because Americans are notorious for being ever on the move. More than rootedness in a homeland, the ideas of frontier and of movement onward and upward have inspired American endeavors. Yet the question of place lies at the heart of the problem of contemporary American Jewishness. How does physical distance from (or closeness to) the Jewish center relate to spiritual and psychological distance from the Jewish people? When you are a citizen of one place and you have a connection to another place, what happens to your identity? Which place is your real place?

We have always supposed, if only for ideological reasons, that no difference regarding Jewishness is more significant than location in Israel or in the Diaspora (i.e., some other place). The Jews of Israel live in the Jewish state, and so their national group identity and their citizenship overlap, whereas for an American Jew or a British Jew, the overlap may never be as complete. Yet there are underlying dimensions that cut across this gap.

The Olmert greeting is amusing because it defines Jerusalem and New York as lying close together along a single continuum, despite the gulf separating our ideas about Israel and the Diaspora. My interest in this chapter is to explore continuities in the "Jewishness of place or locale" that cut across the bolder-faced divisions among nations, or for that matter, between Israel and the Diaspora.

"The New York Effect"

Let me start with the phenomenon—the specific case of "the New York effect." In contrast to the portrait of American Jews that emerged from the 1990 National Jewish Population Survey (Kosmin et al. 1991), the New York Jewish Population Study (Horowitz 1993) showed that New York area Jews are notably more likely to identify themselves as Jewish and to view this as being their religion, not merely their ethnicity or cultural background. The vast majority of New Yorkers with any sort of Jewish background describe themselves as Jewish by religion (83%), while only 53% of the national Jewishly connected population identify this way (and only half of the national Jewish population when New York is excluded) (See table 1). Outside New York, more than three times as many Jews

Table 1
Comparison of Greater New York Jewish Population—1991[1]
and U.S. Jewish Population—1990[2]

Type of Connection to Jewishness	New York Area % of Total Population in Jewishly Connected Households	U.S. National Overall	Excluding New York
		% of Total Population in Jewishly Connected Households	
1. Born Jews: Religion Judaism	81	51	48
2. Jews by Choice—Convents	1	2	3
(Jews by Religion)	(83)	(53)	(50)
3. Born Jews with No Religion (secular)	4	14	15
Core Jewish Population	(87)	(67)	(65)
4. Born/Raised Jewish: Currently not Jewish	1	3	3
5. Adults of Jewish Background with Other Current Religion	1	5	6
6. Children under 18 Being Raised with Other Current Religion	3	9	9
Total Ethnic or Religious Background	(92)	(84)	(83)
7. Gentile Adults Living in Jewishly Connected Households	8	16	17
Total Jewish Connected Households	100	100	100

[1]*Source:* UJA-Federation 1991 New York Population Study. 8 Counties: New York City, Nassau, Suffolk, and Westchester. Does not include the institutionalized or unenumerated population (668,000 households)
[2]*Source:* CJF 1990 National Jewish Population Survey (includes 100,000 institutionalized) (3.2 million households)

answer "none" or "agnostic" or "atheist" regarding their religious affiliation, but still consider themselves to be Jewish. Clearly, although there is no one form of Jewish identity in New York, as a group, they are more at ease in describing themselves religiously as Jewish, compared to Jews elsewhere in America.

In the aggregate, New York Jews are slightly more observant than other American Jews (See tables 2 and 3). New York Jews as a group, whether living in entirely Jewish or in mixed (Jewish-Gentile) households, are more likely to practice religious rituals than

Table 2
Comparisons of Selected Jewish Practices of Households:
New York and the Nation[1]

	New York 1991		National 1990[2]	
	Entirely Jewish	Mixed Jewish-Gentile	Entirely Jewish	Mixed Jewish-Gentile
Households:	(543,000)	(96,000)	(1,111,000)	(867,000)
Percentage Answering "Yes"	(%)	(%)	(%)	(%)
Attends Passover Seder*	93	80	86	62
Never has Christmas tree	93	31	82	20
Lights Hanukkah Candles	83	69	77	59
Lights Shabbat Candles	49	18	44	19
Attended Purim Celebration*	35	15	24	12
Celebrated Yom HaAtzmaut Israeli Independence Day**	20	8	18	6
Current Synagogue Member	43	15	41	13
Contributed to Jewish Charity in 1990	68	38	62	28
Contributed to Secular Charity in 1990	68	67	67	66
Contributed to UJA-Federation in 1990	37	14	45	12

[1]*Source:* UJA-Federation 1991 New York Jewish Population Study. 8 Counties: New York City, Nassau, Suffolk, and Westchester.
Source: CJF 1990 National Jewish Population Survey.
*"Sometimes, usually, always"
**During the past year

are Jews nationally.[1] They are more likely to attend a Seder, not to have a Christmas tree, to light Hanukkah candles, to fast on Yom Kippur, to attend synagogue weekly, and to celebrate Purim than Jews nationally (although the percentage observing Israeli Independence Day is no different). While New York Jews are more likely than other American Jews to contribute to Jewish charities, they are equally likely to contribute to general (non-Jewish) charities,[2] and somewhat less likely to donate to the UJA-Federation. The overall social milieu of Jews in New York is more Jewish in terms of friendship networks and in terms of exposure to Jewish newspapers and magazines. In addition, contact with Israel is more extensive in New York than elsewhere in America: a larger proportion have vis-

Table 3
Comparison of Selected Jewish Practices of Individuals:
New York and the Nation[1]

Percentage Answering "Yes"	New York 1991[2]	National 1990[2]
	%	%
Personal Religious Practice		
Fast on Yom Kippur	68	61
Attend Synagogue on High Holidays	61	59
Attend Synagogue Weekly	16	11
Israel Ties		
Visited Israel	42	31
Has Close Family or Friends in Israel	45	35
Jewish Social Ties		
Most Friends Are Jewish	63	45
Read Jewish Periodicals, Books*	39	28

[1]*Source:* UJA-Federation 1991 New York Jewish Population Study. 8 Counties: New York City, Nassau, Suffolk, and Westchester.

[2]Figures for New York are based on all core Jewish adults whereas the national figures are based on a subset of core Jews—Jews by religion only. *Source:* CJF 1990 National Jewish Population Survey.

*The New York study asked about periodicals and books, "Do you regularly read? . . ." whereas the national study asked about periodicals only, "Do you subscribe? . . ."

ited Israel or have close family or friends there, compared to Jews living elsewhere in America.

Finally, their intermarriage rates are lower. In New York 13% of the spouses of first marriages were Gentile, whereas the percentage is double that (26%) elsewhere is in the nation. Regarding marriages over time, in New York, the percentage of first spouses who were Gentile increased five times in thirty-some years, from 5% in marriages that occurred before 1965 to 25% in post-1985 marriages. Nationally, excluding New York, the incidence rose from 5% to 47% in the same time period. Again, the New York rate is about half the national rate.

Accounting for the "New York Effect"

The contrast between the Jews in New York and Jews living elsewhere in the United States leads us to wonder "why is New York different?" Answering this question forms the bulk of my discussion.

Methodology

Before I tackle the more interesting substantive questions raised by the "New York effect," I want to address briefly some of the methodological issues that arise.

Ideally, an analysis of New York Jews and of those living elsewhere in America would be based on a single dataset. Such a dataset exists, but it has a limitation for our purposes: the sample size of Jewish households in the New York area is sufficient only for the broadest "between group" comparisons of New York and American Jews. However, once we begin to compare subpopulations of New York Jews with their counterparts elsewhere in America, we must take a slightly different tack. Thus in this chapter I draw on two different although very comparable datasets.

A national study of American Jews (the Council of Jewish Federations' National Jewish Population Study [NJPS]) was conducted in 1990, and a study of the Jews of Greater New York was conducted in 1991 by the UJA-Federation of New York (the New York Jewish Population Study [NYJPS]). The studies used the same means of identifying Jewishly connected households, but drew different samples in the New York area. The NJPS included 410 Jewishly connected households in the 8-county New York area (out of a total of 2,441 households surveyed nationally), while the NYJPS is based on 4,008 Jewishly connected households.

For the remainder of this chapter, I will present data both from the NJPS broken out into two subsamples (the New York area and elsewhere in America) and from the NYJPS.

Why Is New York Different?

A first question to raise about the "New York effect" is the possibility that it does not exist at all! In other words, is the effect merely a result of the sampling differences between the two datasets used to look at Jews living in New York and in America? In table 4 it is clear that irrespective of the dataset, New York Jews are more likely to describe themselves as Jewish than are other American Jews. Similarly the "New York effect" remains apparent in both datasets in comparing the Jewish practices of Jews in New York and those elsewhere in America. So the New York effect does not arise merely from differences in the two survey samples. Next we turn to more substantive considerations.

Certainly the "New York effect" as it relates to intermarriage can be explained simply in terms of the propinquity of large masses

Table 4
Comparison of Greater New York Jewish Population—1991
and U.S. Jewish Population—1990

Type of Connection to Jewishness	New York Area				U.S. National Excluding New York	
	NY JPS[1]		NYJPS[2]		NYJPS[2]	
	Number	%	Number	%	Number	%
1. Born Jews: Religion Judaism	1,325,000	81	899,000	66	3,210,000	48
2. Jews by Choice—Convents	21,000	1	14,000	1	169,000	3
(Jews by Religion)	(1,347,000)	(83)	(913,000)	(67)	(3,379,000)	(51)
3. Born Jews with No Current Religion (secular)	72,000	4	130,000	9	992,000	15
Core Jewish Population	(1,419,000)	(87)	(1,043,000)	(77)	(4,371,000)	(65)
4. Born/Raised Jewish: Currently not Jewish	17,000	1	20,000	1	194,000	3
5. Adults of Jewish Background with Other Current Religion	19,000	1	45,000	3	369,000	6
6. Children under 18 Being Raised with Other Current Religion	44,000	3	77,000	6	626,000	9
Total Ethnic or Religious Background	(1,498,000)	(92)	(1,185,000)	(87)	(5,560,000)	(83)
7. Gentile Adults Living in Jewishly Connected Households	134,000	8	173,000	13	1,176,000	17
Total Population Living in Jewishly Connected Households	1,633,000	100	1,358,000	100	6,740,000	100

[1]*Source:* UJA-Federation 1991 New York Jewish Population Study (NYJPS). 8 Counties: New York City, Nassau, Suffolk, and Westchester. Does not include the institutionalized or unenumerated population.

[2]*Source:* CJF 1990 National Jewish Population Survey (NJPS). Does not included the institutionalized or unenumerated population.

of Jews there. In other words, the sheer numbers of Jews who live in the New York City area, coupled with the high density of Jews in relation to the overall population of the area, make it more likely for Jews to interact with other Jews just by chance, which would lead us to expect a lower intermarriage rate (Blau & Schwartz 1984; Rabinowitz 1989). However, propinquity alone does not explain the more extensive Jewish practice among New York Jews.

New York Jewish practice may stand out from the profile of the rest of American Jewry due to other factors: New York's Jewish population may be older, more Orthodox, or more recently arrived in America (thus closer to the "Old Country" or to the experience of overt anti-Semitism) than other American Jews. Yet in fact New York Jewry is remarkably similar to the rest of American Jewry in terms of the basic demographic characteristics of age structure, educational attainment, and household composition. Although New York Jewry is somewhat more recently arrived in America compared to Jews nationwide, the difference in proportions is not large enough to account for the discrepancy in New York and national rates. Within generational strata, New York Jews continue to outscore their national counterparts on most measures of Jewish activity.

More germane to the "New York effect" is the fact that in America people who express their Jewishness as a current connection to the Jewish religion ("Jews by Religion") are more likely to be found in the Northeast (which includes the New York area) than elsewhere in the United States. "It is by far the dominant location" for Jews by religion (Goldstein 1992.) Can the "New York effect" be explained simply on the basis of this regional variation in the nature of Jewishness? To examine this let us look only at the people who see themselves as unequivocally Jewish by religion (I will call them "Jewish Jews"[3]) and compare the New Yorkers with the non-New Yorkers among them. In addition, in order to be as rigorous as possible, we will look only at "Jewish Jews" who are third generation or longer in America (in other words, those whose grandparents were born in America).

Third-generation "Jewish Jews" in New York look very similar to "Jewish Jews" outside New York on key indicators (see table 5). They are equally as likely to have had some Jewish schooling and to have had a Bar Mitzvah ceremony.

However, in terms of current denomination, New York Jewish Jews are almost five times more likely than the non-New Yorkers to be Orthodox (10% vs. 2%), and less likely to be Reform (41% vs. 55%). So although the third-generation "Jewish Jews" in New York resemble their counterparts outside of New York in terms of their sociodemographic characteristics, when it comes to current denomination, a larger proportion of New Yorkers are Orthodox. In addi-

Table 5
Background by Local
Perfect Cases Only* + 3rd Generation or Higher

	New York Area		U.S. National Excluding New York
	NYJPS[1]	NJPS[2]	NJPS[3]
	N = 1011)	N = 142)	(754)
Denomination Raised			
Orthodox	13.5	7.7	10.6
Conservative	44.0	45.1	40.4
Reform	32.6	36.6	44.4
Just Jewish	6.7	7.7	2.9
Something Else	3.2	2.9	2.7
Jewish Schooling			
Ever received Jewish education	79.0	77.5	84.1
Bar/Bat Mitzvah	55.2	62.7	66.1
Current Denomination			
Orthodox	9.7	3.5	2.3
Conservative	34.2	30.9	32.0
Reform	40.6	50.7	54.8
Just Jewish	9.4	9.1	5.3
Something Else	6.1	5.8	5.6

[1]*Source:* UJA-Federation 1991 New York Jewish Population Study (NYJPS). "New York Area" includes New York City, Long Island, and Westchester.
[2]*Source:* CJF National Jewish Population Study (NJPS).
*"Perfect Cases" are those in which people indicate that their religion of birth, religion of upbringing, and current religion are Jewish.

tion to (and perhaps along with) their greater Orthodoxy, as a group the New York "Jewish Jews" appear to be more observant than non-New Yorkers in their practices (see table 6). The "New York effect" remains: among third-generation "Jewish Jews" in America, New Yorkers are still more Jewish.

The conventional wisdom is that New York looks more Jewish due to the preponderance of Orthodox Jews living there. Allowing for the fact that the proportion of Orthodox in New York is nearly five times higher than outside New York, what happens when we compare "Jewish Jews" of each denomination in New York with their counterparts outside of New York? Does the New York difference disappear?

Table 6
Current Jewish Practices by Locale
Perfect Cases Only* + 3rd Generation or Higher

Percentage Answering "Yes"	New York Area		U.S. National Excluding New York
	NYJPS[1]	NJPS[1]	NJPS[2]
	(N = 1011) (%)	(N = 142) (%)	(N = 754) (%)
Religious Practices			
Attends a Passover Seder	93	95	91
Lights Hanukkah Candles	83	81	86
Never has Christmas Tree	80	75	65
Fasts on Yom Kippur	65	61	57
Attend Synagogue on High Holidays	55	49	57
Lights Shabbat Candles	36	30	37
Attended Purim Celebration	30	23	24
Uses Separate Dishes for Milk and Meat	21	18	10
Celebrated Israeli Independence Day	14	6	14
Handles No Money on Shabbat	14	8	7
Attend Synagogue Weekly	10	5	5
Fasts on Fast of Esther	6	2	3
Buys Kosher Meat	(NA)	5	35
Jewish Social Ties			
Most Friends Are Jewish	58	48	34
Participated in Adult Jewish Education in Past Year	22	8	15
Israel Ties			
Visited Israel	32	23	23
Has Close Friends in Israel	34	28	23
Philanthropic/Organizational Ties			
Household Has a Synagogue Member	33	35	41
Household Gave to			
.... Jewish Charity	58	47	52
.... Secular Charity	67	71	70
.... UJA-Federation	28	33	34

[1]*Source:* UJA-Federation 1991 New York Population Study. "New York Area" includes New York City, Long Island, and Westchester.
[2]*Source:* CJF 1990 National Jewish Population Study.
*"Perfect Cases" are those in which people indicate that their religion of birth, religion of upbringing, and current religion are Jewish.

Among Orthodox "Jewish Jews," the New Yorkers are altogether more observant than their national counterparts—on every ritual practice, Jewish social tie, Israel connection, except for giving to general (secular/non-Jewish) charities and giving to the UJA/Federation, where there were no differences. Unfortunately, there are so few cases in the NJPS that these data are merely suggestive of what other studies have shown. The practice of Orthodoxy in New York differs from what counts as "Orthodox" elsewhere in America. Undoubtedly this arises from the concentration of the *Haredi* (ultra-Orthodox) communities in New York (Heilman & Cohen, 1986, 1989).

In contrast to the strength of the "New York effect" among the Orthodox and among third-generation "Jewish Jews" who are Conservative or Reform, the extent of Jewish practice comes across as altogether more homogeneous (compared to the Orthodox) across the nation, except in relation to a few key practices where the New Yorkers excel (see table 7). These include never having a Christmas tree, fasting on Yom Kippur, having mostly Jewish friends, having visited Israel, and having close friends or family living in Israel. Taken together these elements reflect the salience of Jewishness as an aspect of New York City's overall environment. The large Jewish presence in New York is the underlying variable giving rise to each of the specific behaviors that continue to distinguish New York non-Orthodox Jews from their national counterparts. For the non-Orthodox, New York's Jewish advantage arises from the kind of setting it offers, rather than from the greater piety of its populace. While New York's Orthodox Jews are in fact more *frum* or "observant" than Orthodox Jews living elsewhere in America, New York's non-Orthodox Jews appear to be more Jewishly observant in large part because the social context itself appears to activate them.

It is clear that New York provides a distinctive context for religion and ethnicity—for Jewishness—compared to elsewhere in the United States. This may be part of New York's attractiveness to certain types of Jews, whether leading them to migrate there, or keeping them anchored in the city. Another way of expressing it is that Jews who leave the New York City area may be less Jewish than those who stay, or that they may become less Jewish as a consequence of leaving the region.[4]

Being Jewish in New York has implications, just as being Jewish in Israel does. For the most Jewishly active, New York offers a range of Jewish expression, of Jewish subcultures, which is unparalleled in America. New York City is a place that traditionally has allowed for a great variety of Jewish identities (just as all cities

Table 7
New York[1] Compared to Nation[2]: Jewish Practice by Current Denomination
Perfect Cases Only[c] 3rd Generation

Percentage Answering "Yes"	Conservative		Reform		Just Jewish	
	(346)	(241) Non	(410)	(413) Non	(95)	(40) Non
	New York	New York	New York	New York	New York	New York
	(34%)	(%)	(41%)		(%)	(%)
Religious Practices						
Attends Passover Seder (1)	97	94	94	92	80	75
Never has Christmas Tree	90	74	73	63	62	40
Lights Hanukkah Candles	91	88	81	86	62	70
Fasts on Yom Kippur (3)	79	73	61	52	39	20
Attend Synagogue on High Holidays	72	71	44	53	15	28
Lights Shabbat Candles (1)	45	52	22	30	11	20
Attended Purim celebration (2)	32	29	19	22	18	13
Uses Separate Dishes for Milk and meat	26	17	5	5	3	0
Celebrated Israeli Independence Day	18	20	6	11	5	5
Attend Synagogue weekly (3)	6	7	2	3	3	3
Handles No Money on Shabbat	8	8	6	5	4	0
Fasts on Fast of Esther (3)	6	3	4	1	4	0
Social Ties						
Most Friends Are Jewish	63	44	53	28	37	25
Participated in Adult Jewish Education in Past Year	23	20	14	11	7	8
Israel Ties						
Visited Israel	32	33	26	18	24	12
Has Close Friends in Israel	36	28	23	17	27	20
Philanthropic/Organizational Ties						
Household has a Synagogue Member	43	52	22	38	14	10
Household gave to						
.... Jewish Charity (2)	65	66	52	46	30	33
.... Secular Charity (2)	67	71	70	69	67	70
.... UJA-Federation 92)	38	43	25	30	7	18

Source: UJA-Federation 1991 New York Jewish Population Study.
Source: CJF 1990 National Jewish Population Survey.
Religion of upbringing and current religion are Jewish.
Sometimes, usually, or always
During the past year
Asked of respondent only. All other religious practices were asked about household as a whole.

offer wider berth than smaller towns for the expressions of their citizens) so that not only does New York have more Orthodox Jews,
but it also has more Jewish atheists. This leads to a rich array of
Jewish expressions—Jewish tabloid wars, Jewish cultural life, a
real Jewish politics, which were thought to be a possibility only in
the Jewish state. In short, the quality of Jewish life in New York is
superior even if in the eyes of some the quality of general life is
lacking. This would shed some light on the fact that between 1981
and 1991 New York's Jewish population was more apt to remain in
the city than its white non-Jewish population: perhaps for some the
superior quality of life in Jewish terms mitigates the problematic
aspects of New York's quality of life in general.

For the minimally connected or inactive Jewish person, New
York Jewishness resembles Israeli secular identity. It is part of the
culture of the place, in that it is contextual, rather than belief-
based. In this regard the comedian Lenny Bruce remarked,

> If you live in New York or any other big city, you are Jewish. It
> doesn't matter, even if you are Catholic; if you live in New York,
> you're Jewish. If you live in Butte, Montana, you're going to be
> goyish, even if you're Jewish.[5]

Bruce and his generation were hyperaware of the overall Jewish presence in the city—that it was a Jewish place, even if the rest
of America most certainly was not. He held, essentially, that the
place determines style, if not exactly identity.

What is it about New York that makes it conducive to Jewishness? Certainly the structural features of the New York Jewish community give rise to its greater Jewishness, notably its large Jewish
population size and density over a long period of time. Large population size alone means that diversification is possible on many levels. We see this diversity among the many Jewish subcultures and
communities that exist in New York, which support a variety of
types of Jewishness. A broad range of Jewish services is available in
New York, in addition to a wide array of general services offered by
Jews. The presence of this rich, varied Jewish infrastructure in New
York City is itself a consequence of the city's history as a place with
a significant Jewish population.

This diversity carries over into the institutional and organizational aspects of New York. As a result of New York's long-standing
Jewish population size, New York has become the flagship for the
organizational life of the American Jews. Many national and international Jewish cultural, religious, and communal institutions are

based there. The seminaries from three denominations are in New York City, as are the headquarters of major American Jewish communal institutions. Whatever the historical reasons for their location in New York City, these institutions continue to attract the elite of Jewish communal, religious, and cultural life, thus adding to the quality of the population in addition to its quantity.

The Jewish "presence" in New York arises from both the masses of Jews making up a large percentage of the city's total population, as well as from the wide spectrum of Jewish options there. (While the large Orthodox and Haredi (ultra-orthodox) populations are particularly visible, these are not the only signs of a Jewish presence.) The public face of Jewishness is a larger one, and consequently the city's general range of symbols is very likely to include Jewish symbols as well as those of other groups. A major department store tells its customers (via advertising in the *New York Times*) to come celebrate Hanukkah in the store. As a result of New York City's parking regulations (which are suspended on Jewish as well as on other holidays) even non-Jews may be aware of the occurrence of every Jewish holiday. A more significant example relates to the perception by some that there is a Jewish vote that figures into the city's politics.

All in all, in New York, Jews have a higher profile than in other American places. It feels important and acceptable to be Jewish in New York, because there is (and has been) a Jewish presence in the city. Jewish issues get covered by the general press. One feels more comfortable being a Jew in a place where being Jewish is part of the fabric of the life of the city. In other cities where the density of Jews is much lower, Jews have a much lower profile, and thus Jewish identification requires a certain motivation and effort.

Ultimately, "Jewish" and, by extension, "non-Jewish" have become meaningful categories in New York. In part, this arises from the sheer numbers of Jews who live in New York, but it is also the case that the culture of the city heightens awareness about Jewishness as a social category, as groups in the city become aware of one another and of the boundaries around them. In this regard, consider the differences between New York and the rest of the nation in terms of the flows into and out of Judaism—the percentages of converts to and from Judaism (see table 1). The national rates are three times as high, suggesting that whereas nationally the boundary between Jew and non-Jew may be permeable, in New York it is only semipermeable. Thus, Bruce was not exactly accurate. It is not the case that non-Jews in New York are Jewish; rather, they are aware of Jewishness and of its absence. They can meaningfully call themselves "non-Jews."

Jewishness in New York has become a social category of consequence, over and above the private lives of individuals who live
there (Horowitz & Solomon 1992). As such, New York offers a climate that makes it easier for Jewish people to identify with Jewishness and Judaism, in contrast to the social forces that may work
against such identification elsewhere in the nation. With stronger
Jewish identification, we expect more extensive practice of measures of "public Judaism."

Toward a Sociology of "Jewishness of Place"

That Jewishness varies across nations or cultures seems easy
to accept, yet I have argued that Jewishness varies by locale *within*
the same society. To be a Jew in New York City certainly differs
from being Jewish elsewhere in America, but no doubt comparing
the city to generalized American Jewry is itself a false picture. We
need to compare New York to Cleveland, Boston, Washington,
Chicago, or to Los Angeles. At the same time, it is worthwhile to
consider the extent to which the qualities that make New York a
seemingly unique Jewish place cut across national, historical, and
ideological boundaries. Is New York Jewishness closer or farther
from being a Jew in London, or Tel Aviv, or Haifa, or, for that matter
in Warsaw or Vienna at the turn of the century?

To address these questions a more general concept of "Jewish
environment or place" is needed that goes beyond the specifics of the
New York case. This enterprise involves identifying the various combinations of social and historical forces that bolster the retention of
Jewish identity or affect its nature. With regard to the quality of
Jewishness in any given place, there are several key dimensions that
need to be examined. Most basic is the size of the Jewish population;
its density, both in relation to the total population and to the relevant comparison group (i.e., white non-Hispanics in New York, but,
for the Ashkenazic Jewish populace of Montreal, Anglophones are a
more appropriate reference group). When the effect of density is examined, there seems to be a "tipping point" or threshold effect once
the Jewish population accounts for at least around 10 percent of the
total population, suggesting that density is a major social determinant of the Jewish identity of individuals.

Other structural aspects of place that are important to track
are the number of Jewish institutions in a community and the community's age, as well as some evaluation of the place's status as a

Jewish cultural center (or boondocks). In terms of perception and representation there are a range of issues concerning the nature of the local Jewish presence: the extent to which Jewishness is a social category, the content of this social category, and the degree of acceptance (or rejection) of Jews and Jewishness by non-Jews. Are Jews and Jewishness seen as significant factors in the life of the place? Does society view Jews as productive or counterproductive in relation to its collective effort? Are Jews seen as central or marginal in the intellectual life of the place? Regarding the social perception of the place in the eyes of other Jews, we can ask how often do other Jews (of various stripes) visit the place, in other words, to what extent is a place seen as a center for Jewish life and as a center for life in general? To what extent and in what ways do Jews interact with the rest of society? For this, not only should intermarriage rates be considered, but also other measures of interconnection (e.g., number of Jewish members of government, Jewish involvement in the cultural life, public personages who are Jewish, and Jewish penetration of various networks).

Eventually, localities where Jews live can be described and even mapped out in terms of these various social and structural dimensions, with an eye toward analyzing the nature and viability of Jewish life there. For instance, in New York City Jews have high visibility, are accepted by the mainstream, and are seen as playing a positive and productive role in the city's efforts. In contrast, American Jews are less visible nationally, in comparison to Jews in New York City's life, although the prominence of Israel in America's consciousness may act, in part, as a proxy for Jews. Yet Jews in America are both *accepted* by non-Jews and *viewed as productive* in the nation's efforts. As a foil to both of these examples, consider the case of early twentieth-century Viennese Jews: they were highly visible, highly rejected by non-Jews, and seen as pariahs (i.e., as unproductive).

At a time when so much attention in the American Jewish communal world is focused on reaching Jewish individuals—whether getting them to do more Jewish things, protecting them against intermarriage, or attempting to reach out to the unaffiliated individuals—the notable thing about "the New York effect" (or any other local effect, for that matter) is that it redirects our attention to the importance of the Jewishness of the *place*, in addition to that of the *person*. It reminds us that New York Jews and Jewishness are exceptional in America, and that the greater degree of observance and practice of the city's Jews compared to other American Jews is both a cause and a consequence of the prominence of Jewishness in the city. At the same time, by examining the relationship between the practice of Jewish individuals and the nature of Jewishness as a social category in any particular place, I have suggested the value of adopting an analytic stance that is more consciously *social* or contextual rather than relying on an overly atomized or *individual* approach. In this regard the New York case is no exception. In analyzing (and attempting to change) the level of Jewishness, the emphasis should not be only on intervening in the lives of individuals. Rather, it should involve changing aspects of the context in which people make their decisions and that influences their sense of what the options are. This dual focus would improve the thinking and communal policy-making about continuity, outreach, and the issues of "boundary management" between Jews and their neighbors.

Notes

1. Note that in New York only 15% of the households are mixed, whereas nationally nearly three times that amount are mixed (44%).

2. A. Keysar finds a similar pattern in her analysis (see Keysar 1993).

3. "Jewish Jews" are the "perfect cases" in the NYJPS and NJPS in which people indicate that their religion of birth, their religion of upbringing, and their current religion is Jewish.

4. Paul Ritterband has begun to investigate the historical basis of New York's difference. One of his hypotheses is that New York is different because the migrants who chose to settle there were different from other immigrants: The German Jewish settlement was highly dispersed, whereas the Eastern European Jewish settlement was centered in NYC.

5. Lenny Bruce (1981) "Jewish and Goyish," In *The Big Book of Jewish Humor*, edited by W. Novak and M. Waldoks. (New York: Harper), 60.

References

Blau, P. M., and J. E. Schwartz. (1984) *Crosscutting Social Circles: Testing a Macrosociological Theory of Intergroup Relations*. Orlando: Academic.

Goldstein, Sidney. (1992) "Profile of American Jewry: Insights from the 1990 National Jewish Population Survey. *American Jewish Year Book 1992*. Vol. 92.

Heilman Samuel C., and Steven M. Cohen. (1986) "Ritual Variation among Modern Orthodox Jews in the United States." *Studies in Contemporary Jewry* 2: 164–87.

————. (1989). *Cosmopolitans and Parochials: The Many Faces of Orthodox Jews in America.* Chicago: University of Chicago Press.

Horowitz, Bethamie. (1993) *The 1991 New York Jewish Population Study.* New York: UJA-Federation of Jewish Philanthropies of New York.

————. and J. Solomon. (1992) "Why Is This City Different from All Other Cities? New York and the National Jewish Population Survey." *Journal of Jewish Communal Service* 68, no. 4: 312–20.

Keysar, A. (1993) Patterns of Philanthropy: New York versus non-New York Jewry in 1990, Working Papers, Center for the Study of Philanthropy, Graduate Center, CUNY.

Kosmin, B., S. Goldstein, J. Waksberg, N. Lerer, and A. Keysar. (1991) *Highlights of the CJF 1990 National Jewish Population Survey.* New York: Council of Jewish Federations.

Rabinowitz, J. (1989) "The Paradoxical Effects of Jewish Community Size on Jewish Communal Behavior: Intermarriage, Synagogue Membership and Giving to Local Jewish Federations." *Contemporary Jewry* 10, no.1.

Part IV

The Israel Difference

Chapter 12

≈

From Individuality to Identity: Directions in the Thought of J. B. Soloveitchik and Eliezer Schweid

Jonathan Cohen

In analyzing patterns of Jewish identity, social scientists attempt, as much as possible, to avoid coloring their descriptions with desiderata that have their basis in personal ideals. Jewish thinkers, on the other hand, whether philosophers, theologians, or publicists, usually base their discussion of Jewish self-understanding on some normative conception of the ideal Jew. Diagnoses of the condition of the modern Jew are undertaken under the aegis of a well-articulated "ought," with reference to perceived notions of "classical" Judaism as well as to what are considered to be the presuppositions of modernity as such. A philosophical or theological treatment of the issue of Jewish "identity," then, while unavoidably proceeding from a culture-bound polemical context, will attempt to link the so-called modern Jew to some transcontextual reality meant to give his life not only rootedness and coherence, but also truthfulness and authenticity.

Two contemporary thinkers, the late rabbi Joseph B. Soloveitchik, until his recent passing the undisputed leader of American modern orthodoxy, and Professor Eliezer Schweid, the noted Hebrew University scholar who has written extensively on the interrelations between Judaism, Zionism, and the Israeli public ethos, have addressed themselves directly to the problematics of Jewish identity for the modern Jew.[1] From a contextual perspective, one could say that Soloveitchik's well-known essay, "The Lonely

Man of Faith" (1964) grows out of a troubled ambivalence toward American technological achievement and its accompanying ethic of success. By contrast, Schweid's less well-known essay, "Judaism and the Solitary Jew" (1974) grows out of the felt contradiction between the willingness of many Israelis to make heroic sacrifices when the very existence of the Jewish state is threatened from without, and their unwillingness to make the effort to infuse their lives with positive Jewish content by way of a serious confrontation with Jewish sources. But both Schweid and Soloveitchik are ultimately concerned with the problem of modern Jewish "identity" writ large, namely, the inability of atomistic and present-oriented consciousness to appreciate the role of community and tradition in the very constitution of self-understanding. As they guide their readers from a perceived point of departure to what each regards as a more comprehensive perspective, their ideas point to, and are shaped by, quite different educational strategies. Both, from diverse points of view, may well enrich the perspective of contemporary Jewish educators.

Significantly, both Schweid and Soloveitchik begin their essays with an account of the "loneliness" of the contemporary Jew. They then proceed to lead the reader, by steps, to an endpoint which, while not offering a permanent or total solution to "loneliness," has the purpose of expanding his or her "I-awareness" such that loneliness is either mitigated or rechanneled. This common strategy, despite the significant differences between the two thinkers even in matters of first principle, makes them compelling candidates for comparative analysis.

Soloveitchik: Individuality and Identity

According to Soloveitchik, the human person's awareness of radical individuality is existential. Proceeding by way of an analysis and interpretation of the first two chapters of Genesis, Soloveitchik (1964: 10–20) points to the Bible's portrayal of the prototypical human being as having been created alone (or as part of an ancestral couple) rather than as part of a primal horde. Soloveitchik's choice to describe the awakening of human self-consciousness by the vehicle of single ideal-types is no mere stylistic conceit. Both Adam 1, the self-asserting conquering hero of Gen. 1, and Adam 2, the sensitive and receptive homo religiosus of Gen. 2, are described in terms of the structure of their individual experience. It is only afterward that Soloveitchik (1964: 20–33) turns his attention to the kinds of relationships and communities formed by each type.

Adam 1, created in the image of God the Creator, is charged with dominion over the earth. His assertiveness consists of the imposition of numerical and geometric constructs on his elusive experience in order to bring it under his technological control. According to Soloveitchik, this type, though active and dynamic, is still ultimately superficial, meaning that he has not yet become conscious of his radical individuality. His sense of existential uniqueness has been covered over by a utilitarian, collective consciousness defined by the common tasks of civilization.

It is no accident, in Soloveitchik's interpretation, that the account of Adam 2 in the Bible is placed after the tale of the creation of Adam 1. This literary succession reflects successive moments in the awakening of human self-understanding in all individuals who have been sensitized to the human predicament. It is at the very pinnacle of their success as creators and conquerors that humans awaken to their existential quandary: no matter how much they might attain dignity in this world by the subjugation of disease, the amelioration of social injustice, or the rational distribution of wealth, they cannot escape the ineluctable fact of their mortality. The point at which the particular individual has been cast into this world, and the unknown point at which he will depart from it, seem arbitrary and inexplicable. One's attention is turned from what Soloveitchik calls the "how" question, which focuses on the operation of the intelligible laws of nature, to the "why" question concerning the very purpose and meaning of being. The individual realizes that he is not really infinitely perfectible, and he becomes a problem to himself. He yearns to know that his ephemeral life has some ultimate worth.

For Soloveitchik, then, Adam 1 has no real, essential "I-awareness." The sense of "identity" offered by the company or by the secular polity cannot redeem the individual from his need for existential adequacy and security. To really be human does not mean to think or produce. It means to be unique and unrepeatable, to know oneself as such, and to seek an anchor in a "true," and not an illusory, collective, and transcendent framework. Although Soloveitchik (1964: 22-23, 27) insists that both the task-orientation of Adam 1 and the introspective posture of Adam 2 are enjoined by the Bible, and are reflected in two innate drives that inform human thought and activity as a whole, it is clear that he values the "depth-perception" of Adam 2 over the "surface-experience" of Adam 1.

Since what makes people unique is existentially more significant than what makes them alike, they find themselves in a situation of "lonely" self-enclosure. The existential confirmation that people so desperately seek can be bestowed only as a gift of God, and this can come to pass only if both God and humans take part in a gesture of mutual self-transcendence. Humans must turn from self-assertion and dominion and allow themselves to be overpowered by God. They must disinterestedly dedicate themselves to norms perceived as coming from without, and take up a posture of service and sacrifice. Only then will God emerge from his transcendent hiddenness and confirm them in their finitude. When this happens, humans acquire a profound security that can then spill over into genuine empathy and solidarity with their fellow human beings.

While this transformation takes place in the personal-existential sphere, it is not unmediated. Neither does the expansion of "I-awareness" to include empathy with other unique human beings occur between all people indiscriminately. The story of Adam's sacrifice of part of himself so that the other might be together with him and opposite him is a story of intimacy and the foundation of family. Furthermore, the mutual self-revelation of the hiding God and hiding human does not take place in some mystical, esoteric realm. It culminates in a normative message, framed in legal-political categories, addressed to a concrete, particular people called upon to realize existential empathy in all areas of its collective life. It is the covenant that establishes the mutual self-transcendence of God and humans beyond the time of its first emergence. It is the Halakha that "objectifies" unconditioned devotion to God and nonutilitarian concern with the condition of other people (Soloveitchik 1964: 35, 38–40; 1986: 66–68).

The mediation of the expanded I-awareness takes place not only "horizontally," by way of institutions of intimacy such as the family and the Jewish community or by more formal institutions like the Halakha, but also "vertically," by way of tradition and sacred history. The "identity" of the Jew consists of an existential "being-together" not only with family and community but also with past and future members of the people. The substance of such a link, moreover, is not exhausted by the sense of a common fate or by the awareness of the role of inheritance in the constitution of personality and consciousness. It involves a moral commitment to the continuity of a tradition that has been bequeathed in trust, as well as a sense of responsibility to transmit the covenantal calling to those who are as yet unborn. The ground of such a commitment derives from a religious dimension that forms an essential component of the identity and self-concept of the traditional Jew. The covenantal tradition is anchored in an encounter between the individual, his fellow and God—the eternal One who makes self-transcendence possible (Soloveitchik 1964: 45–48).

Toward the end of his essay, Soloveitchik (1964: 56–64) raises the issue of the disposition of the modern Jew to respond to the directions opened up by the tradition. At this point it must be clarified, lest our presentation create a kind of optical illusion, that Soloveitchik does not identify Adam 1 consciousness with Western civilization *in toto*; neither does he see the Jewish covenantal community as the exclusive carrier of Adam 2 awareness. "The Lonely Man of Faith" is written with constant reference to the great philosophers and religious thinkers of the Western tradition, whose work is regarded as illustrative of the universal human quest for redemption in the face of the mysterious and the absurd. Furthermore, there are dimensions within the Jewish tradition itself that indicate a distinctive Adam 1 orientation. Certain traditional insights are partially translatable into the universally intelligible thought-categories of the devotee of reason. The Bible and the Halakha both orient the Jew to participation in the civilization and culture of humanity, called by God to dignity and mastery.

The modern Jew, however, is seen by Soloveitchik as intent upon a flight from loneliness to identity by superficial means. He builds communities and institutions aimed at the propagation of religious culture, rather than at the mediation of the sacrificial faith-gesture. Jewish religious and communal life is cast exclusively in the mold of Adam 1. "Active" Jews pray for uplift, attend lectures that "translate" Judaism into the categories of the disciplines and occupations they inhabit, and cultivate "we-feeling" in aesthetically pleasing environments. The emergence of "civil Judaism" in the Diaspora, from Soloveitchik's perspective, would be yet another import from the world of Adam 1, concerned with Jewish dignity in the face of anti-Semitism, and with communal health, welfare, and political status. The contemporary Jew is joined to other Jews through humanly initiated "projects" and is not interested in subordinating himself to demands from without, issuing from the past, which may clash with his drive for what Leo Strauss (1953: 236) has called "comfortable self-preservation."

Soloveitchik is concerned about contemporary Jews falling prey to an incomplete mode of identity, which, when it becomes an exclusive pattern, turns into a kind of one-sided anesthetic togetherness. Even commitment to the community of the covenant, despite the sense of existential rootedness that it provides, does not put an end either to loneliness or to conflict. First of all, the insecurity of finitude is never finally put to rest. Secondly, since one is called upon to function in the "saeculum" of Adam 1 as well as within the intimate framework of the covenantal community, the committed Jew can never entirely be devoted to either. One is therefore never completely identified with, or at home in, either sphere. The contemporary traditional Jew is, and should unavoidably be, in conflict with self and in conflict with fellow Jews. One's rational, legitimate Adam 1 conscience chides one for the sacrificial leap to obedience, while one's Adam 2 conscience tries to tone down the claims of Adam 1 to sovereignty (Soloveitchik 1964: 50-55, 65). One is both "of" the Western world and not "of" it. While one has learned to translate elements of the tradition into the language of civilization and culture, one cannot make one's posture of surrender to God intelligible to those who are unwilling or unable to make the "leap of faith."

The endpoint of the motion of Soloveitchik's essay, then, is not an arrival at rest or fulfillment. True, the Halakha casts its net over the entire saeculum, striving to gather up all areas of human conquest in a comprehensive gesture of offering to God. This drive toward universal sanctification, however, can never be realized fully in an unredeemed world. In the fragmented reality we live in, the identity of the contemporary Jew will necessarily be composite and disharmonious. He will experience varying degrees of alienation from, or loyalty to, the multiple communities within which he is called upon to function.

Schweid: Beyond Contemporary Individualism

Eliezer Schweid (1974: 15-104) gives us a quite different understanding of contemporary Jewish "loneliness," as well as a different route leading out of the confines of individuality. While he shows sympathy for the loneliness of the modern Jew, and undertakes an extensive survey of the historical, social, and intellectual circumstances that have led up to it, he accords virtually no legitimacy to individuality as such. Soloveitchik sees the awareness of radical individuality as a true and fruitful insight; an inevitable and legitimate reaction to the kind of task-oriented cooperation needed to carry forth the divinely sanctioned human guest for technological and sociopolitical sovereignty. Schweid, on the other hand, views it as a mere negative outgrowth of that doubtful quest. He is much more interested in portraying the negative consequences of secularism as the prelude to a retrieval of tradition than in the legitimation of secularity from a traditional point of view, so central to the Orthodox Soloveitchik. Following A. D. Gordon, Schweid presents modernity and technology as having disintegrated the human being's "natural" organic attachments, replacing them with a rights-oriented atomism.

The postulation of autonomy and the primacy of self-realization have created the illusion that individuals begin and end with themselves, both "horizontally" (vis-à-vis the collective) and "vertically" (vis-à-vis the past). The result has been the gradual loosening of ties with family, people, culture, history, literary sources and, ultimately, with the final "context" and the transcendent source of situation: God. True, modern individuals take what they need and choose from the collective and from the past, perhaps even consenting to make restitution, as one would pay a tax. Still, their connection to peoplehood is experienced more as an unavoidable result of external conditions than as an internally affirmed choice.

Thrown back on the self, the individual can and must emerge from its confines by recourse to the most human of resources: reflective understanding and the possibility of free appropriation. Modern thought (beginning with Descartes) attempts to understand and validate the self from within the self. Having established formal existence, however, one may naturally proceed to ask: "Who am I?" It then becomes clear that the borders of the self are too confining to provide an adequate answer. The person becomes aware of herself as having been brought into being from the outside, without concern for one's will. The question of identity—"Who am I?"—is immediately translated into the question of biography and origin— "Where did I come from?" Moreover, human beings have the freedom to participate in the creation of their subsequent biography by choosing their relationships with other individuals, with society, and with the very past they have inherited. The "Who am I" question, then, also involves an orientation to the future, and a concern with questions of possibilities and valued ends. The crystallization of identity entails self-choice and self-affirmation *within the surrounding context* of past circumstances and future opportunity.

Unlike Soloveitchik, Schweid does not attribute a dimension of "otherness" to the faith-experience. Writing for those, like himself, whose biography does not include a priori commitment to sacred sources and to Halakha, he begins with a discussion of recognizably human phenomena, later challenging the reader to uncover the transcendent dimension underlying them. Schweid thus reflects on the successive biographical, social, and cultural contexts that surround and flow into the individual, in concentric circles that extend outward in space and time: family, people (or nation), culture, history, and the literary-normative sources of national culture and history. Each is examined from three points of view: (1) the philosophical clarification of these phenomena in their relation to the individual; (2) the Jewish orientation, as he sees it, to each (based chiefly on an overview of the biblical perspective); and (3) the implications of self-appropriation or self-rejection by the Jewish individual who has become aware of the inescapable influence of these inherited contexts.

Family: The beginning of one's biography is always given from the outside. First and foremost, it is the family that places the individual in the world—as body, through the biologic process of generation, and as spirit, through education in the direction of valued ends. Knowing oneself as so situated, one must have an attitude—positive or negative—toward this family framework which, on the one hand, is informed by parental awareness of the positive value of having children who will then, in turn, establish families of their own, and, on the other hand, by the children's awareness of their parents' role in their very coming into being. In fact, the context of child-raising is one of those areas in which even the staunchest "autonomist" comes up against a sense of a priori obligation that transcends all personal rights.

Initially, Schweid's only "spiritual" presuppositions are those that assume consciousness and free will as features of human action and decision- making, but he moves from here into an account of the biblical and subsequent Jewish traditional understanding of the family. The Bible has no abstract concept of humanity as such; it knows only families, which then proliferate to become families of families (tribes), families of tribes (peoples), and the overarching family of peoples. Without family, the human group turns into an undifferentiated mass, devoid of social and moral order. The Bible even portrays the relationship between God and humanity, and more especially the relationship between God and the people of Israel, as a fatherhood. Whatever the biblical writers sensed of divine creation and providence was distilled from experiences within family, tribe, and people. This view is expressed in the duties incumbent upon parents and children as articulated in the Jewish tradition. The honoring of father and mother reflects the insight that reality and identity are ultimately a gift from one's parents, and this awareness is seen as a basis for the moral personality. The responsibility to educate one's children is viewed as a kind of spiritual parenting.

As Schweid sees it, the formation of individual personality in relation to the family can take place from one of three orientations: (1) indiscriminate imitation of family norms and behavior patterns; (2) wholesale rejection of the family, along with its national and cultural character; or (3) appropriation of the family framework, while undertaking to correct that which is seen as in need of correction and to offer a personal interpretation of the received. In the first case, however, the free, open, creative aspect of the self is rejected, while the second attitude involves a veritable self-contradiction, since the act of wholesale rejection fixates the individual on his origins and closes options for creativity. The most self-affirming option is the third, since it allows for the kind of self-acceptance that can liberate true creativity. Schweid regards the attitude of "creativity in receptivity" (Scholem 1971: 282) as the most adequate human response to the inescapable human situation of freedom in context and as the posture most typical of the Jewish tradition.

Peoplehood: Once one appropriates one's familial origin, however, one finds that this family bears the indelible stamp of the people, or nation, which is both its extension and its carrier. On the one hand, the family is the smallest cell that quantitatively constitutes the nation. It is the model for the people, which is a family of families, and while the relationships between its constituent individuals and families may be more distant, differentiated, and formalized, they retain something of the organic quality of family life—if only because they are based on a shared collective biography and shared forms of life. On the other hand, the family is constituted by national cultural forms. Just as the people "models" the family by being a more all-inclusive, though less intense, version of it, so the family "models" the people, by being a heightened microcosm of obligations, roles, and relationships enjoined by national-cultural tradition.

As a human phenomenon, the people, or nation, like the family, is not merely a matter of biology or collective self-preservation;[2] it is an expression of will, with consciously determined criteria for membership and deviance. Here, too, feelings of intimacy are informed by awareness of the status of the other as partner in a shared history and culture. Schweid's concept of peoplehood, then, is inextricably bound up with his concept of culture. Human beings are just as naturally situated in a network of national- cultural patterns of interaction as they are placed within a family framework. They develop their personalities in interaction with the culture of their people just as naturally as they become who they are within the context of the family. However, just as one is called upon to undertake a critical affirmation of one's family inheritance, so is one called upon to do the same with regard to the cultural ethos of one's people.

In certain respects, according to Schweid Jewish people exhibit the characteristics of any other people. An external glance at the biblical account shows us a family striking out on its own, establishing its own "family of families" that later becomes a people in its own right. The difference between the biblical people of Israel and the other nations lies not in its structure, but in the way it conceives of its destiny. The Israelite extended family has a rich collective biography that serves to give it a sense of unity. Nevertheless, throughout the biblical account, the people of Israel are never finally and completely a unified people; they must choose and rechoose their peoplehood throughout their history. This strange phenomenon of a perpetually unfinished people can only be explained by an understanding of the unique interconnection between the people of Israel and the Torah, the embodiment and record of its covenant with God. The peoplehood of the Jewish people is defined and constituted by its covenantal commitment to realize the Torah. It disintegrates as a people when it is not loyal to the covenant. When the Torah is implemented in the life of the people, the very existence of the people becomes charged with value. The Jewish people "are" only when they realize their "ought."

Another unique and "strange" feature of Jewish peoplehood, according to Schweid, is the way in which universality and particularity are bound together in its covenantal history. The biblical account shows us the God of the world and of all the nations entering into a covenant with a particular people, the realization of which has universal ramifications. The implausibility and seeming ethnocentricity of this claim lies at the root of the enmity that the nations of the world feel toward the people of Israel. It is also the reason why Jews throughout history have wished to deny the covenant and become like all the other nations.

For the contemporary secularized Jew, however, there are additional reasons why the covenantal claim has lost much of its power. First of all, Jews of today, whether they live in the Diaspora or in Israel, can actually assimilate. Second, the aberrations of latter-day nationalism have given national feeling something of a bad name. Third, the growth of technology and telecommunications seem to be leading to a kind of international standardization and leveling, as national distinctions become blurred. Still, says Schweid, nationalism is hardly on the wane, as attested by the powerful resurgence of national feeling in many parts of the world. Furthermore, the international common denominator said to be evolving out of the communications revolution has no real cultural depth or specificity. Schweid insists that a strong sense of national "selfhood" rooted in a particular culture that runs deep is a condition for genuine openness to other cultures. Lonely individual Jews of today can expand their individuality to include not only family, but also nationality, without denying either their pluralism or their universalism.

Culture: A positive affirmation of peoplehood naturally entails the wish that one's people renew itself and not disappear. It is at this point that the modern Jew must choose his or her orientation to national revival. Schweid does not believe that the ideal of Jewish "normalcy" within a national, sovereign framework has the wherewithal, in itself, to ensure even the physical survival of the Jewish people in the face of the option of assimilation. Affirming Jewish uniqueness, however, leads to a confrontation with the problem of the meaningfulness of Jewish culture and Jewish history. The path leading the "lonely" modern Jew out of his or her self-enclosedness turns now from the "horizontal" direction (outward to family and people) and takes up a "vertical" orientation (through culture backward to history and literary sources).

Schweid's definition of the concept of culture replaces what is often understood as a "classic" phenomenon, beheld as a comprehensive work of art or as a storehouse of products, with a lived ethos-in-process: the dynamic crucible of creativity-in-receptivity. It is the shared life of creativity based on a collective spiritual inheritance. Individuals thus cannot sever themselves from the cultural context within which they find themselves. As is the case with the family context, even rebellion against one's cultural matrix is a kind of continuity by opposition. All cultural creativity begins with the active appropriation of creations that have come down from the past (distant or recent), by exposure to which one's personality takes form. Culture, whether in the form of custom, morality, or even scientific methodology, thus has a conservative pull that draws the modern back in time before she or he can take up the task of reapplication to new conditions. The problem is that moderns have difficulty extricating themselves from their present concerns and giving themselves over, if only temporarily, to a phenomenon that seems at first to have no direct bearing on their interests.

History: History, for Schweid, is a dimension constituted by the conscious choices of humans. Human groups have acted during different periods in the past as the bearers of value-aspirations—for example, the gaining of national independence or the rejuvenation of national culture. The present is the future dimension of that past— the arena in which these aspirations are either realized, negated, or modified. It is for this reason that people ascribe value and continuity to those areas of their past deemed worthy of remembrance: if they were to be regarded as having no lasting meaning or teleological direction, one would have to reach the same conclusion with regard to one's life and values in the present. These events or values are lifted out of the past and carried into the future. It is only by such a move that a people with a culture gains an understanding of the direction or meaning of its collective existence over time.

Schweid again turns to the Bible as the model for the teleological orientation to history that was just presented. Pagan mythologies are based on the circular recurrence of natural processes. The Bible, on the other hand, while it exhibits the mythological tendency to amplify events that may or may not have an historical nucleus, provides the basis, in so doing, for a genuinely historical perspective. The "mythological" literary rendering of the plagues of Egypt transmits a message that spirit and will can triumph over the forces of nature and over human tyrants. The people of Israel embarking upon the Exodus from Egypt is the paradigmatic tale of a people undertaking a planned destiny in the light of valued ends to be realized in the future.

The modern Jew now learns to look upon the present state of Jewish culture as either a reflection or a distortion of valued ends that came to be regarded as the "oughts" of Jewish existence in the past. The past becomes a dimension of what Yosef Chaim Yerushalmi (1982) has called "collective memory." Without jettisoning critical historical consciousness, the modern Jewish individual may see herself as continuous with the Exodus from Egypt, carrying that memory into both present and future while determining at each juncture whether the goals of that Exodus have been realized, discarded, or reinterpreted.

Literary sources: Literary sources reflect a people's quest to understand the origins of the abiding conditions of its life. For this reason, they have an essentially "religious" character. They concern themselves with the ultimate rather than with the proximate. They undertake to think through the relationship between history (created and inherited by humanity) and that which conditions the possibility of any history. Ultimate beginnings cannot be empirically described, only metaphysically and axiologically conceived and told as stories inappropriately termed *myths* by the critical historians. These records come to be regarded as sacred literature, seen as the repository of the nation's self-understanding with reference to the final conditions of its history.

The Jewishness of the individual Jew, then, involves a turning to the metahistorical sources of Jewish history. This orientation need say nothing in advance about the fruits of such an encounter. A "source," by definition, is the beginning-point of a process of continuous flow. Its content is open to constant creative reinterpretation, so that it may serve as the basis for a living, dynamic culture. The unity and continuity of the Torah, notwithstanding the diverse worldviews and normative orientations that it incorporates, lies in its being both the story and formulation of the people's covenant with God, as well as the account of its fulfillment or abrogation in different historical settings. As far as the Jewish people is concerned, the status of the "Torah" has accrued to this corpus by virtue of its continuous study as a normative point of departure for the orientation of lived life. In Schweid's (1974: 93) language, "if a person studies (these sources) as one would study Torah, whatever he should derive from them according to his own understanding within the context of his own unique situation—this is Judaism as far as he is concerned." The "Jewishness" of one's commitment is not to be judged by a priori standards of content, whether related to law or to creed. It is to be determined by one's willingness to bring all the questions of one's individual experience and historical situation to the study of the Torah, with the hope that they will be addressed in the present as they were in the past.

Faith: As we have seen, Schweid describes a process of consciousness-raising, during which individuals come to see just how much their very individuality is affected by such "givens" as family, people, culture, history, and the literary sources. They are called upon to choose themselves within these givens, for it is only in relation to these that they can make any personal, creative contribution. It would seem more difficult, however, to awaken contemporary secular Jews to an awareness that they find themselves within a preexisting dimension of faith. How can such a claim be honestly made when these "lonely" Jews of today either deny faith, or perhaps yearn to believe yet insist that they cannot?

The reason why Schweid dares to make the assumption that faith is an innate human disposition, despite the protestations of the ostensibly faithless, has to do with his characterization of faith itself. Faith, for Schweid, is an attitude of "reliance upon" and "trust in." Human beings express an attitude of reliance on a countless number of things in the very course of living. People rely on other people, especially on family and society. In a broader and deeper sense, when people undertake projects of any kind they rely on circumstances continuing to be such that the project has a chance of realization. These expressions of faith derive from an even more comprehensive reliance on, and trust in, life itself. While knowledge and reflection can deepen and mature faith, the primary faith-orientation proceeds from a dimension of immediate experience within which being itself is affirmed. According to Schweid, such an attitude bespeaks an implied reliance on a first carrier or basis upon which life and being rest. It is this attitude that underlies all the more specific manifestations of faith found in human experience. It is trust in the ultimate reliability of such a first source that is known as faith in God.

The "Who am I?" question is raised to its final power through the question "Where do I ultimately come from?" According to Schweid, the approach to this question must be made on two levels: the personal-individual and the communal-historical. On the first level, the individual thinking subject asks the radical question: How is it that I am this reflecting consciousness, here and now? Beyond the question of the beginning of the body or one's contiguity with one's family or people, one asks: what was there before self-awareness? Before the content of memory? What will there be when awareness is no more? The realization that there must be a situator of consciousness is the beginning of faith. Consciousness, however, is never abstract or impersonal. It is always highly personal and directed toward valued purposes. This understanding leads to the further insight that the One who has situated purposeful consciousness must be purposeful as well. There must have been a teleological will that intended that such value-oriented awareness come into being. It is at this stage that God is conceived not as a neutral or mechanical First Cause, but as a Personal Will.

Religious awakening, then, is on the one hand manifestly personal. It is not, however, exclusively personal, as latter-day Protestantism and liberalism would have it. If individuals are irrevocably placed in a context of community and history, then their religious quest for ultimate identity must lead them to a search for the primary origins of tradition and culture. They must reach back to the realm of metahistory or "myth" as embodied in sacred writings. It is there that they are exposed to the first meetings of their chosen community with the Will that has brought it into being and given it purpose. Self-choice within the framework of a community thus necessarily involves confrontation with the religious dimension that stands at the basis of the cultural ethos of that community.

Whatever the external political and social causes for the loss of faith of the contemporary Jew, the question of whether he or she will repudiate or regain it is one that will be decided from within, by the will of the individual and the community. Those who have continued the life of faith must see to it that the religious culture of Judaism addresses the concerns of all Jews. Jewish individuals who have become estranged from Judaism can renew their connection not through an irrational "leap" to an imagined pair of arms waiting on the other side, but through gradual and critical appropriation of the inescapable "media" within which the immanent dimension of faith can be discovered.

Soloveitchik and Schweid: Points of Comparison

Many of the differences between Soloveitchik and Schweid are attributable to their opposing normative orientations to the Jewish tradition. Soloveitchik begins with an a priori commitment to the content of that tradition. Although the motion of his theologizing proceeds "from the bottom up," from the human situation to the possibility of divine response to that situation, his mode of interpretation is from the sources out. While his analysis of the human predicament is heavily influenced by latter-day existentialist thought, his first move, as a traditional Jew, is to derive his understanding of the human condition from an authoritative revelational source—the Torah.[3] Schweid, on the other hand, speaks out of a biographical and communal context within which this a priori commitment to the sources does not hold. In retracing his own steps back to the tradition, and in attempting to lead other Jews of similar background along the same path, Schweid must take his readers through the known before he conducts them into the unknown. They must be led to see the plausibility of positive reconnection with more proximate, "secular" frameworks such as family, people, culture, and history before they can turn to the Torah as the repository for reflection on the ultimate purpose of these frameworks.

Soloveitchik sees an essential gap between peoplehood, culture, and history, on the one hand, and the kind of faith enjoined by the Torah and exemplified by the great biblical and rabbinic personages, on the other. Addressing himself to the committed traditional Jew, he simultaneously rejects that orientation that would insist that the Jew dwell exclusively in some "wholly other" realm and, conversely, tries to wean his subject away from mere pleasant encounters with religious culture. Thus, while civilization and culture, both general and Jewish, are presented as divinely enjoined directions of human motivation in their own right with their own internal rules, they ultimately become a neutral and passive field awaiting infusion by transcendent normativity. The Jew may be active in the cultural world, but she or he expresses Jewishness most particularly through uncompromising exemplification of those untranslatable elements of the faith experience that those who stand outside it can only be arrested by, but can never really understand (Soloveitchik 1964: 51–52, 60–63). Schweid, coming from the other end of the Jewish spectrum, seeks to expand the horizons of the uncommitted Jew to include hitherto unconsidered aspects of his known experience. Instead of typologically distinguishing between culture and faith, then, Schweid proceeds to redefine "culture" and "history" such that they may be converted into media through which the innate human potential for faith may be discovered.

Soloveitchik's faith involves a relinquishing of identity, rather than a fulfillment of identity. In the moment of surrender to God, even the continuity and integrity of the "I-awareness," with all its enmeshments and entanglements, is sacrificed in favor of an unconditional devotion to God's will. This will is experienced as descending upon one from the outside, as something of an invasion, not as proceeding from an inner activity or awareness of humans. For this reason, any possible transition from "religious culture" to true religiosity is portrayed by Soloveitchik as the result of charismatic inspiration rather than gradual internal growth (Soloveitchik 1969: 61, 65–67).

For Schweid, on the other hand, religious faith is a natural outgrowth of the innate human disposition to trust life and affirm being. This attitude is intrinsically relational and proceeds outward to embrace ever-larger parameters. One comes to rely on God by way of a series of more proximate reliances: on family, on people, on culture and its constitutive sources, and on history and its metahistorical presuppositions. The expansion of individuality does not take place under conditions of surrender. One must bring the very contextual fabric of one's individuality to the confrontation with the sources. One must ask all of one's most radical questions, including those proceeding from contemporary Jewish culture and history, which place the very status of the sources in doubt. There is no discrete realm within which a certainty of another order is revealed. While one cannot approach the Torah with advance assurance that one's deepest existential concerns will necessarily be addressed, a prior attitude of trust in one's people, culture, and history may yet yield vindication in the religious realm as well.

Conclusion

I would like to suggest that the community of Jewish educators can learn from the ways in which Soloveitchik and Schweid approach the issue of the expansion of individual identity to include a communal, historical, and transcendental awareness. It would seem that for Soloveitchik, that expansion can take place only by way of a continuing cycle of crisis and alienation. Initial awareness that nature is not innately "friendly" to human survival and development leads humanity to seek to manipulate the environment. Even as they succeed in this venture, however, they realize that they are ultimately mortal and inadequate, and contract themselves in order to receive norms from the outside. At this point, however, the tradition itself challenges Jews to view their context once more as inadequate, to emerge from communal self-enclosure and to take responsibility for developments in the larger community of both noncommitted Jews and civilized human beings. Once there, however, they will inevitably experience a further sense of alienation as they fail in the attempt to communicate the essence of faith-experience to those who do not share their communal intimacy. In an unredeemed world, this cycle of commitment and alienation must constantly be repeated.

Given such a situation, any educational goad to growth must, at some point, concern itself with the raising of consciousness to appreciate the dimensions of crisis. To be sure, circumstances of developmental readiness, communal context, and the dispositions of educators must all figure prominently in decision-making as to the appropriateness of engendering alienation to counteract superficiality. The undermining of hard-won securities can never be undertaken irresponsibly. Still, it would seem that educators taking their bearings from an orientation like that of Soloveitchik would have to see the challenge to complacency as an essential, not accidental, feature of an overall strategy for the cultivation of a mature Jewish self-understanding.

We have seen that Schweid also begins his essay with an account of the "crisis" of contemporary individualism. For Schweid, however, this crisis is not seen as innate to the human condition. Partially explicable as a result of a certain configuration of historical circumstances, it is ultimately remediable by an act of individual or communal will. It is neither cyclic nor necessarily permanent. Schweid is clearly trying, in the rhetorical context of his essay, to challenge any sense of self-satisfaction that the secular Israeli Jew might have. Still, the deliberate heightening of alienation could not be considered an essential component of an educational strategy undertaken along the lines of his thinking. For Schweid, the path from individuality to expanded identity involves the discovery of organic interconnections that were there all the time. Individual alienation and separation from familial, national, cultural, historical, and even transcendent contexts is an unnatural state. The cultivation of a more comprehensive Jewish self-awareness in keeping with Schweid's system would involve not a periodic, guided "uprooting" but rather a gradual enlargement of perspective leading to a recognition of de facto "rootedness."

Unlike Soloveitchik's ideal Jew, Schweid's ideal Jew is not endemically "homeless," wandering from one fragmented framework to another. He comes to the realization, despite unceasing and unrelenting questioning, that he was "at home" in an organic system of interlocking frameworks all along. It is for the educator to cultivate this awareness of enmeshment and to exemplify the preferability of situated creativity to circumscribed self-assertion.

Notes

1. For a critical assessment of the thought of Joseph B. Soloveitchik see Eugene Borowitz (1983). An evaluation of Schweid's views on Jewish culture, as compared with the views of Nathan Rotenstreich, can be found in Yehudit Ben-Chur (1991).

2. In this respect, Schweid's understanding of peoplehood is very different from that of Soloveitchik, who sees the Hebrew term *am* as signifying a cohesiveness born of a perceived threat to physical survival. See Soloveitchik (1975: 87).

3. In Soloveitchik's words: . . . we must determine within which frame of reference, psychologico-empirical or theologico-Biblical, should our dilemma be described. I believe you will agree with me that we do not have much choice in the matter; for the man of faith, self-knowledge has one con-

notation only—to understand one's place and role within the scheme of events and things willed and approved by God, when He ordered finitude to emerge out of infinity and the Universe, including man, to unfold itself. (Soloveitchik 1964: 9)

References

Ben-Chur, Yehudit. (1991) "Tivah shel tarbut yehudit behagutam shel Nathan Rotenstreich ve-Eliezer Schweid." Ph.D. diss. Hebrew University, Jerusalem.

Borowitz, Eugene. (1983) *Choices in Modern Jewish Thought*. New York: Behrman House.

Erikson, Eric. (1962) "Youth: Fidelity and Diversity." *Daedalus* (winter): 5–27.

Scholem, Gershom. (1971) "Revelation and Tradition as Religious Categories in Judaism." In *The Messianic Idea in Judaism*. New York: Schocken.

Schweid, Eliezer. (1970) *HaYachid: Olamo shel A.D. Gordon*. Tel Aviv: Am Oved.

———. (1974) "HaYehudi HaBoded VeHayahadut." (Judaism and the Solitary Jew) In *Hayehudi HaBoded VeHayahadut*. Tel-Aviv: Am Oved, 15–112. An excerpted version in English was published in *Shefa Quarterly* 2, no. 4 (1981): 38–53. All references in this paper are to the original Hebrew essay.

Soloveitchik, Joseph B. (1964) "The Lonely Man of Faith." *Tradition* 6: 5–67. Recently republished as *The Lonely Man of Faith*. New York: Doubleday (1992).

———. (1975) "Kol Dodi Dofek." In *Ish ha-emunah*. Jerusalem: Mossad Harav Kook.

———. (1986) *The Halakhic Mind*. New York: Seth Press.

Strauss, Leo. (1953) *Natural Right and History*. Chicago: University of Chicago Press.

———. (1965) *Preface to Spinoza's Critique of Religion*. New York: Schocken.

———. (1987) *Philosophy and Law*. Philadelphia: Jewish Publication Society.

Yerushalmi, Yoseph Chaim. (1982) *Zachor: Jewish History and Jewish Memory*. Seattle: University of Washington Press.

Chapter 13

❧

Patterns of Jewish Identity Among Israeli Youth and Implications for Teaching Jewish Texts

Asher Shkedi

This chapter seeks to examine patterns of Jewish identity among Israeli youths in their encounter with Jewish texts and to explore the implications of these identity patterns for educational thought and practice. Without demeaning the value of sociological, psychological, and philosophical studies in the field of Jewish identity, it would be helpful to suggest one more direction in the research on Jewish identity. This direction will focus on education and teaching in order to find direct answers to questions that Jewish educators face.

M. Rosenak (1978) suggests a theoretical educational framework for understanding Jewish identity and identification. In his view the educational reality is characterized by tension between the particularistic Jewish tradition on the one hand and universality and modernity on the other (Schweid 1977; Woocher 1986; Liebman & Cohen 1990). In order to portray the options available to the Jew today, Rosenak suggests a typology of responses (Rosenak 1984; Rosenak & Shkedi 1993), each of which is characterized by the attribution of a different meaning to a variety of Jewish phenomena. For example, the significance of Shabbat is not the same for Jews who observe mitzvoth (commandments) or for Reform Jews or for whoever describes herself as secular. Despite these differences, all three are likely to say that Shabbat is important to them.

Culture, according to C. Geertz (1973), consists not only of symbols through which people express themselves (language, deeds, objects, etc.), but of the meanings that people grant to these symbols. Accordingly, it could be claimed that Judaism is a culture that finds expression in a framework of symbols to which Jews give meaning and definition. Through these symbols, Jews communicate and express their life conception (Liebman & Cohen 1990). According to Geertz's approach, it could be said that the role of education in Jewish identity is in dealing with the meaning of symbols, opinions, and phenomena belonging to the Jewish world or those to which the Jewish world relates.

Our study focused on two major questions:

a. What patterns of Jewish identity characterize the perceptions of youths toward Jewish texts in general?

b. What patterns of Jewish identity characterize the perceptions of youths toward a specific text from the Bible?

We conducted interviews with 27 female and 25 male pupils in the upper grades of junior high school and high school in Israel. This population included representatives of three groupings within Israeli society—secular, traditional, and religious, in relative proportion to their distribution within the population. Nine respondents were religious, 15 traditional, and 28 secular. The Haredi (ultra-Orthodox) were not a part of this study.

In order to guarantee the triangulation of data for the purpose of obtaining greater validation and a deepening of understanding, each respondent underwent two interviews (Kirk & Miller 1986). The interviews were conducted according to the ethnographic-qualitative approach (Spradley 1979). They took the form of an open discussion, and the respondent was invited to raise issues as he or she saw fit. The interviews were analyzed according to principles presented by A. Strauss and J. Corbin (1990). These principles emphasize the dialogue between theoretical knowledge and data that arise out of the phenomenon under study for the purpose of building grounded theory. As stated, the conceptual framework proposed by Rosenak (1984) served as a theoretical-conceptual basis for creating analysis tools, but included some significant changes arising out of the interviews themselves.

The first interview was intended to expose the young people's general sense of Jewish identity and their perceptions toward Jewish concepts and Jewish texts. During the second interview, which was more focused, interviewees were presented with a specific text from the Bible and they were asked to explain their understanding of the text:

> Do not rejoice when thy enemy falls, and do not let thy heart be glad when he stumbles, lest the Lord see it, and it displease him, and he turn away his wrath from him. (Prov. 24, 17)

The choice of this text was not accidental. The selected text is short, relatively easy to understand, and does not present complex language problems. The messages it contains were likely to be familiar to the young people. At the same time, the text does not refer to any specific historical and social context and, as such, sounds as if it speaks directly to people here and now. Moreover, the text has two parts—the first part, which gives clear expression to a humanistic idea; and the second part, which refers to a divine source.

Patterns of Orientation

We classified the meanings attributed to Jewish texts by the informants into seven patterns of orientation.

"Distancing" Orientation

Distancing implies perceptions of Jewish symbols and concepts from a standpoint of foreignness and detachment. A total distancing orientation means a lack of self-identification of the person as a Jew, and his or her detachment from the society of Jews. The complexity of Jewish life today is expressed, among other things, by the fact that Jews may express a desire for Jewish identification and existence and, at the same time, may respond to various Jewish phenomena and concepts from the position of distancing.

Against our expectation (Shkedi 1993) only 4 informants out of a population of 52, expressed perceptions toward Jewish texts in general that can be defined as distancing. The picture changed when the respondents were asked to read the selected biblical text and to relate to it. Then 19 respondents adopted a distancing-oriented stance, and expressed distancing and even rejection. Occasionally, respondents expressed distance from the text because of its being Jewish, and it could be that if it had been a general moral story or a folktale of a different people, the attitude might have changed.

> This is a Jewish text . . . the way the page appears, in
> the phrasing, in the shape of the letters. It is unattrac-
> tive. I wouldn't want to touch a text like this. . . . The
> explanation following is ridiculous. The way it is writ-
> ten is really stupid. . . . It connects directly to Judaism
> and to everything related to it—the hypocrisy. . . . The
> whole idea that everything is to do with God is bull-
> shit. . . . (Efrat, 17, secular)

For some, the fact that they did not believe in God, in his existence, and in his active presence in the world, created a barrier between them and the text. In other cases, the text was rejected
because it denies people their freedom of choice.

> . . . It is really ridiculous in some cases. . . . You have
> choices, but if you pick the wrong one, you'll be pun-
> ished, but it's like you have to choose the right way,
> that's what it says, a bit stupid in my opinion. . . . (Li-
> bat, 17, religious)

However, the religious connotations were not solely responsible
for the feeling of distance. Some respondents rejected the text because its message is so trivial that it need not to be said in the name
of God, and need not be studied at school. For others, distancing
took place from texts in which the command seemed to them to be
impossible to fulfill and inhuman.

"Isolation" Orientation

At the other pole of orientation is the isolation response,
namely, the closure of people within the walls of Judaism, an unwillingness to be exposed to and consider opinions whose source is
not Judaism, and the erection of a barrier between themselves and
expressions of a universal consciousness. The barrier is expressed
through the choice of a particular life-style, dress, neighborhood,
severity in certain mitzvoth (commandments), and is most likely to
be found among the *haredim*. Despite the fact that *haredim* were
not part of this study, we found two respondents whose attitude toward the Jewish texts in general and in the selected biblical text
specifically could be defined as isolation-oriented.

The isolation orientation toward Jewish texts was expressed in
the unwillingness to be exposed to deliberations and doubts that
were viewed as dangerous, and that could adversely affect the feel-

ing of wholeness and security. There was also a tendency to attribute the development of events to supernatural powers.

This relationship toward Jewish texts would not accept non-Jewish points of view even if these do not contradict the Halakha (Jewish religious code of law) and the principle of the holiness of the text. Moreover, belief in the holiness of the texts meant that scientific texts that contradict the Torah must be rejected:

> If we define ourselves as Jews, then we must know
> our sources . . . where we came from . . . God created
> me, and not the monkey. . . . The Torah must be rou-
> tine for every one. (Dan, 18, religious)

An additional expression of the isolation perception was the rejection of any and all developmental perceptions of Jewish texts, especially of the Bible, and an acceptance of the fundamentalist perception regarding the notion that "Moses received the Torah at Mt. Sinai":

> I hate it when they say "The writer" . . . wrote the Bible. . . . What
> do you mean "Somebody wrote"? . . . I don't want to believe that
> somebody came and took a pen and wrote it . . . that someone
> made it up in his head. (Itai, 15, traditional)

"Belonging" Orientation

The belonging orientation entails recognition of an actual belonging to the Jewish group to which texts are related, although without any profound obligation to the significance that is supposed to derive from this belonging. This is in contrast to the "distancing" reaction that expresses a perception of foreignness and detachment from the Jewish world, symbols, events, and texts. Nine respondents expressed a position of belonging toward Jewish texts in their entirety, while only two related in a belonging manner to the text from "Proverbs."

> The Bible is our book, just like there is the Koran for
> Moslems . . . I don't believe in anything that is writ-
> ten there, it all looks like a fairy tale to me, they force
> me to read in school and prepare for exams, and
> that's my only contact with it. (Lital, 17, traditional)

The belonging orientation recognizes that Jewish texts have to be known, but not taken too seriously. Belonging did not necessarily imply an obligataion to the messages in the texts. The texts evoked a surface relationship of interlinked attraction and rejection.

At the basis of the belonging orientation was the recognition of a relationship between the respondents and Jewish texts, at the same time that respondents kept a distance from the texts as much as possible. This position accorded a lukewarm meaning, and sometimes even a cold one to the texts. Respondents adhering to this position accepted the texts, but did not study them in depth; while they did not reject the texts, they were not excited by them. The text exists; it is present; it is no more than a fact to be accepted.

"Identification" Orientation

The identification orientation expresses a belonging relationship to the text, but, in contrast to the belonging orientation, here the identification peception is based upon feelings toward the text; something that gives the text meaning. Twenty-one respondents expressed an identification perception toward Jewish texts. Only eight associated an identification perception to the biblical text.

Characteristic of the identification orientation was the use of words of feeling and expressions of emotion: "Very important," "I love," "I respect," "It pleases me," "It's special," "It is connected to me," and more. But we should not be misled—the identification orientation did not mean an encompassing, a priori acceptance of the truth of these texts, and certainly not of their authority.

> Torah is very holy, very important to Judaism, it is the only remnant left to us from the past . . . I respect it very much, I will never throw the Bible onto the floor. The things that are written are very nice. . . . All in all, everything is connected to you . . . but, I don't know, it seems to me very unrealistic, this whole thing, not very tied to us. I don't know if today someone could do hocus pocus and cross the Nile. There are so many miracles and many tales, it's a bit hard to believe in all that. . . . (Malcha, 18, traditional)

The identification perception entails neither deep study nor great consideration of contents, but, rather, a feeling that the texts contain something meaningful. What exactly? It was not always clear. Many young people expressed a sort of sadness, even apology, for the fact they did not read the texts much. Occasionally, this was accompanied by the resolution that the day would come when they would seriously study Jewish texts. This sometimes sounded like things that people say, but do not actually intend to do.

In the case of the text from "Proverbs" the relation of identification often developed because the respondents felt that an encounter between themselves and Jewish texts was not problematic insofar as the texts did not conflict with things that they do, feel, or think. Some pointed to a greater sense of closeness to this type of text than to others that are taught in school.

"Ideational" Orientation

Those respondents with this type of orientation found ideas in the texts that are beyond people themselves, which transcend the immediate and accessible, beyond time and place. These are ideas whose source can be God-like, belief-based, conscience-related, social, and so forth. Only two respondents expressed an ideational perception toward Jewish texts in general while fifteen did so in response to the text of "Proverbs."

Ideational orientation toward Jewish texts implied neither a necessary a priori commitment to abide by them, nor agreement with all the ideational concepts arising out of the texts. However in most instances those respondents who found ideational significance in the texts held in esteem the ideational foundations found there. Many of those adhering to an ideational position expressed a commitment to the ideational message in the text while rejecting any connection to a divine presence.

The ideational perception also sought to examine the extent to which the messages in the text are relevant today—can the ideas in the text really and entirely be applied?—through dialogue with the texts. Emphasis on the ideational significance within the texts was signaled by the beginning of discussion and deliberation rather than by simple, blind acceptance.

> Yes. I once heard that sentence "Do not rejoice when thy enemy falls," I remember. I accept that . . . the idea yes, but I can't say that I'm sure that I could abide by it. Maybe I'd be happy if I were in that position. It happens to me a lot, "Great, another Arab died," when it happens [people] really are happy. Even though I believe that we shouldn't be happy, I'm really

not against Arabs. . . . But still, when I live in my
country and see what is happening here, and how
many are being killed. . . . (Tzili, 18, secular)

Halakic-Theocentric Orientation

Seven respondents related to Jewish texts in a Halakic-theocentric manner; the same number as those who granted Halakic-
theocentric significance to the passage from "Proverbs," though they
were not necessarily the same respondents in both cases. This manner of perception, like the one preceding, focused mainly on the
ideational aspects of these texts. However the Halakic-theocentric
perception regarded God as the sole source of these ideas and placed
ultimate value in the application of the ideas even prior to understanding (or, in the language of tradition, "observing mitzvoth"). In
this view, the Jew is obligated to observe mitzvoth, not only as an
individual, but as part of the Jewish people. The observance of
mitzvoth originates in a command from God, and, as such, is distinct
from observing laws and customs originating in people or society.

The Halakic-theocentric orientation toward Jewish texts implies that the texts as a whole (and not selective parts of them) have
meaning and place obligations upon their readers. Every word is
meaningful, even if people do not always reach the level where they
are able to understand the meaning of things.

> . . . It is a divine thing, and a normal man, or even a
> genius, is not equipped to write it. It is also one of the
> most important things in Judaism, it is a book that
> will sustain the Jewish people. (Roni, 17, religious)

Some emphasized the difficulty in observing the commandment, and in the promised punishment to whomever does not abide
by the commandment as part of the Torah's need to educate.

> This is an improvement in the behavior of man, it is
> the guidance of rabbis who tell us how we are sup-
> posed to behave in a given situation . . . it is not that
> easy to carry it out because it goes against man's
> character . . . but I think that this is one of the things
> that Judaism demands of us—to overcome, go beyond
> man's "yetzer" (inclination). . . . This is achieved
> through prohibitions. (Libat, 17, religious)

Belief is the key concept by which all the poles are joined and that eases doubts: belief in the obligation implied by the texts and in the meaning of the texts even for those people who do not grasp it, or who are unwilling to admit it.

At this point, it is necessary to explain the difference between the Halakic-theocentric and the isolation orientations. The factor common to both these perceptions is the commitment to Jewish law and tradition. However, whereas the isolation perception seeks to isolate Jews within the Jewish world through estrangement from all things that are not part of the tradition, the Halakic-theocentric perception recognizes that the modern era has the potential for many positive ideas and opportunities that do not contradict the Jewish world and the Halakha, and that occasionally even match the ideas of Judaism.

"Developmental" Orientation

The developmental orientation toward the texts uses academic-scientific methods to find meaning in Jewish texts. While Jewish tradition relates to the texts in an a-historic and a-scientific manner, this approach seeks to subject them to criticism like any other product of human creativity. Seven respondents related to Jewish texts in general in a manner that can be defined as developmental, whereas only three related in this way to the text in "Proverbs." The developmental perception views the development within our world from the point of view of people's wants, deeds, talents, and control over the occurrence of events.

> It's stories that are supposed to explain certain phe-
> nomenon, that are supposed to provide background
> for the development of the Jewish people. I believe
> more in the part about science . . . in the theory of
> evolution, how man was created, how the world was
> created. I mean this gives answers more than the
> Bible, which contains many contradictions. (Lior, 18,
> secular)

The developmental orientation toward the texts is dualistic. On the one hand, Jewish texts and the Bible in particular are seen as shapers and recorders of the history of the Jewish people. On the other hand, the texts are seen as the foundations that guided and unified the Jewish people throughout their history, and thus fulfilled a worthy role.

The developmental perception does not necesssarily mean scientific coldness and estrangement. Moreover, in some instances, the "modern" meaning that people apply to Jewish texts may serve as the means by which to develop an emotional feeling toward them. The developmental perception helps the respondents clarify their feelings toward Jewish texts and toward the possibility of exploring their validity today.

Approaches to Jewish Texts

In the following discussion we will first discuss the findings related to perceptions toward Jewish texts in general. Then we will deal with the findings related to perceptions toward the specific text in "Proverbs," through a comparative discussion with the first part. In the final part, we will address possible implications for Jewish education and for the teaching of Jewish texts.

Perceptions of Jewish Texts in General

In order to characterize the patterns of Jewish identity that arise out of this study, we adopt the approach suggested by S. M. Cohen (1991), in his study on American Jewish identity. Cohen distinguishes between two dimensions according to which patterns of Jewish identity can be categorized. The first dimension consists of the commitment toward the content or ideology, and the second dimension, of the commitment to continuity and identity. It appears to us that this distinction is valid in our case as well. The belonging-identification dimension expresses the desire to belong to a Jewish group. The content-based, ideological dimension shows not only a willingness to belong to the Jewish group, but also a willingness to relate to Jewish contents, expressed through ideational, Halakic-theocentric or developmental responses to the texts. The study findings show that the vast majority of the respondents (thirty) related to the Jewish texts in a belonging-identification manner, while displaying no deep, serious attitude toward the content of the texts. Sixteen of the young people related to the texts in terms of content. Only four did not find any meaning in Jewish texts and related to them in a manner showing alienation and distancing. Two youths expressed an attitude of isolation.

Two findings are surprising insofar as they do not meet the expectations that arise from teachers' reports concerning Jewish texts (Shkedi 1993). The percentage of respondents feeling estrangement and distance from Jewish texts was minimal. At the same time, a significant percentage of youths not only expressed a belonging perception, but also twenty-one of them related in a manner that we defined as identification-based; that is, they held an emotional relation toward Jewish texts. It appears to us that we may conclude from this finding that the majority of the youths not only recognized their belonging to a Jewish group, but that they viewed Jewish texts (and especially the Bible, because that is what they are most familiar with) as intimately connected to the group to which they belong. This can be explained by the fact that people belonging to a particular group generally have a tendency to attribute positive characteristics to the group and to what belongs to that group. Such a tendency may be explained by people's need to reinforce their self-image (London & Frank 1987; Horenczyk 1992).

These findings may be placed in their proper proportions when they are juxtaposed with another prominent finding: only 16 of the young people found content-based significance in Jewish texts. These findings must be considered in light of the fact that of all the respondents, 9 were religious and 15 others came from homes in which tradition was observed. These findings would appear to teach us something about the Jewish identity of the majority of the young people interviewed. While most had a clear sense of Jewish belonging and identification, this did not entail deep knowledge of contents.

Research on Jewish identity among the American Jewish population reveals similar findings: less emphasis on Jewish contents, ideology, and mitzvoth, and greater emphasis on the dimension of belonging (Phillips 1991; Cohen 1991, 1988, 1983; Liebman & Cohen 1990). J. Woocher (1986) sees in this trend the creation of a civil religion, whose characteristics are replacing traditional religiousness. According to C. S. Liebman and S. M. Cohen (1990), a similar trend is developing in Israel, albeit manifesting a unique Israeli variation. Thus, the perceptions revealed toward the texts in this study reflect current trends in Israeli society.

The discussion on findings regarding general perceptions would be incomplete without stressing the fact that the young people interviewed were students in Israel where the Bible is a mandatory subject, starting with kindergarten and continuing until the end of high school. Schools place great emphasis on the precise study of the texts, using traditional and modern methods, with an emphasis on messages and values. Moreover, in a study that examined the views of teachers of Jewish texts, all those interviewed said that they viewed the content-based objectives as central goals (Shkedi & Horenczyk 1995). Despite this, less than one-third of the youth-related to the content aspects of the text as a source of identification. This contradiction may be interpreted either as a failure or as a success on the part of the schools. On the one hand, perceptions toward Jewish contents are meager; on the other hand, the majority of the young people did view Jewish texts as a source of identity, albeit from a belonging-identification angle.

Data gathered through qualitative research receive their significance only in relation to the context within which they were gathered (Lincoln & Guba 1985). Thus, we must understand the perceptions of the young people toward Jewish texts within a context in which they were asked to relate their general approach toward Jewish texts. In order to complete the picture, we called for additional perceptions by the respondents, this time regarding a specific text.

Perceptions of the "Proverbs" Text

The meaning that the respondents found in the "Proverbs" text was different from their general perception of Jewish texts. The prominent findings are that 19 youths expressed a perception that can be defined as distancing and alienation as opposed to 4 who expressed this type of perception in the general context, and that only 10 of the young people expressed a belonging-identification orientation toward the specific text as opposed to 30 who expressed this perception toward Jewish texts in a general context. In our view, these findings do not contradict the conclusion that the respondents' perceptions of the texts are for the most part belonging-identification perceptions, in a manner that does not go in depth into the contents. However, when the young people were faced with an actual text, and they were asked to read it and determine a position toward it, they found themselves forced to relate to the content and to determine a content-based position. In this situation, the belonging-identification perception was in confrontation with the specific messages of the text, and in this context the young people's perceptions underwent great differences.

At the same time, the content-based perceptions toward the patterns of identity prevailed: ideational, Halakic-theocentric, and developmental. Twenty-five respondents found content-based meaning in the "Proverbs" text, versus 16 respondents who expressed a similar perception regarding texts in general. The most significant finding was found in the ideational pattern of perception: 15 respondents so perceived the "Proverbs" text, versus 2 who did so regarding texts in general. It could be that this arose because the complexity and the problematics of the text made it more difficult for them to relate to the text on the content-based level.

We shall now attempt to explain the findings in anthropological terms. An anthropological perspective views the process of the encounter between the young people and the Jewish texts as a process of cultural meeting and of the transfer of culture. According to this explanation, every learning process is a process of the internalization of systems of symbols. In the consciousness of all human beings, there is a "dictionary" of symbols that is a consequence of education that they absorb from birth onward. A learning process occurs when new symbols are absorbed within the existing system of symbols, and find their place. A new symbol that links up with existing symbols is easily assimilated and receives meaning in existing contexts in the consciousness (Geertz 1973; Wurtzel 1983). A new text in its symbolic complexities, connects with existing systems of symbols, and finds its meaning within these systems. The fact that people are different in their systems of cultural symbols explains the different responses to the same texts.

The distancing response to the "Proverbs" text can be explained by inner systems of symbols that do not relate to the text and that capture the messages in it as foreign and distant. The idea presented by the text does not coincide with the way in which that person captures the occurrence of events in the world. It should be emphasized that this was not the first time that these young people encountered such texts. Bible study in school had exposed them to many similar texts. Despite this, or despite the educational experience over the years at school during which teachers presented them with research-based or ideational explanations, the text was perceived as strange, distant, unattractive, and irrelevant. L. A. Cremin (1976) pointed out that the influence of educational forces outside the schools, mainly the family and the community, but also the media, is greater than the influence of formal education in school. In this case the influences outside school moulded the cognitive structure or system of symbols of the youths in a manner in which this type of message appears irrelevant.

A similar explanation may clarify the relatively large number of respondents who attributed to the "Proverbs" text ideational meaning. Such meanings are probably absorbed within the symbols existing in the young people's consciousness. It is possible that this text receives meaning in their eyes because of its value-based messages, and is absorbed as such in their consciousness.

The fact that there was no assigning of developmental meaning to the text should come as a surprise. The nonreligious schools offer students secular-modern explanations that are intended to allow them "to live in peace" with texts that express messages of belief and divine presence. This approach is operational in the perceptions of the "Proverbs" text of a small minority of the young people. It appears to us that this point requires further research.

Up until now, the findings have shown that Jewish identity is very complex, and that people can give positive meaning to Jewish texts in one context and negative meaning in another. This conclusion is a key point in our proposals for educational treatment.

Jewish Identity as a Key in the Encounter with Jewish Texts

If the positions of students toward the texts were a priori distancing, we could have attributed this to the failure to teach Jewish texts. The feeling of belonging and the identification expressed by most of the young people toward the world of Jewish texts indicates a much more complex picture.

These findings may suggest that Jewish education that plays on the belonging-identification chord has a chance of being absorbed and succeeding. Accordingly, we can explain the relative success of seminars that deal with issues of Jewish identity and of "roots" programs that have become very popular in the past few years. However, this education angle raises questions. Does this educational direction have the power to offer the depth that should be given to the construction of Jewish identity? An additional question, and perhaps the most important one for our purposes, is whether such an approach contain the answer to teaching Jewish texts. It seems to us that the findings of this study leave doubt in this regard.

Some educators have proposed disconnecting the teaching of Jewish texts from any intent to educate for Jewish identity, and to present these texts as just another subject that a person needs to know and that a school needs to teach. Thus, students will study

Jewish texts and especially the Bible in the same way that they study Shakespeare or the history of the French Revolution. In our understanding, this is not a realistic option. Our study shows that although the teacher can try to present the texts in an objective-scientific manner, they will be absorbed within the cognitive system, in the inner world of symbols, as a Jewish text that belongs to a Jewish group and as a text that belongs to the same group that the young people belong to. That is, the texts are much more "loaded" than any non-Jewish subjects.

The educational direction that we suggest is completely different. Rather than placing the emphasis on the disciplinary meanings of content, or on teaching the texts in a popularistic manner that does not reach depth of contents, we propose, instead, personalization in teaching Jewish texts. The concept of personalization in teaching texts relates to the "self-actualization" concept of humanistic psychology (Maslow 1968), according to which people have an inner tendency to realize, reinforce, and widen their self. G. Horenzyk (1992) points out the inner need to find meaning. These needs are like "inner whispers." When we speak of the personalization of teaching Jewish texts, we mean an educational way that will be directed toward the inner world of symbols of the young people, and that will respond to their needs for self-actualization.

Personalization of study is in fact what those same respondents who found content-based meaning in the "Proverbs" text did. They related to the text because it answered the moral, value-based, questions with which they were preoccupied. They did not ask themselves whether the questions they were asking were those that the writer intended, and they certainly did not ask whether the answers they defined for themselves were intended by the writer. They brought closer to themselves parts of the text that appeared more significant, and gave meaning of one type or another to the parts of the text that seemed harder to accept. The question: "What does the text mean to me?" was at the center of their perceptions. Or in other words, they read the text from their world of symbols and into their cognitive structures. Questions as to the writer's intent or the authenticity of what is written are undoubtedly an essential foundation in teaching Jewish texts. However, as the saying has it: "The `Torah' has multiple interpretations." Certainly, serious knowledge of contents is necessary, but no less so is in-depth knowledge of the students' world and society.

It is possible that the issue calls for considering a change in teaching approach. We must ask: Does frontal, routine teaching have within its power the ability to encourage students to find meaning in the texts? Do centralized mandatory curricula allow for the discovery of meaning in Jewish texts? Is it a realistic option to adopt S. Fox's (1981) suggestion to combine nonformal education with formal education in Jewish education? While this study raises more questions than answers, the findings are significant for Jewish educational deliberation and action.

References

Cohen, S. M. (1983) *American Modernity and Jewish Identity*. New York: Tavistock.

———. (1988) *American Assimilation or Jewish Revival?* Bloomington: Indiana University Press.

———. (1991) *Content or Continuity: Alternative Bases for Commitment*. American Jewish Committee.

Cremin, L. A. (1976) *Public School*. New York: Basic.

Fox, S. (1981) *Is Jewish Education a Bulwark Against Assimilation?* Jerusalem Shazar Library, Institute of Contemporary Jewry, Hebrew University of Jerusalem (Hebrew).

Geertz, C. (1973) *The Interpretation of Cultures*. New York: Basic.

Horenczyk, G. (1992) "The Actualization of Jewish Identity: Research Findings and Educational Implications." In *Studies in Jewish Education*, edited by A. Shkedi. Vol. 6. Jerusalem: Magnes Press, 100–120.

Kirk, J., and L. Miller. (1986) *Reliability and Validity in Qualitative Research*. Beverly Hills: Sage.

Liebman, C. S., and S. M. Cohen. (1990) *Two Worlds of Judaism: The Israeli and American Experience*. New Haven: Yale University Press.

Lincoln, Y. S., and E. G. Guba. (1985) *Naturalistic Inquiry*. Beverly Hills: Sage.

London, P., and N. Frank. (1987) "Jewish Identity and Jewish Schooling." *Journal of Jewish Communal Service* 64, no. 1: 4–13.

Maslow, A. (1968) *Toward a Psychology of Being*. 2d ed. New York: Van Nostrand.

Phillips, B. A. (1991) "Sociological Analysis of Jewish Identity." In *Jewish Identity in America*, edited by D. Gordis and Y. Ben Hurin. Los Angeles: Wilstein Institute, 1–25.

Rosenak, M. (1978) "Education for Jewish Identification: Theoretical Guidelines." *Forum*, no. 28-29; 118–29.

———. (1984) "Jewish Types: Responses and Educational Options." *Jewish Education* 52, no. 2: 19–29.

———. (1986) *Teaching Jewish Values: A Conceptual Guide.* Jerusalem: Melton Centre for Jewish Education in the Diaspora of the Hebrew University of Jerusalem.

———. (1987) *Commandments and Concerns: Jewish Religious Education in Secular Society.* Philadelphia: Jewish Publication Society.

———. and A. Shkedi. (1993) *Jewish Identity and Jewish Existence: Teacher's Guide, A Program for Teacher Workshops.* Even Yehuda, Israel: Reches Publishing House (Hebrew).

Schweid, E. (1977) *A History of Jewish Thought in Modern Times.* Jerusalem: Hakibbutz Hameuchad and Keter Publishing House (Hebrew).

Spradley, J. P. (1979) *The Ethnographic Interview.* New York: Holt.

Strauss, A., and J. Corbin. (1990) *Basics of Qualitative Research.* London: Sage.

Shkedi, A. (1993) "Teachers' Workshop Encounters with Jewish Moral Texts." *Journal of Moral Education* 22, no. 1: 19–30.

———. and G. Horenczyk. (1995) "The Role of Teacher Ideology in the Teaching of Culturally Valued Texts." *Teaching and Teacher Education* 11, no. 2: 107–17.

Woocher, J. (1986) *Sacred Survival: The Civil Religion of American Jews.* Bloomington: Indiana University Press.

Wurtzel, Y. (1983) "Toward an Applied Antropology of Jewish Education." In: *Studies in Jewish Education*, edited by B. Chazan. Vol. 1. Jerusalem: Magnes Press, 23–38.

Chapter 14

A Social Constructivist Approach
to Jewish Identity

Gabriel Horenczyk and Zvi Bekerman

Identity

The growing importance and use of the term *identity* in scientific and lay discourse have not diminished its vagueness. As stated figuratively by G. M. Breakwell, theorizing about identity is "like traversing a battle-field. Though strewn only with the debris of unconsolidated thought rather than unexploded shells, it is no less deadly" (Breakwell 1986: 10). Serious conceptual and methodological problems also affect the study of ethnic and national identities (Lange & Westin 1985). Reviews of research on ethnic identity within social and developmental psychology (Liebkind 1992; Phinney 1990) portray a wide, rich, but often confused picture of theories, methodologies, and findings. This state of affairs has been attributed in part to insufficient interaction between the various disciplines engaged in the study of national and ethnic phenomena, and a crossing of disciplinary boundaries—mainly psychology, sociology, and anthropology—would seem to be necessary in order to achieve a comprehensive understanding of ethnic identity processes (Liebkind 1992).

Jewish identity fares no better than other ethnic and national identities. As indicated by H. S. Himmelfarb (1982) and by S. N. Herman (1989), during the last decades there has been a major shift from the early study of identity (exemplified by investigations such as D. Elkind's [1967] analysis of children's conception of Jewishness from a Piagetian developmental perspective) to studies of Jewish identification and involvement. This shift is partially attributable to ideological and disciplinary imperatives. C. S. Liebman (1973) claimed that the focus of early studies on identity stem from a concern for integration, while more recent studies are mostly concerned with survival. Himmelfarb (1982) related the shift to the fact that sociologists have taken over what psychologists used to do in the past. Overviews of research on American Jewish identity and identification (Phillips 1991; Schoenfeld 1991a, 1991b) seem to agree on the need to develop better and more varied theoretical and methodological approaches. Although a strong call for the adoption of more interpretative paradigms has been voiced—not only by researchers with anthropological backgrounds (e.g., Bekerman 1986; Schoenfeld 1991b) but also by scholars with a more traditional sociological orientation (Cohen 1988; Phillips 1991)—still the most renowned and influential work on Jewish identity is based on survey research (Cohen 1983, 1988; Herman 1989; Sklare & Greenblum 1979). It has been claimed (Schoenfeld 1991a), however, that although these studies have provided us with much data regarding Jewish behavioral and attitudinal patterns, most of them are not based on solid conceptual frameworks and have not kept pace with new developments in the social sciences.

In light of this, we propose to approach the study of ethnic and national identity in general, and of Jewish and Israeli identities in particular, in terms of the meanings people assign to the stuff of daily social and cultural reality in which ethnicity and nationality are embedded. This orientation calls for interpretative methodologies that allow for the discovery of meaning from within the personal, social, and primarily the cultural worlds of the individual (Bruner 1995). A step in this direction has been taken by the sociologist Steven Cohen (1991), who included in his comprehensive survey of Jewish attitudes items dealing with the meanings attributed by the respondents to Jewish celebrations and holidays.

Social Representations and the Study of Jewish Identity

Recently, the theory of social representations conceived by S. Moscovici (1984, 1988; see also Flick 1995), which is grounded in a social constructivist orientation and advocates the use of interpretative methodologies, is attracting increasing interest among social psychologists, primarily from European countries. Since concepts and methodologies associated with this approach have inspired much of our research, let us describe it in some detail. This discussion will emphasize those central aspects of social representations theory that are highly relevant to the social constructivist study of Jewishness and Israeliness.

Unlike the increasingly individualistic orientation of traditional social psychology, social representations theory locates the individual in the social and cultural context, with heavy emphasis placed on the social anchoring of psychological processes. Social psychology, in Moscovici's (1984) words ". . . is above all an anthropological and historical science." Although Moscovici himself has purposely remained uncommitted to any precise, and therefore limiting, definition of social representations, elsewhere they have been described as shared cognitive systems that originate in everyday social interaction and furnish individuals with a commonsense understanding of their experiences in the world (Hogg & Abrams 1988). Social representations are social in the sense that they are collectively created and collectively maintained, they facilitate and regulate social interaction, and play a major role in the formation and development of social groups (Ibañez 1988). Although the notion of social representations has not been received without criticism (e.g., Jahoda 1988; Parker 1987), Moscovici's ideas have generated fruitful theoretical and empirical developments (see, e.g., Breakwell & Canter 1993).

Social representations theory studies epistemological and cognitive processes at two levels: the interpersonal and the explicitly collective (Moscovici 1988). This social emphasis is akin to paradigms in the field of social constructivism rooted—inter alia—in cognitive studies within sociology and psychology. This approach in sociology seeks to apply phenomenological philosophical ideas to the arena of social life. From an ethnomethodological standpoint, for example, A. Schutz (1970) claimed that intentional acts are not purely individually constructed, but are socially constructed as well. Within the field of psychology, similar propositions were put forward by L. S. Vigotsky (1986), who, departing from the Piagetian framework, shifted constructive processes from the individual mind to the social arena. Vigotsky suggested a strong relationship between the social interactional modes in any culture and the psychological functions of its members, in other words, between culture and cognition.

As for the ways by which social representations are generated, Moscovici highlighted two central, intertwined functions: objectification and anchoring, both of which serve to make the unfamiliar familiar. Objectification allows the representation to become a concrete part of our recognizable world; it effects the "materialization of an abstraction" (Moscovici 1984: 38). Anchoring relates to the ways in which social representations become inserted in their social and cultural backgrounds and structures. This process is rooted in the social sphere; it is from within the shared ideas of a social group and its language that we encounter the first strides toward making the strange familiar.

We would like to suggest that the social representations approach, with its social constructivist orientation and its emphasis on the processes of social and cultural anchoring, can provide us with a renewed theoretical, conceptual, and methodological framework for the study of variations in ethnic or national identity in general, and Jewish or Israeli identity in particular. As indicated by Moscovici (1993), Jewishness can be understood as a social representation, and it therefore may be studied as such. In this chapter we propose to explore the meanings ascribed to Jewishness and Israeliness within the broader context of the social representations of Israeli "culture" or "society." We assume that, for Israelis and Jews living in Israel, the meanings assigned to Jewishness and Israeliness are closely related to the meanings given to other main components of their social and cultural worlds. Moreover, the meanings of each of the elements emerge out of the networks connecting them within the broader context of culture and society. These contextualized and socially construed meanings are what we are after. Our long-term goal is the comprehensive and contextually sensitive mapping of these social and cultural fields, which will eventually show us where, when, and how, Israeli Jews see their Jewishness and their Israeliness.

In the following sections: (1) We present the "associations grid" as a research tool for investigating the associative meanings attached to ethnic and national concepts. (2) We propose the use of Multidimensional Scaling conceptualization and methodology for describing the anchoring of these terms in diverse cultural and social backgrounds. (3) We introduce a constructivist dimension of ethnic or national identity (in our case Jewish or Israeli identity), namely, the extent to which this identity plays a role in the person's construing of his or her social and cultural worlds. Examples from two studies will help us clarify and illustrate these ideas.

Since our theoretical propositions are closely tied to the methodology employed, we will have to describe our research methods in some detail. As indicated earlier, the social representational approach can offer not only an appropriate theoretical and conceptual framework, but it can also provide us with methodological perspectives that are better suited to our research interests. While much of the research on social representations has employed qualitative strategies, an increasing number of studies have opted to describe the structure and contents of social representations employing quantitative methods (Breakwell & Canter 1993). However, the use of these methodologies is primarily descriptive and interpretative, making the traditional distinction between quantitative and qualitative research orientations inappropriate within the context of the social representations perspective (Purkhardt & Stockdale 1993).

Jewishness and Israeliness Within the Social Representation of "Local Culture"

In one of our studies, we adopted quantitative methodologies with the aim of partially mapping the representational field of the Israeli "local culture"; in other words, these methods were aimed at revealing the internal organization of the various components of Israeli culture. In the first stage of the study we asked a small number of respondents to supply associations to various concepts central to the Israeli cultural world (e.g., Israeli, Peace, Arab, Secular, and Judaism). Based on these free association responses, we created an "associations grid." Each of the cultural concepts was placed on a row, and thirty-five of the associations (e.g., "old," "nice," "traditional," and "mine") were located in the columns. This grid was presented, in the second phase of the research, to high school students from various Israeli subpopulations ("Secular," "Religious," newcomers from the former Soviet Union, etc.). Each student was requested to check the words or expressions (columns) which he or she associates with each of the concepts (rows).

The responses to the "associations grid" provided us with rich data that enabled the mapping of variations in the structure and in the content of the social representation of "local culture" among diverse subgroups of Israeli youths. As just indicated, we were especially interested in the locations assigned to aspects of Jewishness and Israeliness within the representational field of "local culture."

Our interpretative efforts followed two main paths, each utilizing a different technique of data analysis—namely, Multidimensional Scaling and Correspondence Analysis. In this chapter we concentrate on the first of these approaches.

MDS (Multidimensional Scaling) techniques (Kruskal & Wish 1978) allow different stimuli to be located along a multidimensional space by preserving the relations of distance between them. For example, if we choose eight Israeli towns from different parts of the country and provide the computer with the distances between each pair of them, a MDS program will produce a spatial display closely resembling the map of Israel. In order to map the representational field of the Israeli local culture among our respondents, we computed a distance measure (like the distance between every two cities in our previous example) between each pair of the cultural concepts included in the grid. Since we were interested in the associative meaning attached to the concepts, we followed B. E. Garskof and J. P. Houston (1963) who suggested that the meaning similarity of two concepts is a function of the number of associations that these concepts have in common. Let's say, for instance, that in the response sheet of one respondent we find that Secular and Israeli have twenty associations in common, while Secular and Judaism have only seven common associations. In this case, we will infer that for this subject Secular is more similar (in terms of associative meaning) to Israeli than to Judaism. In his or her representational map, therefore, Secular will be located closer to Israeli than to Judaism. For each respondent, we thus computed Ellegard's association indexes[1] (Doise, Clemence, & Lorenzi-Cioldi 1993) between each pair of concepts, and constructed a similarity matrix between all the concepts included as rows in the association grid.

These matrices were then subjected to Multidimensional Scaling, which provided us with "representational maps" reflecting the patterns of similarities and dissimilarities in associative meanings between the cultural concepts. Since our sample was purposely heterogeneous, we analyzed the data of each of the subgroups separately (a "points of view" approach; see Tucker & Messick 1963). A close inspection of the two-dimensional maps obtained for the different groups revealed interesting differences in the location of words connected to Jewishness and Israeliness within the cultural representational field. Figures 1 and 2, for example, depict the MDS maps of the "secular" native Israeli respondents and of the newcomers from the former Soviet Union.

Fig. 1. Two-Dimensional Representational Map of "Local Culture"—
"Secular" Respondents

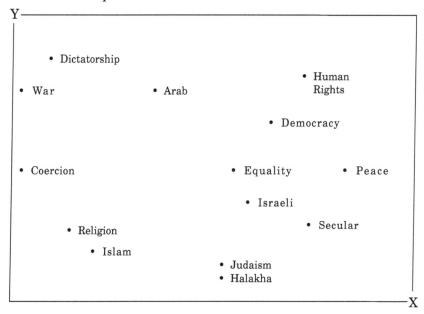

Fig. 2. Two-Dimensional Representational Map of "Local
Culture"—Immigrant Respondents

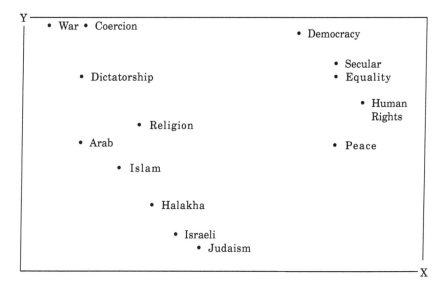

The map in figure 1, although derived only from secular Israeli Jews, appears to reflect the social and cultural struggle taking place in modern Israel between the subgroups of Israeli society over the meaning of Jewishness and Israeliness. As pointed out by R. Paine, this conflict represents an attempt to constitute Jewish and Israeli identity in Israel; " antagonistic versions of these identities become bastions of ideology" (Paine 1989: 123). In another study conducted among secular and religious Jewish adolescents in Israel (Horenczyk & Bekerman 1996), we showed the complex ways in which the social representations of Jewishness and Israeliness are structured by different segments of Israeli society so as to serve the group's purposes in the ideological struggle. As suggested by G. M. Breakwell, social representations are ". . . rhetorics used by groups to engender cohesiveness and maneuver relative to other groups" (Breakwell 1983: 199).

It would seem that our secular respondents sharply differentiate between their Jewish and Israeli identities. The positioning of Israeliness together with other universalistic Western values, which are positively regarded within national democratic societies, reflects the secular view of national Israeli identity as part of the Western culture and perspective that has been adopted and is cherished. The specific national identity, Israeli, is a particular one; but, as poignantly stated by M. Billig "the way 'we' assert 'our' particularity is not itself particular. 'We' have a history, identity and flag, just like all those other 'we's. In this, 'we' (whichever national 'we' is to be proclaimed) speak (or imagine ourselves to speak) a universal code of particularity" (Billig 1995: 72). Jewishness, on the other hand, is strongly connected to Halakha (Jewish Law), and both are left out of the universalistic Western cluster, thus exemplifying the internal dialogue between the Jewish and Israeli subidentities. In this struggle, the secular Israeli seems to ascribe a religious meaning to Jewishness and to locate it close to other religious constructs (such as Religion and Islam), thus creating a "religious other" with whom the argumentation is being carried. But a close inspection of the map also shows that Jewishness becomes part of the secular's "own" within the context of the political struggle. Jewishness joins the ranks of "us" (secular Israelis) located at the right of the map; the "political other" (at the left) is now composed of Arabs and Islam. This configuration thus portrays the complex nature of Jewish identity, with its multiple meanings each activated within its specific argumentative context.

In sharp contrast to this pattern, ethnic, national, and religious concepts appear quite undifferentiated on the map obtained from the immigrant respondents: Judaism, Israeli, and Jewish Law emerge closely arranged, and not very far from Islam and Arab, yielding a "particularistic" cluster located near the "negative" side of the map (also occupied by a cluster of negatively valued terms such as *Dictatorship* and *War*). This "neighborhood interpretation" (Kruskal & Wish 1978) of MDS maps, that is, the identification of "clusters" or differentiable areas within the dimensional space and the comparative examination of their contents, allows for the study of the objectification of ethnic and national concepts and of their anchoring in the various cultural and social backgrounds. This approach may aid us in the understanding of the different meanings attached by subgroups of the Israeli society to aspects of Jewishness and Israeliness, thus shedding light on social and cultural variations in the construal of Jewish and Israeli identities.

The quantitative study of social representations tends to emphasize another type of interpretation of spatial configurations, and we believe that this approach can be of great value in the understanding and assessment of ethnic and national identity. This strategy focuses on the meanings that can be attributed to the underlying dimensions that emerge from the MDS calculations. For example, in our preliminary study on the social representations of local culture, we examined the items located on both sides of each of the dimensions underlying the representational field. For most of the subgroups, the horizontal axis could clearly be interpreted as an "evaluative" dimension (good-bad), and the vertical axis could generally be understood as reflecting a "universalistic-particularistic" dimension. We may therefore suggest that individuals tend to construe their "local culture" in terms, or by means, of these two dimensions.

The "Constructivist" Dimension of Ethnic and National Identity

Recently, social representations have been conceptualized by Willem A. Doise as "reference points in relation to which individuals position themselves according to specific social experiences they share with other individuals" (Doise, Clemence, & Lorenzi-Cioldi 1993: 155). In other words, while a culture as a whole may offer its members a number of tools for construing a certain representational field, different individuals (and different subgroups) will make differential use of these tools. Within the framework of Multidimensional Scaling, the INDSCAL (Individual Differences Multidimensional Scaling) method fits this notion well. It assigns each respondent a weight on every dimension. This weight "indicates the salience or the importance of the dimension for the individual . . . the weight indicates the extent to which an individual uses the dimension in his/her judgments" (Doise, Clemence, & Lorenzi-Cioldi 1993: 92). When the dimension can be interpreted as an ethnic or national identity, the individual weights may help to measure the constructivist aspect of the identity just suggested, namely, the extent to which the individual uses the identity for construing his or her social and cultural world. In order to illustrate this approach, we will briefly describe another study dealing with patterns of ethnic and national identity among high school immigrants from the former Soviet Union.

Using a different MDS technique for eliciting data, we obtained a bidimensional graph in which twelve social categories (a nonreligious Israeli, a religious Israeli, an Ethiopian immigrant, a Jew who stayed in Russia, the respondent herself, etc.) were located. This representational map is displayed in figure 3.

Fig. 3: Two-Dimensional Representational Map of "Social World"— Russian Immigrants

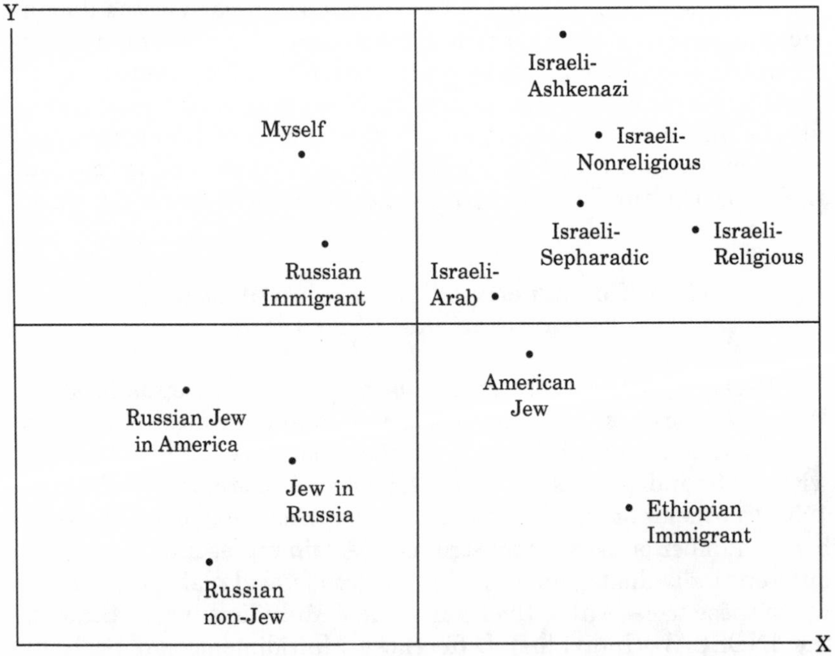

The internal interpretation is straightforward. The horizontal axis (the "Russian" dimension) opposes "Russians" (Russian immigrant, Russian Jew in America, Russian non-Jew, Jew in Russia, and "myself") on the left to non-Russians on the right. The vertical dimension can be labeled "Israeli": it makes a sharp distinction between people living in Israel (religious and nonreligious, Ashkenazi [from European origin], and Sephardic [from Oriental origin], Israeli Arabs, and "myself") with those (Jews and non-Jews) living outside Israel (except for the Ethiopian immigrant). However, not all newcomers are assumed to use these dimensions to a similar extent, and the INDSCAL method provided us with individual weights, reflecting the salience of these dimensions in the personal construal of each respondent. Subsequent analyses revealed some interesting findings; for example, the weight on the Israeli dimension was positively correlated with the number of Israeli friends: immigrants who report having more Israeli friends tend to differentiate more between Israelis and non-Israelis (with themselves included in the Israeli group) than more "isolated" immigrants. The weight on the "Russian" constructivist dimension was found to be negatively related to assimilation attitudes; in other words, Russian immigrants who use this dimension to a greater extent (i.e., distinguish more between "Russians" and "non-Russians," with themselves included among the Russian group) tend to show less willingness to assimilate into Israeli culture (Horenczyk, in press).

We have termed this use of the Russian and Israeli dimensions for the construal of the social world the *constructivist* aspect of the Russian and Israeli identities. Most of us are familiar with the two dimensions of Jewish identity proposed by S. N. Herman (1989)—centrality and valence. The Jewish identity of an individual is central when it affects a wide range of behaviors and attitudes; valence refers to the individual's positive or negative attitude toward his or her Jewish identity. We would like to suggest that the "constructivist" aspect of Jewish identity introduced in this chapter is analytically, methodologically, and empirically distinguishable from centrality and valence. Most of us are familiar, for example, with Jewish people who would score low on most attitudinal and behavioral scales of Jewish identification but who nevertheless tend to categorize people (or ideas) around them in terms of Jew or Gentile. We could characterize the Jewish identity of these individuals as low in centrality but high in "constructive use." And another example of this pattern: In an exploratory study on identity changes following migration, U. Ta'ir (1993) noted that many Russian Jews—who showed

almost no behavioral or attitudinal expression of Jewish identity—
used to wait at the movie theater for the credits at the end of the
film in order to look for Jewish names among the producers and
actors.

A study recently completed shows that this constructivist (or
categorizing) use of Jewish identity is related to the importance attached to this identity. Using the "associations grid" methodology
just described and the INDSCAL procedure for analyzing the data,
we classified each respondent as "high" or "low" in constructivist use
of Jewishness—the extent to which he or she distinguishes between
Jews and non-Jews in the construction of his or her social world. In
addition, we classified respondents as "high" or "low" in centrality of
Jewish identity—the extent to which Jewishness is expressed in behavior (in our study, primarily in Jewish ritual behavior). Three
groups clearly emerged from our data: respondents who scored high
in both centrality and constructivist use, respondents who scored
low on these two dimensions, and a third group of respondents who
showed low levels of centrality but high degrees of constructivist or
categorizing use of Jewish identity (almost no respondents fell into
the theoretically possible fourth category—high in centrality but
low in constructivist use). Subsequent analysis showed, as expected,
that respondents who scored high on centrality (and therefore also
high on constructivist use), attached high the importance to their
Jewishness, while those who scored low both on centrality and constructivist use tended to attach little importance to their Jewish
identity. However, constructivist use was also related to the importance of Jewishness: the respondents in our third group, those who
don't express their Jewishness in daily behavior but who still categorize their social worlds along Jewish/non-Jewish lines, scored
high in importance of Jewishness, almost to the same degree as
those who were also high in centrality of Jewish identity. This group
may represent a relatively wide range of Jewish individuals in different parts of the world, among them those Russian Jews at the
movie theaters described by Ta'ir (1993).

This notion of the constructivist use of Jewishness seems to us
to be thus increasingly relevant for the understanding of modern
Jewish identity. Many of us feel quite helpless and hopeless when
confronting the identity of the "marginally affiliated Jews" (Cohen
1991) armored with the centrality and valence dimensions alone.
Michael A. Meyer (this volume) quotes Magnes who wrote about
"seeing through Jewish eyes." Our notion of the constructivist use of
Jewishness may be part of that Jewish sight.

Conclusion

What are the origins and antecedents of this constructivist dimension of ethnic identity? What are its attitudinal and behavioral consequences? What are the educational implications of this notion and its broader social constructivist framework? In this chapter, we have presented a preliminary sketch of ideas and research findings that may assist in the development of a social constructivist approach to the study of Jewish identity and its cultural variations. In spite of being quantitative, our interpretative methodologies have assisted us in showing Jewish and Israeli identities as social products, taking shape within the broader context of the social representations of Israel's culture and society. The MDS maps describe the meanings assigned to Jewishness and Israeliness as closely related to the meanings given to other main components of the cultural and social worlds among Israeli subgroups. In a sense, as argumentative products within the many voices and conceptual understandings of Israel's communities, Israeli and Jewish meanings emerge through a dialogic act in the context of other socially construed meanings.

If indeed Jewishness and Israeliness are structured to a considerable extent by different subgroups of Israeli society by dialogic maneuvers relative to other groups, we have to ask ourselves which educational strategies and methods can reflect, encourage, and support efforts toward building and strengthening Jewish and/or Israeli identities. We believe that when moving from a perception of these types of concepts as qualities of mind toward an understanding of them as argumentative dialogic social products, we will have to reconsider both our views regarding the possibility of cultural transmission and our perspectives regarding the nature of curricular development geared toward the support of identity development.

We believe that steps toward the improvement of current educational realities regarding identity development could be facilitated by the inclusion of pedagogies that would sensitize youths to the dialogic nature of cultural processes and attune them to a careful listening and managing of the multiple voices emanating from continuously emerging and developing social contexts (Bekerman & Silverman, in press). Such approaches might encourage youths to explore their own biographical narratives (and those of others), to look in them for accounts in which Israeliness and Jewishness are articulated, argumentated, and appropriated.

Jewish and Israeli identities were conceptualized and operationalized in this chapter as being closely related to individual and social constructions of culture. Such a discourse that creates strong connections between identity and culture may also add to the reviewing, and renewing, of our educational approaches. Curriculum becomes then a cultural topic (see Giroux 1994) and not an isolated tool for the creation or strengthening of identity. A cultural understanding of curriculum means, however, much more than just choosing a cultural focus or the preferred cultural values according to present historical constrains; cultural sensitivity toward curricular development implies the conceptualization of curriculum and its repositioning within the given context of social relations, which encompass the pragmatics of those same relations and the interaction of those with the social institutions in their sociohistorical context. The opening of a window through which our students could be able to seriously reconsider themselves and their narratives contextualized in the complex dynamics of institutional and social life within a sociohistorical perspective might help inject new life into our educational enterprise.

In a similar vein, Z. Lanir (1993), after criticizing current curricular efforts to teach value concepts (more specifically, democratic values), suggested that curricular development should direct participants toward "reflective construct thinking" so as to make conscious their own construct system and their social field of representation. This claim follows a well-established line of thought within the philosophical hermeneutical tradition (Gadamer 1976). We believe that our work may contribute both to the justification as well as to the development of such an approach in the area of multicultural, ethnic, and Jewish education.

But immediate practical, applied, objectives are not our only goals. On the methods for exploring social representations, S. Moscovici (cited in Hammond 1993) said: ". . . One should judge them not by 'what can be done with them' but 'what can be thought with them.' " We would like our work to be judged in the same light.

Notes

1. For any two rows, this index was calculated by dividing the number of associations common to both rows by the square root of the product of the number of associations checked for each of the rows.

References

Bekerman, Z. (1986) "The Social Construction of Jewishness." Ph.D. diss., Jewish Theological Seminary, New York.

————, and M. Silverman. (in press) "Are Non-observant Israeli Jews 'Hebrew-speaking Goyim'? Cultural Constructivist Perspectives." *Journal of Jewish Education*.

Billig, M. (1995) *Banal Nationalism*. London: Sage.

Breakwell, G. M. (1986) *Coping with Threatened Identities*. London: Methuen.

————. (1993) "Social Representations and Social Identity." *Papers on Social Representations* 2, 198–217.

————, and D. M. Canter, eds. (1993) *Empirical Approaches to Social Representations*. Oxford: Oxford University Press.

Bruner, J. (1995) "Meaning and Self in Cultural Perspective." In *The Social Self*, edited by D. Bakhurst and C. Sypnowich. London: Sage, 18–29.

Cohen, S. (1983) *American Modernity and Jewish Identity*. New York: Tavistock.

————. (1988) *American Assimilation or Jewish Revival?* Bloomington: Indiana University Press.

————. (1991) *Content or Continuity? Alternative Bases for Commitment*. New York: American Jewish Committee.

Doise, W., A. Clemence, and F. Lorenzi-Cioldi (1993) *The Quantitative Analysis of Social Representations*. Translated by Julian Kaneko. Hertfordshire: Harvester Wheatsheaf.

Elkind, D. (1967) "The Child Conception of His Religious Denomination: I. The Jewish Child." In *The Psychodynamics of American Jewish Life*, edited by N. Kiell. New York: Twayne 197–216.

Flick, U. (1995) "Social Representations." In *Rethinking Psychology*, edited by J. A. Smith, R. Harre, and L. Van Langenhove. London: Sage, 70–96.

Gadamer, H. G. (1976) *Philosophical Hermeneutics*. Translated by D Linge. California: University of California Press.

Garskof, B. E., and J. P. Houston. (1963) "Measurement of Verbal Relatedness: An Idiographic Approach." *Psychological Review* 70, no. 3: 277–88.

Giroux, H. A. (1994) *Disturbing Pleasures: Learning Popular Culture.* New York: Routledge.

Hammond, S. (1993) "The Descriptive Analyses of Shared Representations." In *Empirical Approaches to Social Representations*, edited by G. M. Breakwell and D. V. Canter. Oxford: Oxford University Press, 205–22.

Herman, S. N. (1989) *Jewish Identity: A Social Psychological Perspective.* 2d. ed. New Brunswick: Transaction Books.

Himmelfarb, H. S. (1982) "Research on American Jewish Identity and Identification: Progress, Pitfalls, and Prospects." In *Understanding American Jewry*, edited by M. Sklare.

Hogg, M. A., and D. Abrams (1988) *Social Identifications.* London: Routledge.

Horenczyk, G. (in press) "Conflicted Identities: Acculturation Attitudes and the Immigrants' Construction of their Social Worlds." In *Language, Identity, and Immigration*, edited by E. Olstein and G. Horenczyk. Jerusalem: Magnes Press.

———, and Z. Bekerman. (1996) "Ascription and Culture in the Social Representation of Ethnicity and Nationality," Manuscript submitted for publication.

Ibanez, T. (1988) "Representaciones Sociales, Teoria y Metodo." In *Ideologias de la Vida Cotidiana*, edited by T. Ibanez. Barcelona: Sendai, 15–80.

Jahoda, G. (1988) "Critical Notes and Reflections on 'Social Representations.' " *European Journal of Social Psychology* 18: 195–209.

Kruskal, J. B., and M. Wish. (1978) *Multidimensional Scaling.* Newbury Park, Calif.: Sage.

Lange, A., and C. Westin. (1985) *The Generative Mode of Explanation in Social Psychological Theories of Race and Ethnic Relations.* Stockholm: Center for Research in International Migration and Ethnic Relations.

Lanir, Z. (1993) "Educating for Democratic Behavior in an Intercultural Context." *International Journal of Intercultural Relations* 15: 327–43.

Liebkind, K. (1992) "Ethnic Identity—Challenging the Boundaries of Social Psychology." In *Social Psychology of Identity and the Self-concept*, edited by G. M. Breakwell. London: Surrey University Press, 147–85.

Liebman, C. S. (1973) *The Ambivalent American Jew.* Philadelphia: Jewish Publication Society of America.

Moscovici, S. (1984) "The Phenomenon of Social Representations." In *Social Representations*, edited by R. Farr and S. Moscovici. Cambridge: Cambridge University Press, 3–70.

————. (1988) "Notes Toward a Description of Social Representations. *European Journal of Social Psychology* 18, 211–50.

————. (1993, December) "Jewishness Matters." Paper presented at the Conference on National and Cultural Variations in Jewish Identity, Jerusalem.

Paine, R. (1989) "Israel: Jewish Identity and Competition over 'Tradition.' " In *History and Ethnicity*, edited by E. Tonkin, M. McDonald, and M. Chapman. London: Routledge, 121–36.

Parker, I. (1987) "Social Representations: Social Psychology's (mis)use of Sociology." *Journal for the Theory of Social Behaviour* 17. 447–70.

Phillips, B. A. (1991) "Sociological Analysis of Jewish Identity." In *Jewish Identity in America*, edited by D. M. Gordis and Y. Ben-Horin. Los Angeles: Wilstein Institute, 3–25.

Phinney, J. S. (1990) "Ethnic Identity in Adolescents and Adults: Review of Research." *Psychological Bulletin* 108: 499–515.

Purkhardt, S. C., and J. E. Stockdale. (1993) "Multidimensional Scaling as a Technique for the Exploration and Description of a Social Representation." In *Empirical Approaches to Social Representations*, edited by G. M. Breakwell and D. V. Canter. Oxford: Oxford University Press, 272–97.

Schoenfeld, S. (1991a) "Interpretive Social Science and the Study of Jewish Identity: Inside the Black Box." Paper presented at the the Third Israel-Canada Conference on Social Scientific Approaches to the Study of Judaism, Bar Ilan University, Israel.

————. (1991b) "Three Survey Approaches to Jewish Identity and Their Implications for Research on Jewish Education." Paper presented at the Conference of the Research Network on Jewish Education, Cleveland.

Schutz, A. (1970) *Collected Papers: The Problem of Social Reality*. Hague: Martinue Wishoff.

Sklare, M., and J. Greenblum. (1979) *Jewish Identity on the Suburban Frontier*. 2d. ed. Chicago: University of Chicago Press.

Ta'ir, U. (1993) "Patterns of Ethnic and National Identity among Soviet Immigrants at Different Phases of the Migration Process." Master's thesis, Hebrew University. (Hebrew)

Tucker, L. R., and S. J. Messick. (1963) "An Individual Differences Model for Multidimensional Scaling." *Psychometrika* 38: 333–68.

Vigotsky, L. S. (1986) *Thought and Language*. Translated by Alex Kozulin. Cambridge, Mass.: MIT Press.

Chapter 15

Jewish and Other National and Ethnic Identities of Israeli Jews

Stephen Sharot

Jewish identity in Israel, like Jewish identity elsewhere, is an ethnic identity. It is an identity with a people that meets the criteria of most recent definitions of an "ethnic group." These criteria are distinctive cultural and symbolic characteristics (in the Jewish case the major element is religion), and a sense of kinship and community, the "we" feeling that relates to a belief in a common ancestry and group history. This ethnic identity is a national identity in the sense that there is also an emphasis on the relationship of the group to a particular territory, a homeland.

Jewish identity in Israel is differentiated from, but interpenetrates and overlaps with, other national and ethnic identities. This chapter looks at the interrelations of Jewish identity with Israeli identity, with identities based on countries of origin, and with identities based on a broad distinction between Jews from the European Diaspora and Jews from the North African and Asian Diaspora.

Among Israeli Jews, the Israeli identity has both a civic component and an ethnic-national component. The civic component relates to the legal definition, rights, and obligations of all citizens, Jews and non-Jews, of the Israeli state, a legal-geographic unit. However, when Israeli Jews emphasize their Israeli identity, the ethnic-national component is normally the most prominent in their consciousness. When they think of the term *Israeli*, more than half of Israeli Jews do not include Arabs (Smooha 1992), and the fundamental distinction made between Jews and Arabs at the level of national identity is reflected in the use of different terms when referring to the plurality of non-Jewish and of Jewish ethnic groups in Israeli society. The term *miutim* (minorities) is used with respect to non-Jewish groups, whereas the term *edot* (plural of *edah*) is used to denote Jewish populations from particular countries of origin or regions within countries. However, the term *edah* is used more commonly by Israelis to refer to Jewish groups from North Africa and Asia (Moroccan *edah*, Yemenite *edah*, etc.) who are often referred to collectively as *edot ha'Mizrach* (communities of the East), *Mizrachim* (Easterners, Orientals), or *Sephardim*. Less commonly the term *edah* is applied to Israelis from Europe and America (Poles, Anglo-Saxons, etc.) who are collectively known as *edot Ashkenaz* or *Ashkenazim*.

Identities with particular *edot* and with *edot ha'Mizrach* or Ashkenazim are identities with Jewish populations from particular geographic-cultural backgrounds, and are not identities with the countries of origin, their non-Jewish populations, and their cultures. Some Israeli Jews do identify with their countries of origin, or have at least a positive orientation toward certain cultural components of those countries, and some hardly differentiate between identity with the country of origin and identity with the Jewish group from that country. But where a differentiation is made, several patterns of identity are possible. Where there were high levels of segregation and tension between a comparatively cohesive and culturally distinctive Jewish community and the non-Jewish population in the country of origin, a negative orientation toward the country of origin may coexist with a strong identity with the Jewish group of origin. Where there was little segregation of Jews, cultural distinctiveness or community organization, or where Jews were relatively assimilated, an Israeli-Jewish identity may coexist with a positive orientation toward the country and culture of origin and little special identity with the Jews from that country. Identity with Jews from a particular country of origin may relate to their common participation in that country's wider culture rather than to any distinctiveness they might have had as Jews.

Whereas identities of Israeli Jews with their countries of origin may be similar to ethnic identities in other societies of immigrants, the *edah* ethnic identity is of a special kind. It is of a type particular to a "returning Diaspora," of a people who, prior to their immigration, felt bound to and part of the nation linked to the country or state in which they wish to settle. The special nature of edah identity has made some sociologists question the translation of the term *edah* into English as "ethnic group." Ernest Krausz (1986), for example, admits that *edot* are characterized by primordial attributes, particular sociocultural features, and a consciousness of constituting a group different from others in the same setting, but he argues that, with respect to all three attributes, what unites Israeli Jews is stronger and more important than what divides them. He writes that Israeli Jews share a common religion, trace their origins to a common source and, in addition to the ancient history of their common ancestors, they share parallel historical experiences of dispersion and persecution. These commonalities represent the deepest level of primordialism upon which are superimposed differences in communal histories, languages, and culture that were brought from the more immediate countries of origin.

Krausz implies that the common Jewish ethnic identity of Israeli Jews rules out the possibility of ethnic identities based on communities of origin. My position is that people may have more than one identity based on common descent. National and ethnic identities contain cultural definitions of kinship, and they can vary, like biologic kin, in terms of "closeness" and "distance," as will as in their relative importance with regard to loyalty, pride, social activities, and cultural orientations. National-ethnic identity, encompassing the entire "extended family," may readily coexist with ethnic or subethnic identities that encompass branches of that "family."

Within the more encompassing Jewish identity, Israeli Jews may feel a close kinship to members of their own *edah*. As Israelis, they may feel closer ties to other Israelis than to Jews in the Diaspora, including those Jews who remain in their country of origin. Indeed, many Israeli Jews will report that their Israeli identity, in its ethnic-national sense, is more important to them than their Jewish identity. The extent to which Israelis distinguish their Israeliness from their Jewishness and from the relative importance of one or the other is not always clear, and certain expressions such as *am Yisrael* (the people of Israel) are often understood to encompass all Jews. The emphasis placed on these interpenetrating and overlapping identities (Jewish, Israel, *edah*, and *edot ha'Mizrach*/Ashkenazim) will vary from context to context, but certain generalizations can be made about their relative importance among different sectors of the Jewish Israeli population.

Few studies of ethnic and national identities among Israeli Jews have investigated the relationships between the identities that I have distinguished. Most have either focused on the relationship between the Jewish and Israeli identities or on the relationship between Israeli and *edah* identities. An example of the former are the studies of Simon N. Herman (1989) who reported on the identities of high school students (16-17 years) in surveys carried out in 1964 and 1974 and of an adult sample (over age 20) in 1985. Most Israeli Jews were found to have positive feelings toward both the Jewish and the Israeli identities. Herman wrote that the exceptions, very small in number, were the "Canaanites" who rejected a Jewish identity in favor of a new Israeli or "Hebrew" identity, and the ultra-Orthodox, anti-Zionist Neturei Karta who rejected any Israeli identity. He found that most Israeli Jews say that, when they feel more Jewish, they also feel more Israeli. Jewish citizens of other countries are more likely to feel that there is no relationship between their feeling Jewish and their feelings for their nationality (e.g., American) or that there is an incompatibility between their feeling Jewish and their feelings for their nationality (e.g., Argentinean). There are very few Israeli Jews who feel that their Jewish and Israeli identities are incompatible, but there was a significant minority (over one-fifth) who reported that there was no relationship between their feelings of being Jewish and their feelings of being Israeli.

The Israeli Jews who compartmentalized their Jewish and Israeli identities displayed somewhat weaker orientations to both identities and were found more frequently among those who defined themselves as "nonreligious" rather than "traditional" or "religious." The crucial variable in Jewish identity was, in fact, religious observance as operationalized by self-definition as "religious," "traditional," or "nonreligious." Israeli Jews from North African and Asia had a stronger Jewish identity than those from Europe because they included greater proportions of the "religious" and "traditional." However, when respondents were faced with a question where they had to favor one identity over the other, a greater proportion of religious and traditional students originating from North Africa favored the Jewish side in comparison with religious and traditional students originating from Europe.

Yair Auron (1993) also found that religiosity was the crucial factor in accounting for the relative emphases on Jewish and Israeli identities in a survey, carried out in 1990, of students in teacher-training colleges. Sixty-six percent of those who identified themselves as "nonreligious" put their Israeli before their Jewish identity compared with 19 percent of those who identified themselves as

"traditional," and less than 1 percent of those who identified themselves as "religious." Auron found that the Israeliness of this sample
of young Israelis (most were between the ages of 21 and 26) was expressed *principally* in relation to the Israeli state and to the Land of
Israel, whereas Jewishness was expressed *principally* in relation to
the religion of Israel and to the people of Israel. The majority of the
haredim or "ultra-Orthodox" did not accept an Israeli identity and
had negative feelings toward the Israeli state, but the "nationalist
religious" and the traditionalists expressed strong positive feelings
for the Israeli state as well as for the Jewish religion and people.
The nonreligious expressed either lack of interest or negative orientations toward religion and only weak feelings in their belonging to
the Jewish people. The meaning that they attributed to *the people of
Israel* appeared to be narrowed to those Jews who lived within the
boundaries of the State of Israel, whereas among the traditionalists
and the religious the term referred to the worldwide Jewish people.

Like Herman, Auron did not find that differences in origin
(North Africa-Asia or Europe-America) had an effect on identity beyond the differences in religiosity between the two categories. Jewish identity tended to be stronger among North Africans-Asians
because this category included the majority of traditionalists. An intergenerational decline in religiosity, which was especially evident
in the North African-Asian category, suggests a decline in the importance of Jewish identity, but this might be balanced out by a
trend among the nonreligious to put a greater emphasis on their
Jewish identity. The significance, if any, of this trend is difficult to
interpret. The pattern among secular Israelis up to the Six Day War
of denying a Jewish identity in favor of an Israeli or "Hebrew" identity has almost disappeared, but Auron suggests that Jewishness
may have only appeared to have strengthened because of a weakening of Israeliness. Although the Holocaust has become a central element in the Jewish consciousness of all Israelis, among the
nonreligious, this development does not appear to have changed attitudes toward Diaspora Jews or Jewish Diaspora history. Most of
the nonreligious expressed their differences from Diaspora Jews
when they argued that although religion should not play an important part in the public and private lives of Israelis, it should play an
important part in the lives of Diaspora Jews.

The disappearance of the self-proclaimed non-Jewish Jewish Israeli should not be taken to signify a revival of Jewish consciousness. The greater readiness to proclaim a Jewish identity may
reflect changes in the Israeli civil religion with its more extensive

nationalization of traditional religious symbols. This does not mean either deeper understandings of what it means to be a Jew in Israel or growth in the existential meaning and value of Israel as a Jewish state (Liebman and Don-Yehiya 1983; Diamond 1986).

Studies of the relationships between Jewish and Israeli identities have tended to be quite separate from studies of identities based on country or continent of origin. The latter have focused on either an *edah* identity or an identity with the broad categories of *edot ha'Mizrach* or Ashkenazim. In general, those who have focused on the *edah* identity have been anthropologists who approach the subject from a perspective that emphasizes the cultural, primordial, expressive, nonrational components of ethnicity (Shokeid & Deshen 1982; Deshen & Shokeid 1984; Weingrod 1985). Those who have focused on the *edot ha'Mizrach* identity have been sociologists who have emphasized the socioeconomic, political, instrumental, rational components of ethnicity (Smooha 1978, 1987; Swirski 1981). Neither of these approaches have paid much attention to the ethnic identities of Israelis of European origin. The cultural-anthropological perspective finds little interest in them because they do not emphasize distinctive cultural heritages of their communities of origin. From the socioeconomic perspective, Shlomo Swirski (1981) argues that there is less need to analyze Ashkenazi consciousness than the *edot ha'Mizrach* consciousness; the Ashkenazi consciousness is expressed openly in the mass media, in literature, in the educational system, and by official propaganda. Swirski argues that, although there are clear signs of mutual recognition among Ashkenazim, they do not express their commonality in particularistic terms but by such terms as the *state* or *society*.

A prominent example of the anthropological cultural approach is to be found in the work of Shlomo Deshen (1972, 1976) who presents persistence and change of religious and cultural practices as outcomes of a conflict between an identity with the *edah* and with an identity as an Israeli. The tension and accommodation of the *edah* and Israeli identities was the focus of a study of ritual changes in a synagogue of Jews from Tunisia. Deshen wrote that the Tunisian immigrants were bound by the cohesive factors of common culture and origin but that they also wished to acknowledge the new bonds of Israeli nationhood. There has been some change in Israel from a melting pot to a more pluralist ideologist, "yet ethnic loyalties and adherence to ethnic practices on the one hand, and Israeli nationalism, patriotism, and citizenship on the other, still remain uneasy bedfellows." Deshen showed how changes or adjustments in the prayers and symbols of the synagogue represented an infusion of new content that related the immigrants' evolving Israeli identities to traditional themes. For example, a memorial prayer that was traditionally confined to deceased rabbis was said for two nonlearned men who had died when they tried to save a girl from drowning. The original reference of this symbol of commemoration was the traditional criteria of scholarship and piety, but it was bestowed on men who were evaluated according to new criteria of universal human virtues. Over some issues, particularly those that encroach upon focal aspects of cultural heritage, a separatist stance was taken; but in most cases compromises were made that allowed for the continuation of a separate *edah* identity within the broader compass of the national Israeli identity.

When the Tunisian Jews lived in Tunisia they identified themselves principally as Jews and conceived of their religious culture as *the* Jewish religion (rather than as one particular local version of it). Their identity as an *edah*, as Tunisian Jews, developed in Israel, and their concern in preserving their heritage took on the meaning of the preservation of a specific Tunisian Jewish heritage. This newly formed identity could not be divorced from, or seen to be in conflict with, their continuing identity as Jews. Deshen's analysis implies, therefore, that tension between *edah* and Israeli identities is a tension between Jewish and Israeli identities. In contrast to the works of Herman and Auron, religious Jews, rather than secular Jews, experience tension between Jewish and Israeli identities.

An exception to the focus of Israeli anthropologists on the ethnicity of Jews from North Africa and Asia is Rina Neeman's (1994) study of an ethnic association founded in 1980 by veteran immigrants from Rumania. Unlike the Tunisian Jews, whose identity as Jews and as an *edah* were anchored in their religious heritage, the members of the Rumanian association, who were all aged fifty-five or over, defined themselves as irreligious and were reluctant to employ ethnic terminology in identifying themselves and their association. They referred to Rumanian Israelis, not as an *edah* but as an aliyah, an immigration or literally *ascent*, a term with clear positive connotations in Israel. The members' orientation toward their country of origin or toward the Rumanian people as a whole was ambivalent; references to Rumania as motherland and nostalgia for the scenery and culture of their youth existed alongside feelings of antagonism and hostility toward a people whom they saw as their oppressors and persecutors. The feelings of ambivalence that association members also expressed toward Rumanian Jewry, both in the past and in contemporary Israel, were related perhaps to their perceptions that Rumanian Jewry lacked solidarity and were ignored and discriminated against in Israeli society, especially in comparison with other Ashkenazi populations.

Neeman interprets the activities of the association as the means by which members are able to transform their identity as Rumanian Jews from one with negative associations to one in which they can be proud. The concerns of the association to promote the cultural distinctiveness, sociocultural integration, and status of Rumanian Jewry are seen as ways of bridging their identities as Rumanian Jews and as Israelis. Members are deeply committed to the State of Israel, but their problems with the Hebrew language and with Israeli patterns of behavior, including those of their children, are seen by them as indications of their lack of integration into the society. Within the association, they are able to feel belonging and solidarity, to restructure their personal biographies around ethnic themes, and to integrate their Rumanian ethnicity with both their Jewish and Israeli identities.

The relationships between *edah* identities and the broader Jewish and Israeli identities have tended to be ignored by those sociologists who are inclined toward socioeconomic interpretations of ethnicity in Israel. Shlomo Swirski (1981) has presented the most explicit socioeconomic interpretation of *edot ha'Mizrach* as the basis of an emergent ethnic identification in Israel. He argued that the common experiences of Jews from North Africa and Asia created a new ethnoclass and identity. Their subordinate position within the ethnic division of labor, their subjection to discrimination, and the "colonialist" orientation of the Ashkenazim have erased the differences among the *edot* from North Africa and Asia and created a common consciousness. In this analysis, Swirski simply takes the wider Jewish and Israeli identities for granted; they do not appear to impinge on the *edah* identity or the *edot ha'Mizrach* identity.

The relationship between Jewish identity and *edah* identity is a central part of Eliezer Ben-Rafael's analysis of ethnicity in Israel. In his book *The Emergence of Ethnicity: Cultural Groups and Social Conflict in Israel* (1982), he treated ethnicity primarily as a cultural phenomenon and argued that the form that it has taken in Israel was the consequence of an encounter of the cultures of Jews originating from Europe and from North Africa-Asia. Ben-Rafael wrote that an *edah* identity did not develop among the dominant category of Jews from Europe. Their cultural orientations were largely formed by Zionists who immigrated from Eastern Europe prior to the establishment of the State of Israel. They had already undergone a process of secularization prior to their migration, and they understood their migration as "a denial of history," as a break from the religio-cultural and social features of the Jewish communities of the Diaspora. They were committed to a secular notion of nationhood that was justified in terms of the universal right of all nations to autonomy and emancipation. Religion, their "Judaism," and "Jewishness," was but a reflection of the national principle. Ben-Rafael did not explicitly discuss the relationship between the Jewish and Israeli identities, but he implied that, for Ashkenazim, the Israeli identity would be the most encompassing one.

Most immigrants from North Africa and Asia had undergone comparatively little secularization, and they conceived of their immigration as a fulfillment of messianic prophecies or as a means of expressing and continuing their sacred culture. They did not distinguish Judaism from their "parochial" cultural legacy, and they were not, therefore, ready to abandon those cultural attributes that they had adhered to in the Diaspora. Their contact with secularized Jews in Israel came as a shock to many, and their consciousness of the need to defend their primordial attributes led many to strengthen their traditional ways during their first years in the new society. This meeting led to the emergence of the *edot* as distinct sociocultural entities and distinct identities ("Moroccan," "Yemenite," etc.), even though these identities continued to be bound to the broader identity of Jew. Although not explicitly stated, this implied that for Jews from North Africa and Asia, the Jewish identity would continue to be more encompassing than the Israeli identity.

Ben-Rafael denied that the term *edot ha'Mizrach* referred to an ethnic group or identity. It is, like the term *Ashkenazim*, a term referring to a "sociocultural category" and emerged in order to signify the de facto pluralism between the two Jewish sociocultural categories. The term does not denote a major focus of ethnic self-identity because, unlike the *edah* identity, it does not have an ascriptive basis or have much meaning within the wider frame of Jewish identity.

The absence of an awareness of kind based on country of origin among European immigrants was congruent with the ideology of *mizug ha'galuyot* (fusion of the exiles). In its traditional formulation, the gathering and amalgamation of Jews from different parts of the world referred to the future messianic kingdom, but it was secularized as part of the modern Zionist ideology. This fusion was to be implemented by the unconditional acceptance of all Jewish immigrants as full citizens of Israel. Among North African and Asian immigrants, the absence of differentiation between Jewishness and the cultural legacy of the community of origin meant not only that they were concerned with maintaining their particular religio-cultural expressions, but also that they conceived of themselves as part of a larger whole in which they would amalgamate. In comparison with European immigrants, Middle Easterners experienced a tension between the belief in the fusion of the exiles and their emergent ethnic identities.

Ben-Rafael drew on his samples of middle-class Moroccan and Yemenite Jews in Israel to demonstrate that the fusion ideology, when combined with the openness of the dominant European category, encourages mobile Jews from North African and Asian origins to assimilate and undergo a process of "de-ethnization." At the same time, the very openness of the European category contributes to the continuation of cultural distinctiveness in the "ethnoclasses" of the lower strata of Jews from North Africa and Asia. Because the upwordly mobile from the *edot* assimilate into the predominantly European middle class, they distance themselves from their origins and exert little cultural influence on the majority who remain in the lower strata. Thus, ethnicity is likely to remain an important feature of the "truncated ethno-classes" in Israel.

The restriction of Ben-Rafael's sample to middle-class Jews from Morocco and Yemen meant that he was not able to substantiate that the *edah* identity among Israelis from North Africa and Asia was far more important, especially among the lower strata from these origins, than among Jews from Europe. Nor was he able to show that an identity based on the label *edot ha'Mizrach* had not emerged among at least the lower strata of Israelis from North Africa and Asia.

In the book that I coauthored with Ben-Rafael (1991), and in the articles that we wrote together with Hanna Ayalon (1985, 1986), we analyzed a large and more comprehensive sample of middle-aged males, most of whom had migrated to Israel in their childhood or youth, from four countries of origin: Morocco, Iraq, Poland, and Rumania. The sample was stratified so that, in each group of origin, half of the respondents were in blue-collar work and half were in white-collar work. Among the hypotheses we tested were those suggested in Ben Rafael's previous book: that an *edah* identity is more important among North Africans-Asians than among Europeans; that this identity is convergent with the broader Jewish and Israeli identities; and that this identity is more important among the lower strata of North African-Asians.

We revised, however, Ben-Rafael's former expectations with respect to an identity of *edot ha'Mizrach*. We recognized that the term *edot ha'Mizrach* was not related to a cultural entity that existed prior to immigration, and that the communities in North Africa and Asia varied greatly with respect to their Judeo-Arabic dialects, religious customs, and other cultural features. However, in their confrontation with Israelis from Europe, many North African and Asian Israelis felt that, despite their differences, they were closer culturally to other *edot ha'Mizrach* than to Ashkenazim. The label *edot ha'Mizrach* may have originated as a stereotypical device used by Israelis from Europe, but North African-Asians appear to have rejected its negative connotations and adopted it as a source of identity. Insofar as it was based on a feeling of cultural similarities, we did not expect it to be an alternative to the *edah* identity (as Swirski suggested), but rather to accompany and possibly reinforce it.

We did not expect the Ashkenazi identity to have as much meaning for the European Israelis as the *edot ha'Mizrach* identity had for North African-Asian Israelis. However, the integration of the European groups in Israel and their perceptions of differences, both cultural and socioeconomic, between themselves and North African-Asians may have made the Ashkenazi identity more significant than the more specific *edah* identity.

In order to tap ethnic identities, we asked respondents to rank four identities in order of their importance for them: community of origin (*edah*), Ashkenazi or *edot ha'Mizrach*, Jewish, and Israeli. The great majority placed the Jewish and Israeli identities in first or second place. The Moroccan and Iraqi respondents split evenly in placing Israeli or Jewish identity in first or second place. In constrast, two-thirds of the Poles and Rumanians placed the Israeli identity before the Jewish. Regarding the edah and Ashkenazi/*edot ha'Mizrach* identities, more than twice as many Poles and Rumanians (over 40 percent in these groups) as Moroccans and Iraqis refused to accept these identities. Of those that did rank the labels, the majority placed the *edah* identity in fourth place. Moroccan and Iraqi respondents were split in about equal proportions in placing the *edah* or *edot ha'Mizrach* identities in third or fourth place.

A second set of questions on ethnic identity asked respondents to indicate their level of pride, if any, in the four identities. On all four identities, the Moroccans and Iraqis indicated greater pride than the Poles and Rumanians, and only on the Israeli identity was there little difference. Consistent with the data on the hierarchy of identities, Moroccans and Iraqis did not indicate a clear preference for the Israeli or Jewish identities, and Poles and Rumanians tended to express greater pride in the Israeli identity. Differences were especially prominent with respect to the orientations toward the edah and Ashkenazi/*edot ha'Mizrach* identities: many more Moroccans and Iraqis expressed pride in these identities than did Poles and Rumanians.

Levels of pride in Jewish and Israeli identities were highly correlated for all four groups. There was also a high correlation for all groups, but especially for the Moroccan and Iraqis, between the *edah* and Ashkenazi/*edot ha'Mizrach* identities. However, only the Moroccans and Iraqis demonstrated high correlations between their Israeli-Jewish identities and their *edah* and *edot ha'Mizrach* identities. Among Poles and Rumanians these relationships were weak or nonexistent. We found, as expected, that both the *edah* identity and the *edot ha'Mizrach* identity were more important among the lower stratum of Moroccans and Iraqis than among the higher stratum. However, class differences within the Moroccan and Iraqi groups with respect to ethnic identity were of a lower magnitude that the differences between the Moroccan-Iraqis and the Poles-Rumanians.

In analyzing the prominent division in the level of ethnic identity between North African-Asian and European Israelis, we pointed to an avenue of investigation that has been neglected not only in Israel, but also in the general literature on ethnic identity: the relationship between ethnic identities and the wider identities of nationality and citizenship. The finding that Israelis from Europe were disposed to place their Israeli identity before their Jewish identity and to reject or place only minor importance on the identity associated with the Jewish community of origin may indicate the continuing influence of the cultural orientations of the early Zionist "pioneers" who viewed their Zionism and aliyah as "rebellions" against the Jewish tradition and the way of life of the Diaspora. Such negative orientations toward Diaspora "Jewishness" were less important among later Ashkenazi immigrants and they have lost the prominence they once had, but there has been no ethnic revival of Ashkenazi *edot* and it is clear that associations of elderly immigrants, such as the one studied by Rina Neeman, will not continue into the second generation. Among North African-Asian Israelis, Israeliness is a source of great pride, but it has not yet overtaken Jewishness as the most encompassing identity; and the wider identities have not become differentiated from the "subethnic" identities of the communities of origin. This fusion of the broader and specific identities among *edot ha'Mizrach* is demonstrated by the revival of ethnic festivals (the largest and best known is the Mimuna of the Moroccans) which are multigenerational and that celebrate both the specific customs and the Jewishness-Israeliness of the *edot*.

This research bears implications for the evolving identities among recent immigrants from the former Soviet Union. Since these groups have been subjected to limited research on issues of ethnicity, my discussion from this point will be somewhat speculative. Three categories of immigrants from the former Soviet Union should be distinguished: firstly, those from the Baltic countries and from other areas, such as Moldovia, which were annexed by the former Soviet Union in the West; secondly, those from Georgia and the Islamic republics; and thirdly, those from the Russian "heartland," most of whom lived in Moscow and Leningrad.

The Baltic Jews had been subject to a process of secularization that started later and was that less intensive than the process in the Russian heartland. Although distinctive Jewish cultural forms became highly attenuated, many retained a contact with Judaism and a positive Jewish identity (Rabkin 1989). Their emergent pattern of ethnic identities in Israel should resemble those that we found among Polish and Rumanian immigrants. The Israeli identity will become the somewhat more prominent identity of the interrelated Israeli and Jewish identities, and their identities as *edot* or as Ashkenazim will not be strong. In contrast, the pattern of ethnic identities among Israeli Jews from Georgia and the Islamic republics appears to resemble that of *edot ha'Mizrach*. They had retained relatively high levels of religious observance in their countries of origin, and in Israel the majority continue these levels and describe themselves as *masoriti* (traditional). The greater opportunities for religious practice in Israel allow a significant minority to increase the number of their religious observances. Very few admit to becoming less religious in Israel, but it is probable that the second generation will follow the *edot ha'Mizrach* pattern of intergenerational decline in religiosity.

Prior to their emigration, the Jews from Georgia and the Islamic republics were strong supporters of Zionism. As among the Jewish communities from North Africa and Asia, Zionism did not take predominantly secularist forms but fitted well into the religious tradition of praying for a return to Zion. In Israel the strong Jewish identity continues as the more encompassing of the interrelated Jewish and Israeli identities. Other Israelis identify them as members of a distinctive Jewish group of origin ("Georgian" or "Bukharan") and this pattern contributes to the emergence of a strong *edah* identity that is not differentiated from their Jewish identity. In addition to their Jewish identity, Georgian Jews had a strong sense of Georgian patriotism, and in Israel some maintain an identity and cultural ties with Georgia (Gitelman 1991).

The cultural background of the Jews from the metropolitan Russian centers was entirely different. They had been exposed to the full impact of Sovietization from the 1920s and 1930s, and religious observance all but disappeared among the majority. A survey conducted in 1993 in the towns of Moscow, Kiev and Minsk found that 57% of the one thousand Jews interviewed said that Jewish culture had been nonexistent in their families of origin and only 15% said that they were raising their children in the spirit of the Jewish tradition; 65% had never attended synagogue, and only 1% went regularly or often to synagogue (Ryvkina 1995). A Jewish community in an organizational sense had ceased to exist in the former Soviet Union, and when a Jewish identity was retained it was largely divorced from specifically Jewish cultural content. For many Russian Jews of the 1970s and 1980s, Jewishness took on the meanings of cosmopolitan intellectualism and a strong achievement drive to overcome the barriers to occupational mobility (Markowitz 1995).

The negative associations of Jewish identity with state imposition (the designation "Jewish nationality" in the internal passport) and with discrimination and anti-Semitism were countered somewhat by the pride associated with the Israeli victory in 1967, and the positive connotations of a Jewish identity may have been unwittingly reinforced by Soviet propaganda that blurred the distinction between Zionism and Jewish peoplehood (Rabkin 1989). However, the association of Jewish identity with Israel did not lead, in most cases, to a desire to settle in Israel. Many of those who managed to emigrate in the early 1970s chose to come to Israel, but from 1977 the majority did not come to Israel and from 1980 to 1982 only about one-quarter chose Israel. With respect to the large immigration from 1988, it can be assumed that, if they had had a choice, a large proportion would not have made Israel their country of destination. The 1993 survey in Moscow, Kiev, and Minsk found that, although Israel was the intended destination of the one-third of the sample who intended to emigrate, only one-fifth said that Israel was their historic homeland (Ryvkina 1995; see also Pohoryles-Drexel & Pohoryles 1991). Among the recent immigrants, several do not intend to settle in Israel; they are waiting in a self-imposed cultural ghetto until another state is willing to accept them.

A small proportion of Russian Jews developed a strong Jewish identity in Russia, and in the 1970s a few adopted a traditionally religious Jewish identity and became associated with ultra-Orthodox Judaism, particularly the Lubavitch Hasidim. At the other end of the spectrum were many more who changed their national designation and hid their Jewish background even from their children. Although a significant number experienced obstacles to their full participation in Soviet society and had predominantly Jewish social networks, by certain measures, such as intermarriage, assimilation was extensive. In 1988, of the Jews who married in the former USSR, 58% of the males and 48% of the females entered into a mixed marriage; in the Russian republic the figures were 73% for men and 64% for women, and the proportion of children with at least one Jewish parent who were born to mixed couples possibly approached 80% (Tolts 1995). The high proportion of non-Jews, about 20%, among the Russian immigrants of the last few years was made possible by Israeli law that gives the right of immigration to non-Jewish spouses, children, and grandchildren.

Given the background of most Russian Jews, it is evident that a Jewish identity with positive sentiments and content is a recent and emergent phenomenon that is associated with the process of migration and accommodation to Israeli society. Most do not adopt a Jewish identity with an important religious component; a Brookdale Institute survey found that only 2% of Russian Jews in Israel identified themselves as religious, 19% identified themselves as "traditional," 66% as nonreligious, and 13% were unable or did not wish to define themselves. In comparison with the almost total absence of religious observance in Russia, many now participate in the Passover Seder or fast on Yom Kippur. Such practices are not seen as having religious significance but indicate a belongingness to the Jewish state. The Israeli identity probably will become the more encompassing of the two broad ethno-national identities. Russian Jewish immigrants say that, whereas in Russia they felt Jewish because of the official designation and discrimination, in Israel they feel Jewish because they live in a Jewish state.

Like other immigrations, Jews from Russia are identified by other Israelis by reference to their country of origin. Russian and Jewish state-imposed national designations had been mutually exclusive in the former Soviet Union, and it is not surprising that the immigrants at first rejected being labeled as Russians. The immigrants began to adopt the label as they came to understand that this was just one of many country of origin terms that were tied to a Jewish identity in Israel (Markowitz 1995). The Russian Jewish identity could not, however, refer back to memories of a Jewish culturally distinctive or communally organized group; its cultural references are the Russian language and Russian "high" culture. Some compare their appreciation of literature, ballet, and opera with the "low" tastes and materialism among Israelis. Some see a resemblance between the "uncultured" Asian peoples of the former Soviet Union and Israelis from North Africa and Asia, but Israel as a whole is often seen as a "Levantine" culture. In all likelihood an emphasis on high culture will be insufficient as a basis for the transmission of ethnicity from one generation to another.

To conclude: As a consequence of different religio-cultural backgrounds and socioeconomic encounters in Israel, five distinguishable patterns of national and ethnic identities have emerged.

1. Rejection of a Jewish identity and any *edah* or ethnic identity based on country or region of origin in favor on one national identity, Israeli or Hebrew. This was the "Canaanite" position and is rarely found today.

2. Rejection of Israeli identity and an overlap and mutual reinforcement of Jewish identity, a wider categorization (Ashkenazim) and, possibly, a more specific religious community of origin (e.g., the Litvak *mitnagdim*). This pattern is common among ultra-Orthodox or *haredi* Jews, especially those from Europe.

3. Rejection of, or relatively low attachment to, specific *edah* or ethnic identities in favor of a broad Israeli-Jewish identity, with the Israeli component being the greater source of pride. This is common among Israelis who define themselves as secular, especially of European origins.

4. Overlap and mutual reinforcement of identities based on Jewish community of origin (*edah*), a wider categorization (*edot ha'Mizrach*), and Jewish-Israeli identities with the Jewish identity being the most encompassing and greatest source of pride. This pattern is particularly common among Jews who describe themselves as "religious" or "traditional" from North Africa and Asia.

5. Compartmentalization between an ethnic (but not *edah*) identity, based on language and certain additional cultural components of the country of origin, and Israeli-Jewish identities, with the Israeli identity being the most encompassing. This is common among recent immigrants from Russia.

Not every group from a particular country of origin can be fitted neatly into this categorization. Not only will different groups from a particular country of origin be found in different categories, but certain groups will demonstrate a combination of patterns. Ambiguity of ethnic identities is no doubt pervasive. However, I hope that I have shown that an understanding of Jewish identity in Israel requires that it be investigated and analyzed in relation to other national and ethnic identities of Israeli Jews.

References

Auron, Yair. (1993) *Jewish-Israeli Identity*. Tel Aviv: Sifriat Poalim Publishing House. (Hebrew).

Ayalon, Hannah, Eliezer Ben-Rafael, and Stephen Sharot. (1985) "Variations in Ethnic Identification among Israeli Jews." *Ethnic and Racial Studies* 8: 389–407.

———. (1986) "The Costs and Benefits of Ethnic Identification." *British Journal of Sociology* 37: 550–68.

Ben-Rafael, Eliezer. (1982) *The Emergence of Ethnicity: Cultural Groups and Social Conflict in Israel*. Westport, Conn.: Greenwood.

———, and Stephen Sharot. (1991) *Ethnicity, Religion, and Class in Israeli Society*. Cambridge: Cambridge University Press.

Deshen, Shlomo. (1972) "Ethnicity and Citizenship in the Ritual of an Israeli Synagogue." *Southwestern Journal of Anthropology* 28: 68–82.

———. (1976) "Ethnic Boundaries and Cultural Paradigms: The Case of Tunisian Immigrants in Israel." *Ethos* 4: 271–94.

———, and Moshe Shokeid, eds. (1984) *Jews of the Middle East: Anthropological Perspectives on Past and Present*. Tel Aviv: Schocken. (Hebrew)

Diamond, James S. (1986) *Homeland or Holy Land? The "Canaanite" Critique of Israel*. Bloomington: Indiana University Press.

Gitelman, Zvi. (1991) "Ethnic Identity and Ethnic Relations among the Jews of the Non-European USSR." *Ethnic and Racial Studies* 14: 24–54.

Herman, Simon N. (1989) *Jewish Identity*. 2d ed. New Brunswick: Transaction Publishers.

Krausz, Ernest. (1986) "Eda and "Ethnic Groups' in Israel." *Jewish Journal of Sociology* 28: 5–18.

Liebman, Charles S., and Eliezer Don-Yehiya. (1983) *Civil Religion in Israel*. Berkeley: University of California Press.

Markowitz, Fran. (1995) "Emigration, Immigration and Cultural Change: Towards a Transnational 'Russian' Jewish Community." In *Jews and Jewish Life in Russia and the Soviet Union*, edited by Yaacov Ro'i. Newbury Park: Frank Cass, 403–13.

Neeman, Rina. (1994). "Invented Ethnicity as Collective and Personal Text: An Association of Rumanian Israelis." *Anthropological Quarterly* 67: 135–49.

Pohoryles-Drexel, Sabine, and Ronald J. Pohoryles. (1991) "Soviet Jews in Vienna: A Case Study." In *Soviet-Jewish Emigration and Resettlement in the 1990s*, edited by Tanya Basok and Robert J. Brym. Toronto: York Lane Press, 91–103.

Rabkin, Yakov M. (1989) "Cultures in Transition." In *The Soviet Man in an Open Society*, edited by Tamar Horowitz. Lanham: University Press of America.

Ryvkina, Rozalina. (1995) "Conflicting Values among the Jewish Population of Moscow, Kiev and Minsk." In *Jews and Jewish Life in Russia and the Soviet Union*, edited by Yaacov Ro'i. Newbury Park: Frank Cass, 391–402.

Shokeid, Moshe, and Shlomo Deshen. (1982) *Distant Relations: Ethnicity and Politics among Arabs and North Africans in Israel*. New York: Praeger.

Smooha, Sammy. (1978) *Israel: Pluralism and Conflict*. London: Routledge & Kegan Paul.

———. (1987) *Social Research on Jewish Ethnicity in Israel, 1948–1986*. Haifa: Haifa University Press.

———. (1992) *Arabs and Jews in Israel*. Vol. 2. *Change and Continuity in Mutual Intolerance*. Boulder: Westview Press.

Swirski, Shlomo. (1981) . . . *Lo Nehkshalim Ela Menuhksahlim* (Orientals and Ashkenazim in Israel: Ethnic division of labor). Haifa: Mahbarot Le'Mehkar U'Lebikoret. (Hebrew)

Tolts, Mark. (1995) "Trends in Soviet Jewish Demography since the Second World War." In *Jews and Jewish Life in Russia and the Soviet Union*, edited by Yaakov Ro'i. Newbury Park: Frank Cass, 365–82.

Weingrod, Alex, ed. (1985) *Studies in Israeli Society: After the Ingathering*. New York: Gordon and Breach.

Contributors

GEOFFREY ALDERMAN, pro vice-chancellor and professor of politics and contemporary history at Middlesex University, England, has written extensively on the history of Anglo-Jewry, and wrote a monograph, "Modern British Jewry."

ZVI BEKERMAN, a cultural anthropologist and instructor at the Melton Centre for Jewish Education and at the School of Education of the Hebrew University, is engaged in research on ethnic, national, and religious identity, primarily from sociohistorical and cultural perspectives. He is also interested in the application of this knowledge in educational settings, both formal and informal.

JONATHAN COHEN, an instructor at the Melton Centre for Jewish Education and at the School of Education, at the Hebrew University, specializes in the implications of trends in Jewish thought for Jewish education, and is the author of a book on contemporary trends in the study of Jewish thought.

STEVEN M. COHEN, associate professor at the Melton Centre for Jewish Education at the Hebrew University, has written among other books, *Two Worlds of Judaism: The Israeli and American Experiences* (with Charles Liebman), *American Modernity and Jewish Identity*, and *American Assimilation or Jewish Revival?*

SERGIO DELLAPERGOLA, professor and head of the Harman Institute of Contemporary Jewry, at the Hebrew University, has written extensively on Jewish population trends including *La transformazione demografica della diaspora ebraica*, *La population juife* *de France* (with Doris Bensimon), and *La poblacion judia de Mexico* (with Susana Lerner).

DANIEL ELAZAR, president of the Jerusalem Center for Public Affairs, Senator N. M. Paterson Professor of Intergovernmental Relations, Bar-Ilan University, and professor of political science and director of the Center for the Study of Federalism, Temple University, has written numerous books including *Community and Polity: The Organizational Dynamics of American Jewry, Israel: Building a New Society,* and *The Other Jews: The Sephardim Today.*

HENRY L. FEINGOLD, professor of history at Bernard Baruch College and at the Graduate Center of CUNY, is the author of *A Time for Searching: Entering the Mainstream, 1920–1945* and volume 4 of the series he edited, *The Jewish People in America.* His most recent book is *Lest Memory Cease: Finding Meaning in the American Jewish Past.*

HARVEY GOLDBERG, professor in the Department of Sociology and Anthropology at the Hebrew University, is the author of *Jewish Life in Muslim Libya: Rivals and Relatives* and has edited two collections entitled *Judaism Viewed from Within and from Without: Anthropological Studies,* and *Sephardi and Middle Eastern Jerwis: History and Culture in the Modern Era.*

GABRIEL HORENCZYK, an instructor at the Melton Center for Jewish Education and at the School of Education at the Hebrew University of Jerusalem, has done research on the psychological study of ethnic, cultural, and Jewish identity; identity, acculturation, and adaptation of immigrant and minority youths.

BETHAMIE HOROWITZ conducted the 1991 Greater New York Jewish Population Study for the UJA-Federation, where she was director of research from 1992 to 1996. Currently, she is principal investigator of the Connections and Journeys study, an inquiry into what being Jewish means to younger American Jews, funded by the UJA-Federation. She is a senior scholar at the Center for Jewish Studies, the Graduate Center, CUNY.

PAULA E. HYMAN, Lucy Moses Professor of Modern Jewish History at Yale University, she is the author of *From Dreyfus to Vichy: The Remaking of French Jewry, 1906–1939,* and, most recently, of

The Emancipation of the Jews of Alsace: Acculturation and Tradition in the Nineteenth Century and *Gender and Assimilation in Modern Jewish History*. She is also the coauthor of *The Jewish Woman in America*, and coeditor (with Steven M. Cohen) of *The Jewish Family: Myths and Reality*. She has recently completed a book on the Jews of modern France, and is the coeditor of the two-volume, *Jewish Women in America: An Historical Encyclopedia*.

MICHAEL A. MEYER, Adolph S. Ochs Professor of Jewish History at Hebrew Union College-Jewish Institute of Religion in Cincinnati, is the author of, among other books, *Response to Modernity: A History of the Reform Movement in Judaism*, and editor of the four-volume *German-Jewish History in Modern Times*.

DEBORAH DASH MOORE, professor of religion at Vassar College, is the editor (with Paula Hyman), of *Jewish Women in America: An Historical Encyclopedia,* and the author of *To the Golden Cities: Pursuing the American Jewish Dream in Miami and L.A.*

RIV-ELLEN PRELL, an anthropologist, is associate professor of American Studies at the University of Minnesota, and is the author of *Prayer and Community: The Havurah in American Judaism* and the forthcoming, *Fighting to Become Americans: Jewish Women and Men in Conflict in the Twentieth Century*.

STUART SCHOENFELD, associate professor of sociology at York University and chair of the Research Network in Jewish Education, has written extensively on the religious and social significance of the Bar and Bat Mitzvah.

STEPHEN SHAROT, professor in the Department of Behavioral Sciences at Ben-Gurion University, and author of *Messianism, Mysticism, and Magic: A Sociological Analysis of Jewish Religious Movements* and the coauthor of *Ethnicity, Religion and Class in Israeli Society*. He is the coeditor of the journal, *Israel Social Science Research*.

ASHER SHKEDI, head of the Teaching and Curriculum Department at the School of Education at the Hebrew University of Jerusalem, teaches at the Melton Center for Jewish Education in the Diaspora. His research areas are teacher education, curriculum development and the teaching of Jewish texts; and he published several articles on these topics.

Index